MATRIX COMPUTATIONS AND MATHEMATICAL SOFTWARE

McGraw-Hill Computer Science Series

Allen: *Anatomy of LISP*
Bell and Newell: *Computer Structures: Readings and Examples*
Donovan: *Systems Programming*
Feigenbaum and Feldman: *Computers and Thought*
Gear: *Computer Organization and Programming*
Givone: *Introduction to Switching Circuit Theory*
Goodman and Hedetniemi: *Introduction to the Design and Analysis of Algorithms*
Hamacher, Vranesic, and Zaky: *Computer Organization*
Hamming: *Introduction to Applied Numerical Analysis*
Hayes: *Computer Architecture and Organization*
Hellerman: *Digital Computer System Principles*
Hellerman and Conroy: *Computer System Performance*
Kain: *Automata Theory: Machines and Languages*
Katzan: *Microprogramming Primer*
Kohavi: *Switching and Finite Automate Theory*
Liu: *Elements of Discrete Mathematics*
Liu: *Introduction to Combinatorial Mathematics*
MacEwen: *Introduction to Computer Systems: Using the PDP-11 and Pascal*
Madnick and Donovan: *Operating Systems*
Manna: *Mathematical Theory of Computation*
Newman and Sproull: *Principles of Interactive Computer Graphics*
Nilsson: *Problem-Solving Methods in Artificial Intelligence*
Rice: *Matrix Computations and Mathematical Software*
Rosen: *Programming Systems and Languages*
Salton: *Automatic Information Organization and Retrieval*
Siewiorek, Bell, and Newell: *Principles of Computer Structures*
Stone: *Introduction to Computer Organization and Data Structures*
Stone and Siewiorek: *Introduction to Computer Organization and Data Structures: PDP-11 Edition*

Tonge and Feldman: *Computing: An Introduction to Procedures and Procedure-Followers*
Tremblay and Bunt: *An Introduction to Computer Science: An Algorithmic Approach*
Tremblay and Bunt: *An Introduction to Computer Science: An Algorithmic Approach, Short Edition*
Tremblay and Manohar: *Discrete Mathematical Structures with Applications to Computer Science*
Tremblay and Sorenson: *An Introduction to Data Structures with Applications*
Tucker: *Programming Languages*
Watson: *Timesharing System Design Concepts*
Wiederhold: *Database Design*
Winston: *The Psychology of Computer Vision*

McGraw-Hill Advanced Computer Science Series

Davis and Lenat: *Knowledged-Based Systems in Artificial Intelligence*
Feigenbaum and Feldman: *Computers and Thought*
Kogge: *The Architecture of Pipelined Computers*
Lindsay, Buchanan, Feigenbaum, and Lederberg: *Applications of Artificial Intelligence for Organic Chemistry: The Dendral Project*
Nilsson: *Problem-Solving Methods in Artificial Intelligence*
Watson: *Timesharing System Design Concepts*
Winston: *The Psychology of Computer Vision*
Wulf, Levin, and Harbison: *Hydra/C.mmp: An Experimental Computer System*

MATRIX COMPUTATIONS AND MATHEMATICAL SOFTWARE

John R. Rice

Professor of Mathematics and Computer Science
Purdue University

McGraw-Hill Book Company

New York St. Louis San Francisco Auckland Bogotá Hamburg
Johannesburg London Madrid Mexico Montreal New Delhi
Panama Paris São Paulo Singapore Sydney Tokyo Toronto

This book was set in Times Roman.
The editors were Charles E. Stewart and Frances A. Neal;
the production supervisor was John Mancia.
New drawings were done by VIP Graphics.
R. R. Donnelley & Sons Company was printer and binder.

MATRIX COMPUTATIONS AND MATHEMATICAL SOFTWARE

1234567890 DODO 8987654321

Library of Congress Cataloging in Publication Data

Rice, John Rischard.
Matrix computations and mathematical software.

(McGraw-Hill computer science series)
Includes bibliographical references and index.
1. Matrices—Data processing. I. Title.
QA188.R52 512.9′434 80-17016
ISBN 0-07-052145-X

CONTENTS

PREFACE

This book integrates two very different but complementary subjects: matrix computations and mathematical software. Solving linear equations is a standard item of numerical computation that dates from antiquity. It is a basic building block for algorithms in science, engineering, manufacturing, and every field in which mathematical models are used. Mathematical software has become a standard tool of numerical computation because of the greatly improved reliability and dramatically reduced costs of packaged software. Matrix computation is an ideal vehicle for introducing mathematical software concepts because it is a clean, simple (yet not *too* simple) field useful for all technical areas.

In the matrix computations part of this book the object is to present the basic algorithms for the solution of linear systems and least squares (statistical regression) problems. The more difficult topics of eigenvalue and singular value computations are omitted. However, we directly confront the most difficult problem of all in numerical computation: *How do you know you have the right answers?* Again, matrix computation is an ideal vehicle for studying this central problem.

Five aspects of mathematical software are emphasized: the human interface, software performance evaluation, software parts technology, student practice in writing software, and algorithm design. These are topics from general software engineering and again matrix computation provides a good vehicle for studying them. Software performance evaluation is most easily done on well-understood, standardized problems; at least in matrix computations one knows what the software is supposed to do. But even here such evaluation is not easy since there are conflicting goals and incommensurate costs. The long history in numerical computation of attempts to develop a software parts technology led to many more failures than successes. Nevertheless, we must persevere if we are ever to escape the very high costs of handcrafted software production. Furthermore, use of software parts can give access to the proven ideas and skills of an expert even to those who are relatively unfamiliar with the particular techniques involved.

The projects in Chapter 12 provide three things for students: (1) practice in using other people's software, (2) experience in systematically evaluating realistic questions in software engineering and algorithm design, and (3) experience with a more significant programming project. A well-organized and reasoned report should be required for each project. It is suggested that if most of the projects are assigned to groups of two to four students, not only can they gain experience in working with others but this will also make a more substantial effort on the projects feasible.

The background required for this book is a basic introduction to linear algebra or matrix theory and a solid background in programming—preferably Fortran, since that is where the existing software parts are. Thus the book can be used at the junior/senior level, but it is also appropriate for more mature students at the beginning graduate level. At the higher level one expects, for example, more sophisticated analyses of the projects assigned.

The amount of material is sufficient for a one-quarter or one-semester course. The book is also suitable as a building block for a broader or more specifically focused course. The book originated from a course where part of the material was covered in 8 weeks and then the course went on to linear programming and nonlinear optimization, using a second text.

I thank Carl de Boor, Richard Hanson, Robert Lynch, and Harold Stone for valuable suggestions on the details and organization of this book. I also thank John Reid for providing the sparse matrix examples in Chapter 4. Permission for the use of excerpts in the Appendix was given by Academic Press, The Association for Computing Machinery, Prentice Hall, and the Society for Industrial and Applied Mathematics.

John R. Rice

MATRIX COMPUTATIONS AND MATHEMATICAL SOFTWARE

CHAPTER

ONE

INTRODUCTION

The reason for studying applied mathematics and computer science is primarily to learn to use tools for the analysis of mathematical models arising from the physical or organizational worlds. This book considers how to analyze (solve) models of the simplest kind, those based on linear systems of equations. Matrix computations are studied not only in the algorithmic sense but also in the software sense. Thus we not only study the algorithmic tools but also the question of how to make these tools easily available for others to use. To place this material in context we briefly outline the roles of theory, methods, and software in the solution of problems.

Mathematical models Mathematical models come in two varieties: static (or analytic) and dynamic. A *static model* is a collection of equations, formulas, definitions, tables, relationships, and data which mathematically describe a situation or phenomenon, presumably with completeness. A *dynamic model* is a collection of the same objects which describe how a situation changes from one state to the next. Simulation models are usually of this type and one hopes to apply iteratively the dynamic model starting at an initial state and observe what happens at some later state. Most, but not all, dynamic models are rather explicit in their state transition descriptions, and this approach often is easy compared to the analysis required to get the same information from a static model (if one exists).

The aim of much of mathematical and scientific analysis is to transform a given model into an *explicit* model:

$$\text{Answer} = \text{formula (data, parameters, variables)}$$

Unfortunately, this is frequently impossible and some of the simplest static models have the answer A determined implicitly. Simple examples are (B and C are data)

$$A^2 + A \cos A + 6.1 = 4.2\sqrt{B^2 + 1} - \frac{2.4}{C - 5}$$

$$\frac{dA(t)}{dt} = 2A(t) \sin t - B + \frac{\cos t}{A(t)} \qquad A(0) = 1.0$$

Note that this second static model is in fact an old mathematical equivalent of a dynamic model.

There are two things one does with such a model: First, one solves it. That is, one manipulates it and makes approximations until the answer is in an explicit form. This manipulation may make use of specific values for the data and parameters and thus does not result in an explicit mathematical model; instead one just has a particular solution. This typically happens in applying numerical methods.

The second thing one does is *optimize*. Thus some of the parameters or variables are free and they are to be adjusted to obtain the "best" value for some other variable. A simple unrealistic case is

$$\text{Salary} = H * R - R^2 + T * (R - 5) - \min(0, 1.0 - 1.5R * H)$$

and you believe (dreamer!) that you can control R (which is rate of pay). You can apply calculus to obtain an equation to *solve* for the optimum value of R:

$$d(\text{salary})/dR = H - 2R + T * R - \frac{d}{dR}[\min(0, 1 - 1.5R * H)] = 0$$

The value of R which solves this equation should be the highest or lowest salary. In this case it is easy to see that it is the highest.

We note five facts pertinent to this process: (1) The optimization of an explicit analytic model leads to another mathematical model. The second model is rarely explicit. (2) Almost *all* optimization is accomplished by setting the derivative equal to zero. The exceptions tend to be certain trivial cases or where enumeration (examination of all cases) can be applied. This fact is often hidden because the mathematical items to be differentiated are not differentiable in the usual sense (recall the "min" that appeared in the salary formula earlier). (3) Optimization tends to substantially increase the complexity of a model, and thus models which are optimized tend to be less complex than those which are merely solved. (4) Most of the tools for the analysis of static models also apply to dynamic models. (5) It is easy to obtain models whose solution or optimization is incredibly difficult. There are examples of critical national importance whose complete solution (by currently known methods) would require *all* the technical capability (human and otherwise) of the country for many years. We cite: What happens when various components in a nuclear power plant fail and cause the core to melt? What is the effect on the economy of a particular $10 billion government "pump-priming" tax cut?

The fact is that models are simplified so they become tractable. The trick is to make the simplifications so that one does not lose contact with reality. This is often difficult to do; it is often difficult even to know if contact is lost.

Tools for analysis This book is not concerned with modeling itself. We are interested in the *tools* for solving and analyzing models. The tools fall into three general categories:

Theory gives a general understanding of the model and of the problem-solving process. This is one way to obtain qualitative and intuitive understanding of what is actually going on.

Methods give something to try on the problem. A method is a set of general guidelines or steps to attempt for the solution of a problem. Sometimes (perhaps often) one can solve a problem or model without either completely understanding the method or the problem.

Software is someone else's method made complete and all wrapped up in a computer program. In the best of all possible worlds, you just push the SOLVE button and out come the answers.

CHAPTER
TWO
LINEAR ALGEBRA BACKGROUND

2.A LIST OF THINGS STUDENTS SHOULD KNOW

There are three common sources of linear algebra background for matrix computations: A mathematics junior level course entitled "Linear Algebra," an introductory course in "numerical analysis," or an introduction to "linear analysis." Linear algebra courses are usually the least satisfactory, as they emphasize the algebraic rather than analysis aspects of the subject; linear analysis courses provide the best background. Most students feel their background in linear algebra is less than that needed for a reasonable (but not deep) understanding of matrix computations. This background material is deliberately condensed here and the reader is expected to have access to some reference books.

2.A.1 Vectors

Vectors are *directed lines* (they have length, direction, and position) in N-dimensional space. They are considered to be *column vectors* unless otherwise stated, and thus

$$\mathbf{y} = \begin{pmatrix} y_1 \\ y_2 \\ \vdots \\ y_N \end{pmatrix}$$

The *transpose* is indicated by the superscript T, which changes columns into rows and vice versa. Vectors are usually expressed in terms of a *basis;* a standard set $\mathbf{b}_1, \mathbf{b}_2, \ldots, \mathbf{b}_N$ of vectors is chosen and all other vectors are expressed in terms of the basis $\mathbf{b}_i$, i = 1, 2, ..., N:

$$\mathbf{y} = y_1\mathbf{b}_1 + y_2\mathbf{b}_2 + \cdots + y_N\mathbf{b}_N$$

The coefficients y_i of this representation are the *components* of **y** and the representation is commonly written in the compact form

$$\mathbf{y} = (y_1, y_2, \ldots, y_N)^T$$

The basis vectors define a *coordinate system* and the components y_i are the coordinates of the point at the end of the vector. The standard *arithmetic* operations are (for vectors **x**, **y**, **z** and scalar a)

Addition: $\mathbf{x} + \mathbf{y} = \mathbf{y} + \mathbf{x} = (x_1 + y_1, x_2 + y_2, \ldots, x_N + y_N)^T$

$$\mathbf{x} - \mathbf{y} = -(\mathbf{y} - \mathbf{x}) \qquad (\mathbf{x} + \mathbf{y}) + \mathbf{z} = \mathbf{x} + (\mathbf{y} + \mathbf{z})$$

Multiplication by scalar: $a\mathbf{x} = (ax_1, ax_2, \ldots, ax_N)$

$$a(\mathbf{x} + \mathbf{y}) = a\mathbf{x} + a\mathbf{y}$$

A set $\mathbf{x}_1, \mathbf{x}_2, \ldots, \mathbf{x}_m$ of vectors is *linearly independent* if no *linear combination* $\sum_{i=1}^m \alpha_i\mathbf{x}_i$ of them is zero except for the zero combination; that is,

$$\sum_{i=1}^{m} \alpha_i\mathbf{x}_i = 0 \quad \text{implies} \quad \alpha_i = 0 \quad \text{for all i}$$

A set of vectors $\mathbf{x}_1, \ldots, \mathbf{x}_m$ *spans* a space if every vector in that space can be written as a linear combination of the set $\mathbf{x}_1, \ldots, \mathbf{x}_m$. The *dimension* of a vector space is the minimal number of vectors required to span the space; each basis of an N-dimensional space must have N vectors in it. N-dimensional vector spaces are often called *N-spaces* for short, and *N-vectors* are vectors in N-space.

The *dot product* or *inner product* of two vectors **x** and **y** is

$$\mathbf{x}^T\mathbf{y} = \mathbf{x} \cdot \mathbf{y} = (\mathbf{x}, \mathbf{y}) = \sum_{i=1}^{N} x_i y_i$$

where the x_i, y_i are the components of **x** and **y**. Two vectors are *orthogonal* (perpendicular) if $\mathbf{x}^T\mathbf{y} = 0$. The size of a vector may be measured by $\|x\|$ where

$$\|\mathbf{x}\|^2 = \mathbf{x}^T\mathbf{x} = \sum_i x_i^2$$

This is the usual Euclidean length in the case of three dimensions. The double bar denotes a *norm* and two other norms are frequently convenient

$$\|\mathbf{x}\|_\infty = \max_i |x_i|$$

$$\|\mathbf{x}\|_1 = \sum_i |x_i|$$

and the *Euclidean norm* is denoted by $\|\mathbf{x}\|_2 = [\sum x_i^2]^{1/2}$. The angle θ between two vectors is defined from

$$\cos\theta = \frac{\mathbf{x}^T\mathbf{y}}{\|\mathbf{x}\|_2\,\|\mathbf{y}\|_2}$$

The format for vectors must match that of matrices, so vectors are normally written as *column vectors*. That is $\mathbf{x} = (2, 1, 4, -2)^T$ is actually

$$\mathbf{x} = \begin{pmatrix} 2 \\ 1 \\ 4 \\ -2 \end{pmatrix}$$

This complicates the format of the text, so we write vectors horizontally with the transpose T unless the column format is necessary for clarity. At times we also use *row vectors*, which are vectors whose matrix format is actually horizontal, e.g., a row from a matrix.

We introduced vectors as abstract entities and then turned to a concrete representation using a basis. A basis which defines a coordinate system is essential for computation (because our computers do not manipulate vectors directly), but the abstract geometric view is often more useful for gaining insight into what is going on in a computation.

Problems for Sec. 2.A.1

1 Compute $\|\mathbf{x}\|_1$, $\|\mathbf{x}\|_2$, and $\|\mathbf{x}\|_\infty$ for each of the following vectors:
(*a*) $(1, 2, 3, 4)^T$ (*b*) $(0, -1, 0, -2, 0, 1)^T$
(*c*) $(0, 1, -2, 3, -4)^T$ (*d*) $(4.1, -3.2, 8.6, -1.5, -2.5)^T$

2 Compute the angle θ between the following pairs of vectors:
(*a*) $(1, 1, 1, 1)^T$, $(-1, 1, -1, 1)^T$ (*b*) $(1{,}0, 2, 0)^T$, $(0, 1, -1, 2)^T$
(*c*) $(1, 2, -1, 3)^T$, $(2, 4, -2, 6)^T$ (*d*) $(1.1, 2.3, -4.7, 2.0)^T$, $(3.2, 1.2, -2.3, -4.7)^T$

3 Find the Euclidean norm of $(2, -1, 4)$ and the dot product of the vectors $(2, -3, 4, 1)^T$ and $(4, -3, 2)^T$.

4 Determine if the vector $(6, 1, -6, 2)^T$ is in the space spanned by the vectors $(1, 1, -1, 1)^T$, $(-1, 0, 1, 1)^T$, and $(1, -1, -1, 0)^T$. What is the dimension of the space spanned by these three vectors?

5 Do the vectors

$$\mathbf{b}_1 = (1, 0, 0, -1)^T \qquad \mathbf{b}_2 = (0, -1, 1, 0)^T$$
$$\mathbf{b}_3 = (0, 0, -1, 1)^T \qquad \mathbf{b}_4 = (1, 1, 0, 0)^T$$

form a basis for vectors of dimension 4?

6 Prove that the three vectors

$$\mathbf{b}_1 = (1, 2, 3, 4)^T \qquad \mathbf{b}_2 = (2, 1, 0, 4)^T \qquad \mathbf{b}_3 = (0, 1, 1, 4)^T$$

are linearly independent. Do they form a basis of the indicated space?

7 Suppose that $\mathbf{x}_1, \mathbf{x}_2, \ldots, \mathbf{x}_m$ are linearly independent, but $\mathbf{x}_1, \mathbf{x}_2, \ldots, \mathbf{x}_m, \mathbf{x}_{m+1}$ are not. Show that $\mathbf{x}_{m+1}$ is a linear combination of $\mathbf{x}_1, \mathbf{x}_2, \ldots, \mathbf{x}_m$.

8 Let $\mathbf{x}_1 = (1, 2, 1)$, $\mathbf{x}_2 = (1, 2, 3)$, $\mathbf{x}_3 = (3, 6, 5)$. Show that these vectors are linearly dependent but that they span a two-dimensional space. Find a basis for this space.

9 For any two vectors **x** and **y** and any of the three norms (1, 2, and ∞) show that we have

$$\big|\|\mathbf{x}\| - \|\mathbf{y}\|\big| \le \|\mathbf{x} - \mathbf{y}\|$$

This inequality holds for all vector norms.

10 For two nonzero vectors **x** and **y** show that $\|\mathbf{x} + \mathbf{y}\|_2 = \|\mathbf{x}\|_2 + \|\mathbf{y}\|_2$ if and only if $\mathbf{y} = a\mathbf{x}$ for some nonnegative constant a.

11 For any two n-vectors **x** and **y** show that $\|\mathbf{x} + \mathbf{y}\| \le \|\mathbf{x}\| + \|\mathbf{y}\|$ for any one of the three norms (1, 2, and ∞). *Hint:* Do 2-vectors first and then use induction for the 1 and ∞ norms.

2.A.2 Matrices

The abstract entities that lead to matrices are *linear mappings*, *transformations*, or *functions* between vectors. Once coordinates are introduced for the vectors, then these linear functions can be concretely represented by a two-dimensional array of numbers, a *matrix*:

$$A = \begin{pmatrix} 1 & 6 & -2 \\ 4 & 17 & -12 \\ 0 & 42 & 6.1 \end{pmatrix} = (a_{ij})$$

If **y** is a linear function of **x**, then each component y_k of **y** is a linear function of the components x_j of **x**. Thus we have for each k that

$$y_k = a_{k1}x_1 + a_{k2}x_2 + \cdots + a_{kN}x_N$$

The coefficients are collected into the matrix A, which then represents the linear function (mapping, transformation, or relationship) between **x** and **y**. The linear function is denoted by A**x**.

The rules for manipulating matrices are those required by the linear mappings. Thus A + B is to be the representation of the sum of the two linear functions represented by A and B. One has $A + B = C$ where $c_{ij} = a_{ij} + b_{ij}$. The *product* AB represents the effect of applying the mapping B, then applying the mapping A. The following calculation shows that

$$AB = C$$

where $c_{ij} = \sum_k a_{ik}b_{kj}$. We have $\mathbf{y} = A\mathbf{x}$, $\mathbf{z} = B\mathbf{y}$ and want to determine C so that $\mathbf{z} = C\mathbf{x}$. We express the relationship in terms of components:

$$y_k = \sum_{j=1}^{N} a_{kj}x_j \qquad z_i = \sum_{k=1}^{N} b_{ik}y_k$$

Thus

$$z_i = \sum_{k=1}^{N} b_{ik}\left(\sum_{j=1}^{N} a_{kj}x_j\right) = \sum_{j=1}^{N}\left(\sum_{k=1}^{N} b_{ik}a_{kj}\right)x_j$$

and so c_{ij} is given by the above formula. The i, jth element of C is the dot product of the ith row of A with the jth column of B. We have the *arithmetic* rules

$$A + B = B + A$$

$$AB \ne BA \qquad \text{except in special cases}$$

The transpose A^T of A is obtained by reflecting A about its *diagonal* (the a_{ii} elements). That is, $a_{ij}^T = a_{ji}$. The *identity* matrix is all zeros except for 1s on the diagonal:

$$I = \begin{pmatrix} 1 & 0 & 0 \\ 0 & 1 & 0 \\ 0 & 0 & 1 \end{pmatrix}$$

An identity matrix is necessarily *square* (has the same number of rows and columns). One sees that $IA = AI = A$. The *inverse* A^{-1} of A is a matrix so that $A^{-1}A = I$. Not all matrices have an inverse and, indeed, one can have $AB = 0$ without either A or B being the zero matrix:

$$\begin{pmatrix} 1 & 1 \\ 1 & 1 \end{pmatrix} \begin{pmatrix} 1 & 1 \\ -1 & -1 \end{pmatrix} = \begin{pmatrix} 0 & 0 \\ 0 & 0 \end{pmatrix}$$

If A has an inverse, then we say A is *nonsingular*. We have the following equivalent statements:

A is nonsingular

A^{-1} exists

The columns of A are linearly independent

The rows of A are linearly independent

$\mathbf{Ax} = 0$ implies that $\mathbf{x} = 0$

The *linear equations* problem is given A and b, find the vector $\mathbf{x}$ so that $\mathbf{Ax} = \mathrm{b}$. If A is nonsingular (this makes A square), then this problem always has a unique solution for each $\mathbf{b}$. If A has more rows than columns (there are more equations than variables) then the problem is usually unsolvable, and if A has more columns than rows there are usually infinitely many solutions. The oldest and standard method for solving this problem is by *Gauss elimination* (please forget *Cramer's rule* as it is terribly inefficient). A system of equations is *homogeneous* if the right side is zero, e.g., $\mathbf{Ax} = 0$.

Example 2.1: Gauss elimination for a 3 × 3 system The original system

$$\begin{aligned} 2x_1 + 2x_2 + 4x_3 &= 5 \\ 6x_1 - x_2 + x_3 &= 7 \\ 4x_1 - 10x_2 - 12x_3 &= -4 \end{aligned}$$

becomes $2x_1 + 2x_2 + 4x_3 = 5$

$-7x_2 - 11x_3 = -8$ Subtract 3 times row 1 from row 2

$-14x_2 - 20x_3 = -14$ Subtract 2 times row 1 from row 3

which becomes

$$\begin{aligned} 2x_1 + 2x_2 + \ 4x_3 &= 5 \\ -7x_2 - 11x_3 &= -8 \\ 2x_3 &= 2 \qquad \text{Subtract 2 times row 2 from row 3} \end{aligned}$$

The matrix of this system of equations is *upper triangular* (*lower triangular* means all elements above the diagonal are zero). This system can be solved quickly by *back substitution:*

$$x_3 = \tfrac{2}{2} = 1$$

$$-7x_2 = -8 + 11x_3 = 3 \qquad \text{so } x_2 = -\tfrac{3}{7}$$

$$2x_1 = 5 - 2x_2 - 4x_3 = \tfrac{13}{7} \qquad \text{so } x_1 = \tfrac{13}{14}$$

The analogous process applied to a lower triangular system is called *forward substitution.*

The matrix U is *orthogonal* if its columns $\mathbf{u}_1, \mathbf{u}_2, \ldots, \mathbf{u}_N$ are orthogonal and of length 1. That is

$$\mathbf{u}_i^T\mathbf{u}_j = 0 \qquad \text{if } i \neq j \qquad \text{and} \qquad \mathbf{u}_i^T\mathbf{u}_i = 1$$

Such matrices lead to an easy solution of $U\mathbf{x} = \mathbf{b}$ because U^TU is the identity since the rows of U^T are columns of U. If $U\mathbf{x} = \mathbf{b}$, then $U^TU\mathbf{x} = \mathbf{x} = U^T\mathbf{b}$ and $\mathbf{x}$ is found immediately. Thus if we can find a way to transform a matrix A into an orthogonal matrix, we can use this method to solve $A\mathbf{x} = \mathbf{b}$.

A matrix is a *permutation matrix* if each element is a 0 or 1 and there is exactly one 1 per row or column; for example:

$$\begin{pmatrix} 0 & 1 & 0 & 0 \\ 1 & 0 & 0 & 0 \\ 0 & 0 & 1 & 0 \\ 0 & 0 & 0 & 1 \end{pmatrix} \qquad \begin{pmatrix} 1 & 0 & 0 \\ 0 & 0 & 1 \\ 0 & 1 & 0 \end{pmatrix}$$

Multiplication by a permutation matrix, on the left or right, has the effect of permuting or interchanging the rows or columns of the matrix (see Probs. 5 and 6 below). This property gives them their name and they are useful in formulas to indicate interchanges of rows and columns; they are rarely used in actual calculations.

On a few occasions we refer to the *eigenvalues* of the matrix A. This is a number λ such that $A\mathbf{x} = \lambda\mathbf{x}$ for some nonzero vector $\mathbf{x}$; the vector $\mathbf{x}$ is called an *eigenvector*. The effect of the linear mapping on an eigenvector is simply to multiply it by the constant λ, the eigenvalue. An $N \times N$ matrix has N eigenvalues and normally, but not always, has N eigenvectors. The *spectral radius* $\rho(A)$ of A is the largest of the absolute values of the eigenvalues of A. The spectral radius plays a fundamental role in the convergence of iterations involving matrices.

There are various ways to measure the size or *norm of a matrix*. We use only one, as follows:

$$\|A\| = \max_{\|x\|=1} \|Ax\|$$

The norm is the maximum amount a vector of length 1 is magnified by applying A. This norm is defined in terms of a vector norm, and different vector norms give different norms for A. This norm can be expressed explicitly for the three vector norms introduced earlier. The results are

$$\|A\|_1 = \max_{\|x\|_1=1} \|Ax\|_1 = \max_j \sum_{i=1}^{N} |a_{ij}| = \textit{column-sum norm}$$

$$\|A\|_2 = \max_{\|x\|_2=1} \|Ax\|_2 = \sqrt{\text{max eigenvalue of } A^TA}$$

$$\|A\|_\infty = \max_{\|x\|_\infty=1} \|Ax\|_\infty = \max_i \sum_{j=1}^{N} |a_{ij}| = \textit{row-sum norm}$$

The column-sum and row-sum norms are widely used because they are easy to calculate. It is easy to show that $\rho(A) \le \|A\|$ for any norm, so the column-sum norm and row-sum norms provide simple estimates of the spectral radius of a matrix.

The interest in matrices arises from their relationship to linear functions of several variables (such functions are natural choices for simple mathematical models of things involving several variables). Such *multivariate linear functions* "exist" as abstract functions, just as vectors "exist" as abstract entities. For vectors we obtained something we can manipulate and calculate with by introducing coordinate systems; the same holds for multivariate linear functions, as illustrated in Fig. 2.1. If we express **x** and **y** in terms of some coordinate system, then there should be a formula to get the coordinate $(y_1, y_2, \ldots, y_N)^T$ from those of $\mathbf{x} = (x_1, x_2, \ldots, x_N)^T$. That formula involves a double array of numbers, say $A = (a_{ij})$ and, in fact,

$$\mathbf{y} = A\mathbf{x}$$

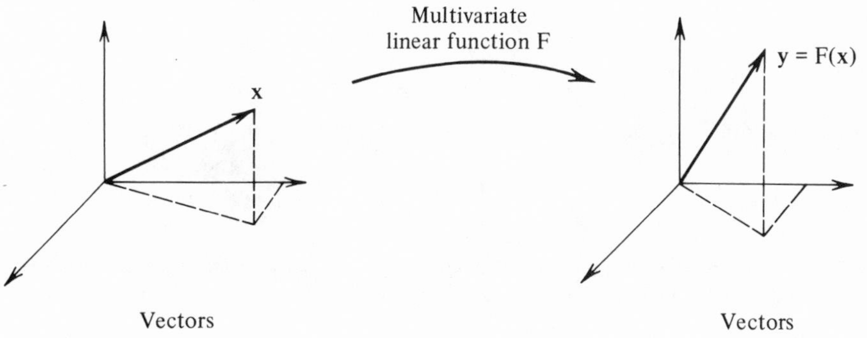

Figure 2.1 Diagram of the effect of a multivariate linear function.

Thus, *a matrix is a concrete representation of a multivariate linear function derived from introducing coordinate systems for the vectors.* Different choices of coordinate systems give different matrix representations for the same function.

If $B = C^{-1}AC$, then A and B are *similar matrices;* this formula expresses the effect of changing coordinate systems (or basis vectors). Thus *all* properties of a matrix A which are properties of the underlying linear function F are unchanged by the *similarity transformation* $B = C^{-1}AC$. Such properties include eigenvalues and eigenvectors.

As an example of the usefulness of eigenvalues and eigenvectors, consider what happens when the eigenvectors are chosen as basis vectors (assuming that there are enough of them). Then the matrix representation of the multivariate linear function is just a diagonal matrix! Further, the components of $A\mathbf{x}$ are simply those of $\mathbf{x}$ multiplied by the corresponding eigenvalue. Thus matrix analysis and computations are dramatically simplified if one can obtain the eigenvectors of A and use them as a basis.

Problems for Sec. 2.A.2

1 Show that $A = \begin{pmatrix} 1 & 2 \\ 2 & 4 \end{pmatrix}$ is singular.

2 Find a nonzero solution to the system

$$x_1 - 2x_2 + x_3 = 0$$

$$x_1 + x_2 - 2x_3 = 0$$

3 Let

$$A = \begin{pmatrix} 1 & 2 & 3 \\ 0 & -1 & 2 \\ 2 & 0 & 2 \end{pmatrix} \qquad B = \begin{pmatrix} 1 & 1 & 2 \\ -1 & 1 & -1 \\ 1 & 0 & 2 \end{pmatrix} \qquad C = \begin{pmatrix} 1 & 0 & 1 \\ 0 & 1 & 2 \\ 2 & 0 & 1 \end{pmatrix}$$

(*a*) Compute AB and BA and show that $AB \neq BA$.
(*b*) Find $(A + B) + C$ and $A + (B + C)$.
(*c*) Show that $(AB)C = A(BC)$.
(*d*) Show that $(AB)^T = B^T A^T$.

4 Show that the matrix A is singular:

$$A = \begin{pmatrix} 3 & 1 & 0 \\ 2 & -1 & -1 \\ 4 & 3 & 1 \end{pmatrix}$$

5 For A of Prob. 4, compute PA and AP where P is the permutation matrix

$$\begin{pmatrix} 0 & 1 & 0 \\ 1 & 0 & 0 \\ 0 & 0 & 1 \end{pmatrix}$$

6 Find the permutation matrix P_1, so that the second and fourth columns of AP_1 are interchanged for a 4×4 matrix A. Find P_2 so that the first and third rows of P_2 are interchanged for A.

7 Write the following system of linear equations in matrix form $Ax = \mathbf{b}$ and identify the matrix A and right side vector $\mathbf{b}$:

$$2x_1 + x_2 - 3x_3 + 4x_4 - 2 = 0$$
$$x_1 + x_2 - x_3 = 1$$
$$2x_2 + x_4 - 7x_3 = 8$$
$$1 + x_1 + x_2 + x_3 + x_4 = 5$$

8 Show that the matrix norm defined here can also be calculated as

$$\|A\| = \max_{\|x\| \neq 0} \frac{\|Ax\|}{\|x\|}$$

9 An $N \times 1$ matrix is a column vector. Show that the transpose of a column vector is a row vector.

10 Suppose that B is diagonal. Show that BA is found by multiplying the first row of A by b_{11}, the second row by b_{22}, etc. How is AB found?

11 Test the following systems of equations for *consistency* (the existence of at least one solution).

(*a*)
$$x + y + 2z + w = 5$$
$$2x + 3y - z - 2w = 2$$
$$4x + 5y + 3z = 7$$

(*b*)
$$x + y + z + w = 0$$
$$x + 3y + 2z + 4w = 0$$
$$2x + z - w = 0$$

12 Show that

$$A = \begin{pmatrix} 1 & 1 \\ 0 & 2 \end{pmatrix}$$

is nonsingular by finding its inverse.

13 Compute the inverses of

$$A = \begin{pmatrix} 1 & 1 \\ 0 & 1 \end{pmatrix} \qquad B = \begin{pmatrix} 1 & 0 \\ 1 & 1 \end{pmatrix}$$

and AB. Show that $A^{-1}B^{-1}$ is not $(AB)^{-1}$ but $B^{-1}A^{-1}$ is $(AB)^{-1}$. Explain this from the definition of the product of matrices representing the composition of two linear functions.

14 Find one solution of

$$x_1 + 2x_2 = 3$$
$$2x_1 + 4x_2 = 6$$

and then find a solution of the corresponding homogeneous system

$$x_1 + 2x_2 = 0$$
$$2x_1 + 4x_2 = 0$$

Show that any multiple of the solution of the homogeneous system can be added to the first solution to obtain yet another solution of the first system.

15 Write a program which carries out matrix addition and/or multiplication. The input is two square matrices A and B, their order is N, and there is a mode switch MODE with MODE = 1 for addition, MODE = 2 for multiplication. The output is to be the matrix C = A + B or C = AB.

16 Calculate the number of additions and multiplications necessary to multiply an $N \times N$ matrix by an N-vector, to multiply two $N \times N$ matrices.

17 Compute $\|A\|_1$ and $\|A\|_\infty$ for the matrix

$$A = \begin{pmatrix} 1 & 0 & 2 & -1 \\ 6 & -4 & 3 & 0 \\ 4 & 0 & -4 & 2 \\ 1 & 5 & 1 & 6 \end{pmatrix}$$

18 Find a 3×3 matrix $A \neq 0$ and a vector $\mathbf{x} \neq 0$ so that $A\mathbf{x} = 0$.

19 Let $A = I - 2\mathbf{x}\mathbf{x}^T$, where $\mathbf{x}$ is a column vector. Show that A is orthogonal and $A^2 = I$.

20 Show for a nonsingular matrix A that $\mathbf{x}^T A^T A \mathbf{x} = 0$ if and only if $\mathbf{x}^T \mathbf{x} = 0$.

21 Let $\mathbf{x}$ be a row vector. Show that $\mathbf{x}\mathbf{x}^T = \mathbf{x} * \mathbf{x} = (\|\mathbf{x}\|_2)^2$. What is $\mathbf{x}^T\mathbf{x}$?

22 Suppose for every vector $\mathbf{x}$ we define the function F as follows:

(*a*) $$F(\mathbf{x}) = (x_3, x_1)^T$$

(*b*) $$F(\mathbf{x}) = (x_1 + x_2, 0, x_3)^T$$

(*c*) $$F(\mathbf{x}) = (x_2, 0, x_1 - x_2, x_3, 0)^T$$

Show that each of these definitions makes F a linear function.

23 Find the matrix that represents each of the linear functions defined in Prob. 22.

24 Consider

$$A = \begin{pmatrix} \cos\theta & -\sin\theta \\ \sin\theta & \cos\theta \end{pmatrix}$$

Give a geometric interpretation of the function represented by A. Show that A is orthogonal.

25 Geometrically describe the effects of the linear functions represented by the following matrices:

(*a*) $\begin{pmatrix} \cos\theta & 0 & \sin\theta \\ 0 & 1 & 0 \\ -\sin\theta & 0 & \cos\theta \end{pmatrix}$ (*b*) $\begin{pmatrix} 5 & 0 & 0 \\ 0 & 5 & 0 \\ 0 & 0 & 5 \end{pmatrix}$

(*c*) $\begin{pmatrix} 1 & 0 & 0 \\ 0 & 0 & 0 \\ 0 & 0 & 1 \end{pmatrix}$ (*d*) $\begin{pmatrix} -1 & 0 & 0 \\ 0 & 1 & 0 \\ 0 & 0 & -1 \end{pmatrix}$

26 Suppose A is orthogonal and $A\mathbf{x} = \lambda\mathbf{x}$ where $\mathbf{x} \neq 0$. Show $|\lambda| = 1$.

27 Suppose $\mathbf{x}$ has components $(x_1, x_2)^T$ for the standard Euclidean coordinate system in the plane [i.e., basis vectors are $(1, 0)^T$ and $(0, 1)^T$]. What are the components of $\mathbf{x}$ in terms of the basis $\mathbf{b}_1 = (1, 1)^T$, $\mathbf{b}_2 = (1, -1)^T$? Give a geometric interpretation of the relationship between the coordinate system defined by $\mathbf{b}_1$ and $\mathbf{b}_2$ and the standard coordinate system.

28 Show that the matrices A and B are equal if and only if $A\mathbf{x} = B\mathbf{x}$ for all vectors $\mathbf{x}$.

29 Suppose that the matrix A has at most one linearly independent column vector. Show that A then has only one linearly independent row vector. Further show that A can be written as $\mathbf{x}\mathbf{y}^T$ for some column vectors $\mathbf{x}$ and $\mathbf{y}$.

30 For the matrix norm defined in this chapter show that $\|AB\| \leq \|A\| \, \|B\|$. This relationship is not true for all matrix norms.

31 Prove that the formula given for the row-sum norm $\|A\|_\infty$ is correct.

32 Prove that the formula given for the column-sum norm $\|A\|_1$ is correct.

33 For an N × N matrix A show that

$$\max_{i,j} |a_{i,j}| \le \|A\| \le N \max_{i,j} |a_{i,j}|$$

34 Consider

$$A = \begin{pmatrix} 6 & 13 & -17 \\ 13 & 29 & -38 \\ -17 & -38 & 50 \end{pmatrix} \qquad A^{-1} = \begin{pmatrix} 6 & -4 & -1 \\ -4 & 11 & 7 \\ -1 & 7 & 5 \end{pmatrix}$$

(*a*) Geometrically describe the set $S = \{A\mathbf{x} \mid \|\mathbf{x}\| = 1\}$ which is the image of the unit sphere under the linear mapping represented by A.

(*b*) What are $\|A\|_\infty$, $\|A^{-1}\|_\infty$, $\|A\|_1$, and $\|A^{-1}\|_1$?

35 Suppose each determinant in *Cramer's rule* were evaluated as the sum of $(n-1)!$ products of n factors each. Estimate how many multiplications are then required to solve $A\mathbf{x} = \mathbf{b}$ for $n = 10$, 100, and 1000. How much computer time would this take if each multiplication (and associated other operations) takes 1 microsecond (μs)?

36 Redo Prob. 35 where each determinant is evaluated by a process that requires $n^3/3$ multiplications.

37 Show that if the rows of A are linearly independent and so are the columns, then A is a square, nonsingular matrix.

38 Suppose that A represents the linear function F [i.e., $\mathbf{y} = F(\mathbf{x})$ can be calculated by $\mathbf{y} = A\mathbf{x}$]. Suppose that changes of coordinates are made in each of the two vector spaces so that the coordinates $(w_1, w_2, \ldots, w_n)^T$ of $\mathbf{x}$ in the new coordinate system are related to $(x_1, x_2, \ldots, x_n)^T$ by $\mathbf{w} = B\mathbf{x}$ and similarly the new coordinates $(z_1, z_2, \ldots, z_m)^T$ of $\mathbf{y}$ are calculated by $\mathbf{z} = C\mathbf{y}$. Show that CAB^{-1} is the matrix which represents F in the two new coordinate systems.

39 Let D be a diagonal matrix. Show that DA = AD for *all* matrices A if and only if D = aI for some constant a.

40 Define e^A by $I + A + A^2/2! + A^3/3! + A^4/4! + \cdots$. Prove the following properties about this *matrix exponential function:*

(*a*) $$\|e^A\|_\infty \le e^{\|A\|_\infty}$$

(*b*) $$e^{A+B} = e^A e^B \qquad \text{if and only if } AB = BA$$

(*c*) $$e^A e^{-A} = I$$

(*d*) $$B = e^{At} \qquad \text{satisfies } \frac{dB}{dt} = AB$$

CHAPTER

THREE

TYPES AND SOURCES OF MATRIX COMPUTATIONAL PROBLEMS

3.A LINEAR SYSTEMS OF EQUATIONS, $\mathbf{Ax} = \mathbf{b}$

3.A.1 Models of Physical Systems

There are numerous physical systems which naturally lead to linear equations. Consider, for example, the balance of forces on a structure (bridge, building, aircraft frame) as illustrated in Fig. 3.1. There are forces from the weight of the bridge and truck which are balanced by the forces at the ends of the bridge. These forces are propagated along the iron beams, and at every node they must balance out to zero (otherwise the bridge would begin moving). If we break the forces into horizontal ($\mathbf{x}$) and vertical ($\mathbf{y}$) components, then at each node we have two equations:

$$\text{Sum } \mathbf{x} \text{ forces} = 0$$

$$\text{Sum } \mathbf{y} \text{ forces} = 0$$

These equations are assembled into one large linear system which one can solve to find the unknown forces in the various beams. Some of the forces are known (weights of beams and truck), which give terms to be moved to the right-hand side so the system is not homogeneous.

Similarly, an electrical network (Fig. 3.2) satisfies Kirchhoff's laws for the balance of currents at the nodes and voltages around the loops. These formulas are linear in the values of the resistances and power sources and lead to a system of linear equations for all the unknown values.

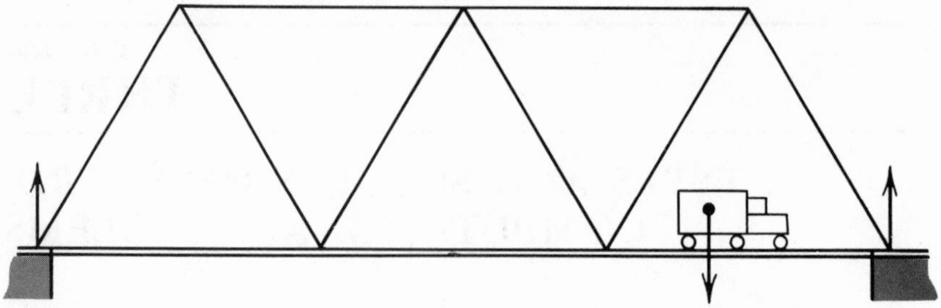

Figure 3.1

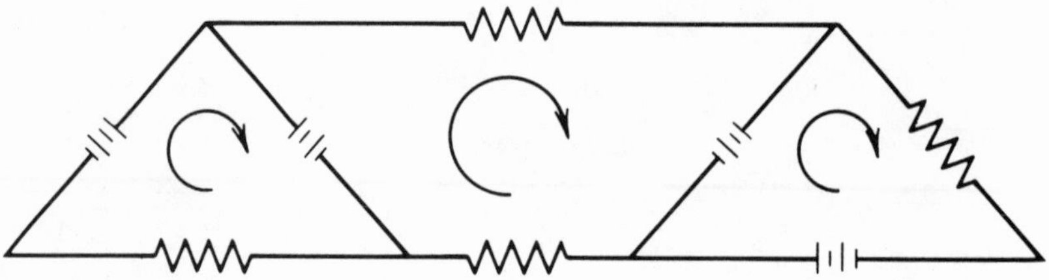

Figure 3.2

The three steps in solving a problem of this type are

1. Formulate the *mathematical model* of the system (building structure, electrical network, etc.). One explicitly computes the a_{ij} based on physical principles of the system.
2. Compute the *forcing function* (external forces on the structure, external loads and inputs to the network). One explicitly computes the b_j based on an analysis of the particular external circumstances of the situation.
3. Solve the linear system $\mathbf{Ax} = \mathbf{b}$ to obtain the values of the solution $\mathbf{x}$.

The first two of these steps depend on knowledge of the physical situation (structural engineering, physics, etc.). The third step uses a numerical computation algorithm; one objective of mathematical software is to provide a reliable, efficient tool for this part of the computation.

Many physical systems are modeled by differential equations, e.g.,

$$\frac{d^2y}{dx^2} + \cos(x)y = \log(x+4) \qquad \begin{matrix} y(0) = 0 \\ y(1) = 1 \end{matrix}$$

which cannot be solved by formulas.The finite difference approach is to discretize the interval [0, 1] as shown here:

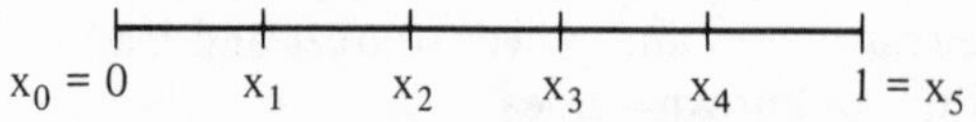

Figure 3.3

and replace the derivative by a simple difference, e.g.,

$$\left.\frac{d^2y}{dx^2}\right|_{x=x3} = \frac{y(x_2) - 2y(x_3) + y(x_4)}{(0.2)^2} \qquad (0.2 = \tfrac{1}{5} = x_4 - x_3)$$

The approximating difference equation at x_3 is then

$$\frac{y(x_2) - 2y(x_3) + y(x_4)}{(0.2)^2} + \cos(x_3)y(x_3) = \log(x_3 + 4)$$

There is one such equation at each discretization point which leads to a linear system for approximate values of the solution of the differential equation. If one multiplies each equation by $(0.2)^2 = 0.04$, then the linear system of four equations is [with $y_i = y(x_i)$]

$$\begin{bmatrix} -2 + 0.04\cos(x_1) & 1 & 0 & 0 \\ 1 & -2 + 0.04\cos(x_2) & 1 & 0 \\ 0 & 1 & -2 + 0.04\cos(x_3) & 1 \\ 0 & 0 & 1 & -2 + 0.04\cos(x_4) \end{bmatrix} \begin{bmatrix} y_1 \\ y_2 \\ y_3 \\ y_4 \end{bmatrix} = \begin{bmatrix} 0 + 0.04\log(x_1 + 4) \\ 0.04\log(x_2 + 4) \\ 0.04\log(x_3 + 4) \\ 1 + 0.04\log(x_4 + 4) \end{bmatrix}$$

The boundary conditions $y_0 = 0$ and $y_5 = 1$ were used to eliminate these variables; they produced terms for the right-hand side of the first and last equations.

As in the previous situation, we see there is an analysis stage (deriving the differential equation and then finding an approximating difference equation) which may be quite complicated. Then there is the numerical computation algorithm to solve **Ax** = **b**, which might be done with a standard piece of mathematical software.

If the differential equation is not linear, then a nonlinear system of equations results. Suppose, for example, that the physical situation led to the differential equation model

$$\frac{d^2y}{dx^2} + \cos(x)y^2 = \log(x + 4).$$

A simple minded but sometimes effective strategy for such a problem is as follows:

Guess at $y(x)$ and call this $y^0(x)$
For $i = 1, 2, \ldots,$ limit do
    Solve $d^2y/dx^2 + \cos(x)y^{i-1}y = \log(x + 4)$ for $y(x)$ and set $y^i(x) = y(x)$
    If max $|y^i(x) - y^{i-1}(x)|$ is sufficiently small, exit loop
End loop

With this approach the procedure outlined for the linear differential equation becomes the inner loop of the computation. It is clear that certain steps can be taken to make the inner loop solution more efficient than just repeating the linear problem solution over and over. Two points are noteworthy here:

1. A standard tool like "solve $Ax = \mathbf{b}$" can become part of the inner loop of a large calculation, and thus it is essential that it be done efficiently.
2. The same standard tool can become "buried" in relation to the total problem solution, and it is essential that this tool be reliable. It could be buried so deep that the programmer is not really aware that the tool is being used and an error in it would be very difficult to diagnose.

3.A.2 Least-Squares Fitting or Regression

Suppose you have 100 observations (data points) $d(t_k)$ which are assumed to be modeled by the formula

$$d(t) = c_1 g_1(t) + c_2 g_2(t) + \cdots + c_7 g_7(t)$$

where the $g_j(t)$ are known functions of the variable t. The coefficients or parameters $c_1, c_2, \ldots, c_7$ are to be determined so the model fits the data. So, theoretically, one has

$$d(t_k) = \sum_{j=1}^{7} c_j g_j(t_k) \qquad \text{for } k = 1, 2, \ldots, 100$$

but, because of observation errors or a bad assumption or both, exact equality in these 100 equations does not hold for any choice of the seven c_j. One can, however, determine the c_j so the sum $\sum_{k=1}^{100} r_k^2$ of the squares of the residuals

$$r_k = d(t_k) - \sum_{j=1}^{7} c_j g_j(t_k)$$

is a minimum. That is, the coefficients c_j are optimized to minimize the least-squares error. Applying calculus to the problem: Find c_j so that

$$E(c_1, c_2, \ldots, c_7) = \sum_{k=1}^{100} r_k^2$$

is a minimum by setting

$$\frac{\partial E}{\partial c_i} = 0 \qquad i = 1, 2, \ldots, 7$$

We get

$$\sum_{k=1}^{100} \left[d(t_k) - \sum_{j=1}^{7} c_j g_j(t_k) \right] g_i(t_k) = 0 \qquad i = 1, 2, \ldots, 7$$

or, by rewriting

$$\sum_{j=1}^{7} c_j \sum_{k=1}^{100} g_j(t_k)g_i(t_k) = \sum_{k=1}^{100} d(t_k)g_i(t_k) \qquad i = 1, 2, \ldots, 7$$

This gives us a system of equations

$$\mathrm{G}\mathbf{c} = \mathbf{d}$$

where G is the matrix with elements

$$g_{ij} = \sum_{k=1}^{100} g_i(t_k)g_j(t_k)$$

d is the vector with components

$$d_i = \sum_{k=1}^{100} d(t_k)g_i(t_k)$$

and **c** is the vector of unknown coefficients. This is the system of *normal equations*.

3.A.3 Organizational Models

Two of the physical systems (bridges and electrical networks) are organizations of physical quantities and many other organizations also lead to linear models. In economics, for example, payment of a bill results in a simple increase in one person's money and reduction in another's. Money is "created" in various ways (finding a gold mine, painting a picture, building a desk from lumber) and one can visualize writing down the equations for the balance of the flow of money (or equivalent forms of wealth) for an economic unit (village, city, country). While there are many uncertainties in actually doing this, economists have made many large mathematical models of such economic operations. These often are large linear systems of equations in the steady-state case (that is, when there are no changes due to the passage of time).

A similar situation exists for the inventory balance of an automobile company. The company has cars at factories, at warehouses, in transit, and at retail dealers. There are simple linear relationships which model the changes in this inventory. While one does not want to "solve for the inventory," there are various manipulations that one may want to perform on this linear model. For example, the company may want to *minimize* its storage costs and try to find the distribution of the car inventory that does this. The obvious solution is to put everything at the cheapest place, but, if that place turns out to be the factory, then there would be no cars sold. So certain *constraints* must be placed on the minimization. This is an example of a problem in *linear programming*, a topic that is closely related to matrix computation.

The formulation, analysis, and manipulation of linear systems of equations are ingredients in all such problems.

3.B MATRIX EQUATIONS, AX = B

A matrix equation AX = B is really just a multiple set of linear systems:

$$A\mathbf{x}_1 = \mathbf{b}_1,\ A\mathbf{x}_2 = \mathbf{b}_2,\ \ldots,\ A\mathbf{x}_m = \mathbf{b}_m$$

for different solution vectors $\mathbf{x}_i$ and right-hand sides $\mathbf{b}_i$. Matrix equations arise frequently because A of the equation $A\mathbf{x} = \mathbf{b}$ usually represents the model (bridge structure, network layout, regression model) and **b** represents the forcing function or external things (loads on the bridge, loads on the electrical network, experimental data observations). Thus for a fixed model (A), one may want to consider many different forcing terms (**b**'s). The significance of this is that, if one has to solve a linear system with one A matrix and many right-hand sides, then it may be very worthwhile to manipulate the matrix A into a particularly simple form so as to make the solution of the many linear systems very easy.

The steps in the solution of such a problem might be:

1. Compute the matrix A which models the system.
2*a*. Compute the forcing function $\mathbf{b}_1$.
3*a*. Solve the linear system $A\mathbf{x}_1 = \mathbf{b}_1$.
2*b*. Compute the forcing function $\mathbf{b}_2$.
3*b*. Solve the linear system $A\mathbf{x}_2 = \mathbf{b}_2$.
Etc.

This can be reorganized as follows:

1. Compute the matrix A which models the system.
2. Compute the forcing functions $\mathbf{b}_1, \mathbf{b}_2, \ldots$ and form the matrix B.
3. Solve the matrix equation AX = B where X has columns $\mathbf{x}_1, \mathbf{x}_2, \ldots$.

The advantage of the latter approach is that at step 3 one knows that a larger computation is to be made and one can arrange to do it efficiently. The first approach can also be done as efficiently, but it requires more care on the part of the programmer to avoid repeating work at step 3*b* which has already been done at step 3*a*. Good matrix computation software will provide a program to solve AX = B efficiently without forcing the programmer to consider just how it is done.

3.C MATRIX INVERSES, A^{-1}

In mathematical and engineering texts one very frequently sees formulas like

$$\mathbf{x} = A^{-1}\mathbf{b} \qquad \mathbf{y} = B^{-1}(I + 2A)\mathbf{b} \qquad \mathbf{z} = B^{-1}(2A + I)(C^{-1} + A)\mathbf{b}$$

which naturally suggests that you would invert some matrices to compute **x**, **y**, or **z**. *This is a very inefficient approach; one almost never needs to invert matrices to compute other things.* In Chap. 5 it is shown that computing an inverse matrix requires about three times as much computation and perhaps twice as much storage as solving a linear system of equations. In particular, any matrix expression applied to a vector can be evaluated efficiently without inverting any matrices, no matter how many inverse matrices there are in the expression. In most cases, actually inverting the matrices is a *computational waste*.

Suppose you want to solve AX = B; you might say "Well, A^{-1} is expensive to compute, but once I have it, then I can find all the $\mathbf{x}_i$ quickly by $\mathbf{x}_i = A^{-1}\mathbf{b}_i$." Even this reasoning is wrong because there is something else (the LU factorization of A) which is much cheaper to compute than A^{-1} and which allows you to find each $\mathbf{x}_i$ from the $\mathbf{b}_i$ just as fast as multiplying $\mathbf{b}_i$ by A^{-1}.

There are, however, certain problems in statistics and engineering where the object of the computation is to see the inverse matrix and not just to use it to find something else. In these problems the elements of A^{-1} have meaning such as being "influence coefficients" that show how forcing terms affect the model. If you are not actually examining the elements of an inverse matrix, then it is very unlikely that you should be computing the inverse.

3.D DETERMINANTS, det (A)

Determinants serve no useful purpose in linear algebra computation. Historically, they were introduced into the mathematical and scientific terminology in the last century, and they are now a standard part of the educational system and language. There are only a very few places where determinants are needed in the theory of matrix computations and it is rare that one needs to compute the actual value of a determiminant. Cramer's rule, for example, is grossly inefficient for solving linear systems of equations (see Prob. 35 of Chap. 2). For example, one commonly hears "I can't solve the system because the determinant is zero." For any sensible way to compute determinants, one discovers whether the system can be solved or not *before* one knows the value of the determinant. The size of the determinant itself has no bearing on the validity of a computation. You may be perfectly safe when det (A) = 10^{-48} and you may obtain complete garbage when det (A) = 6.2. To see this, just consider multiplying each of the equations in a 20 × 20 system by a factor of 100. This increases the determinant by a factor of 10^{20} without affecting the numerical difficulty or singularity of the system.

CHAPTER

FOUR

TYPES OF MATRICES THAT ARISE

4.A SPECIAL MATRICES THAT ARISE FROM APPLICATIONS

4.A.1 Sparse Matrices

Matrices where most of the elements are zero are called *sparse*. The basic source of sparsity is models where a local connection or local influence principle exists. Thus in a bridge, the equations at a node only involve the beams that meet there. Their number is the same whether the bridge is 50 feet in length with 10 beams or 5 miles long with 10,000 beams. Thus, for a big bridge, most coefficients in any particular equation are zero. The same reasoning applies to models of buildings and other physical structures.

The sparseness for bridge models follows from the obvious physical fact that no one beam goes the length of a long bridge. This fact does not apply to electrical networks, yet in practice the models of these networks are also sparse—and the bigger they are, the more sparse they are. Thus, even though in principle one can join two distant points in an electrical network by a wire, in most networks very little of this is done. Again, when differential equations are approximated by difference equations, the difference approximations are entirely local; in the differential equations example of Sec. 3.A.1, there are only three nonzero coefficients in any one equation no matter how many equations there are.

Linear systems with 100,000 unknowns have been solved. The matrix for such a system has 10^{10} elements and, if it were full, it could not be stored in existing computer systems (never mind solving the equations). Such a large system can be solved only if it is sparse (or some very special formulas are applicable). Again, there are linear programming problems with 1 million inequalities and 50,000 unknowns that have been solved. The matrix for such a problem has $5 * 10^{10}$ elements; they must have almost all been zero for this problem to have been solved.

Figure 4.1 shows the pattern of nonzero elements that occurs in two large, square matrices from real applications.

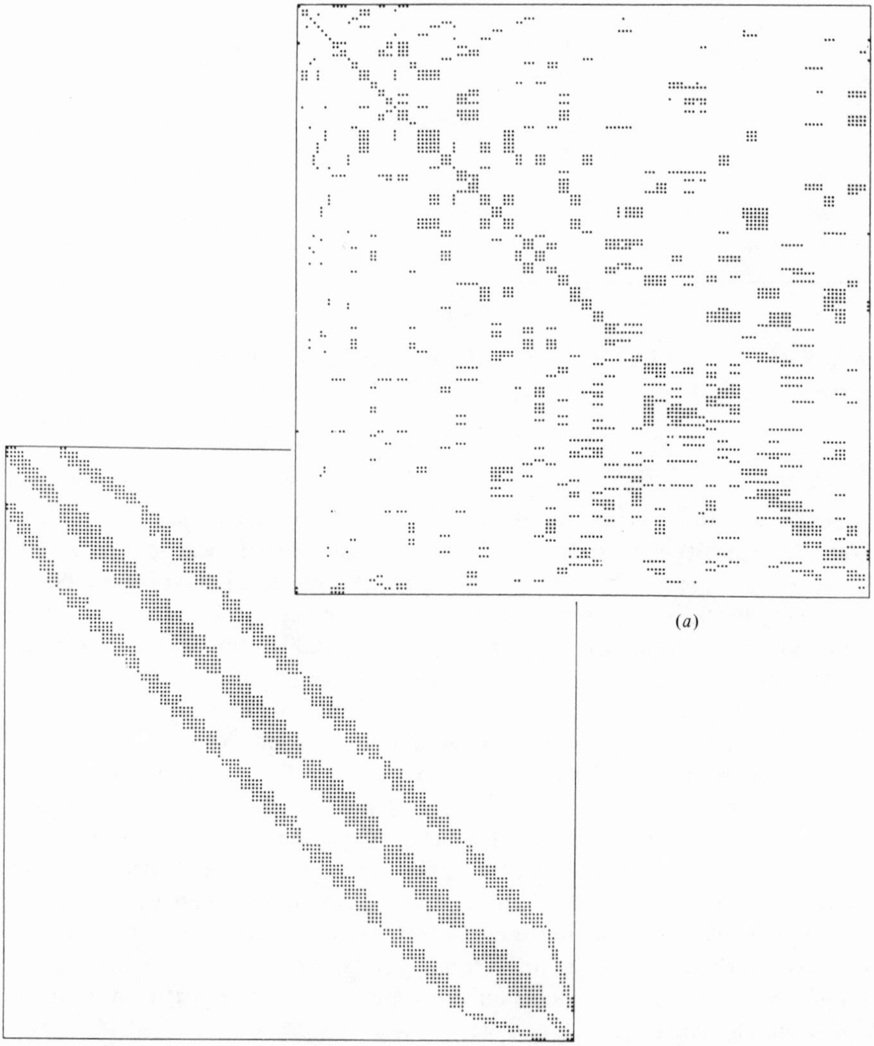

(a)

(b)

Figure 4.1 The pattern of nonzero elements in two large sparse matrices. Each dot indicates a nonzero element. Much larger sparse matrices occur in practice, but one cannot see the dots if the pattern is reduced to this size. (*Courtesy of John Reid, A.E.R.E. Harwell.*)

4.A.2 Organized Sparseness

Many applications lead to matrices that are not only sparse, but have a particular pattern in the nonzero elements. The most common of these is the *band matrix* where $a_{ij} = 0$ if $|i - j| >$ bandwidth (Fig. 4.2). For example, the finite difference matrix in Sec. 3.A.1. has a bandwidth of 1. Such a matrix is called *tridiagonal.* Any model where there is a local influence principle will lead to a band matrix if the equations and unknowns are numbered properly. Consider a regular rectangular pattern such as that shown in Fig. 4.3, where the equation at each node just involves the variables "attached to" the node (four of them). The pattern of nonzero elements is shown in Fig. 4.4. If the underlying physical object being modeled is not quite so regular, then the matrix is still banded, but the pattern of nonzero elements is not so regular.

In general, finite difference matrices tend to be very regular and banded; physical structure models like bridges and buildings tend to be banded but with a less regular pattern; and network matrices are less regular yet.

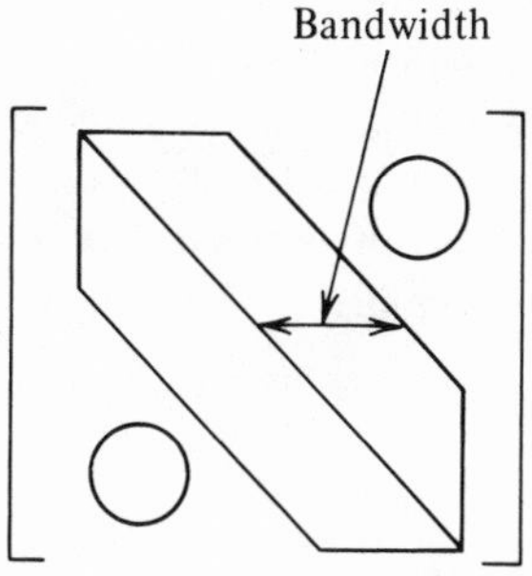

Figure 4.2

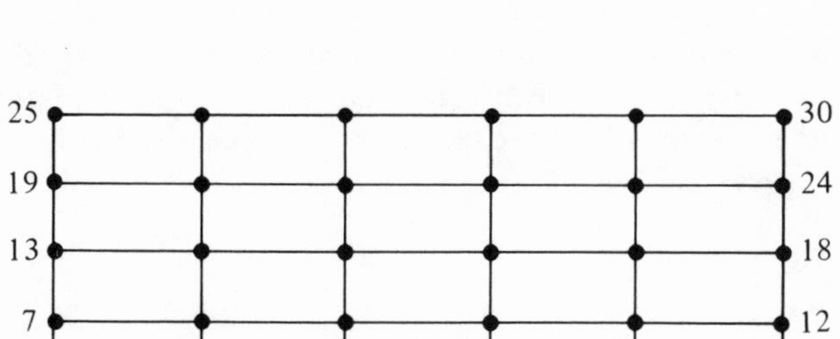

Figure 4.3

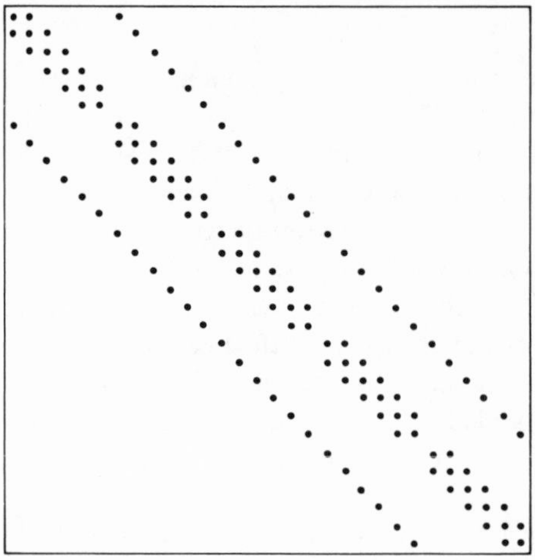

Figure 4.4

4.A.3 Symmetric Matrices

A matrix is *symmetric* if $a_{ij} = a_{ji}$ for all i, j or, equivalently, $A = A^T$. The normal equations are symmetric and many physical equilibrium problems also lead to symmetric matrices. The advantage of working with symmetric matrices is that only half the storage is required and, for most things, only half the work is needed for computations. The properties of *positive definite* ($\mathbf{x}^T A\mathbf{x} > 0$ for all nonzero vectors $\mathbf{x}$) and *positive semidefinite* ($\mathbf{x}^T A\mathbf{x} \geq 0$ for all $\mathbf{x}$) are often associated with symmetric matrices.

4.B SPECIAL MATRICES THAT ARISE FROM ANALYSIS

The analysis for numerical computation focuses on matrices whose special form allows one to do the computation easily. Thus the goal of Gauss elimination is to obtain a simple matrix where the equations can be solved easily. Some of these special matrices are listed here:

4.B.1 Diagonal Matrices

Here $a_{ij} = 0$ except for $i = j$. It is trivial to do calculations with diagonal matrices. The reason that eigenvectors are of interest is that, with them as basis (or coordinate vectors), the representation of the associated multivariate linear function is a diagonal matrix.

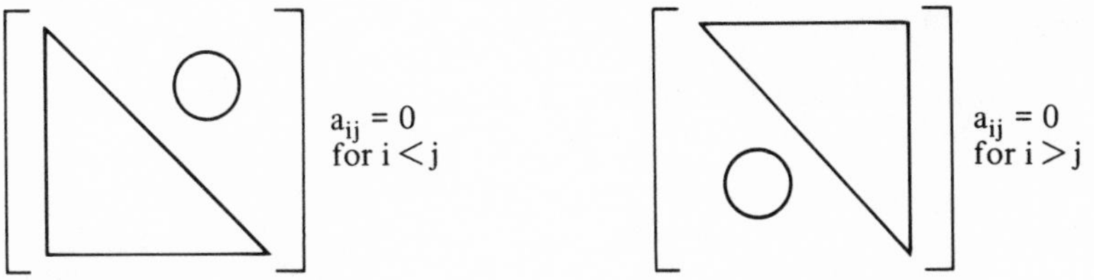

(*a*) Lower triangular (*b*) Upper triangular

Figure 4.5

4.B.2 Triangular Matrices

The two types are shown in Fig. 4.5 and they are both easy to work with. Linear equations can be solved by forward or backward substitution; the eigenvalues are the diagonal elements.

4.B.3 Orthogonal Matrices

If A is orthogonal, then $A^TA = I$ or $A^T = A^{-1}$, and it is easy to solve the linear system $A\mathbf{x} = \mathbf{b}$ as $\mathbf{x} = A^T\mathbf{b}$. Orthogonal matrices do not change the length ($\|\mathbf{x}\|_2$) of any vector. We see that if $\mathbf{y} = A\mathbf{x}$, then

$$\|\mathbf{x}\|_2^2 = \mathbf{x}^T\mathbf{x} = \mathbf{x}^T I\mathbf{x} = \mathbf{x}^T A^T A\mathbf{x} = (A\mathbf{x})^T A\mathbf{x} = \mathbf{y}^T\mathbf{y} = \|\mathbf{y}\|_2^2$$

This is important in numerical computation, where we do not want our manipulations to magnify any errors present (either from the original problem or round-off during the calculation).

4.B.4 Tridiagonal Matrices

This special band matrix has $a_{ij} = 0$ for $|i - j| > 1$, and it arises both in applications and analysis. Many techniques for computing matrix eigenvalues (a topic not considered in this book) involve reducing a matrix to an equivalent tridiagonal form.

4.B.5 Permutation Matrices

A permutation matrix P has only 0s or 1s and there is exactly one 1 in each row and column of P. The product PA has the same rows as A but in a different order (permuted), while AP is just A with the columns permuted. They are mainly used in making the theory look nice; in practice one uses a pointer vector (indirect addressing) instead of permuting rows or columns of a matrix.

4.B.6 Reducible Matrices

The square matrix A is reducible or decomposable if the rows and columns of A can be permuted to bring it into the form:

$$A = \begin{pmatrix} B & C \\ 0 & D \end{pmatrix}$$

for some square matrices B and D. This property allows one to break the problem into two smaller ones, usually with a very substantial savings in work. Unfortunately, such matrices do not arise often in practice; note that diagonal matrices are reducible.

PROBLEMS FOR CHAP. 4

1 Prove that the sum and product of two lower (upper) triangular matrices are lower (upper) triangular.

2 Prove that the inverse of a lower (upper) triangular matrix is lower (upper) triangular.

3 Let A be an $N \times N$ band matrix with bandwidth $K < N/2$. Show that A^2 has bandwidth 2K.

4 Suppose the tridiagonal matrix A is factored so $A = LU$ where L is lower triangular and U is upper triangular. Show that L and U must also be tridiagonal.

5 Show that a symmetric triangular matrix is diagonal.

6 Construct an example which shows that the product of two symmetric matrices need not be symmetric.

7 Let A be symmetric and B another matrix. Show that B^TAB is symmetric.

8 Show that the product of two symmetric matrices is symmetric if and only if they commute, i.e., $AB = BA$.

9 Assume A is lower triangular and is orthogonal. Show that A is diagonal. What are the diagonal elements of A?

10 Show that, if the columns of A are linearly independent, then A^TA is positive definite (that is, $\mathbf{x}^TA^TA\mathbf{x} > 0$ for all $\mathbf{x} \neq 0$). Consider the matrix

$$A = \begin{pmatrix} 1000 & 1020 \\ 1000 & 1000 \\ 1000 & 1000 \end{pmatrix}$$

and compute $B = A^TA$ using four-digit decimal arithmetic. Show that B is *not* positive definite by considering $\mathbf{x} = (1, -1)^T$. Explain this apparent contradiction.

11 Recall the system of equations obtained by the discretization of the differential equation in Sec. 3.A.1. Show that the corresponding linear system is tridiagonal for discretizing any differential equation of the form

$$a(x)y'' + b(x)y' + c(x)y = f(x) \qquad \begin{matrix} y(x_0) = y_0 \\ y(x_1) = y_1 \end{matrix}$$

12 Show that the normal equations derived in Sec. 3.A.2 have a symmetric coefficient matrix.

13 Give an intuitive argument that the organizational models should be sparse for each of the following organizations: (*a*) electrical power network for a public utility; (*b*) regional sewage disposal and water treatment system; (*c*) U.S. Post Office; and (*d*) assembly line operation for building cars.

14 Show how to compute the vector

$$\mathbf{z} = B^{-1}(2A + I)(C^{-1} + A)\mathbf{b}$$

without computing any matrix inverses, just using the vector-matrix arithmetic operations and solving linear systems of equations.

15 Consider the systems of equations

(*a*) $$ix_i = b_i \qquad i = 1, 2, \ldots, M$$

(*b*) $$x_i/i = c_i \qquad i = 1, 2, \ldots, M$$

(*c*) $$x_i/10 = d_i \qquad i = 1, 2, \ldots, M$$

Display the coefficient matrix and compute its determinant for M = 5, 10, 20, and 50. Do you anticipate any trouble in solving these systems of equations?

CHAPTER

FIVE

GAUSS ELIMINATION AND LU FACTORIZATION

5.A THE BASIC ALGORITHM AND THEOREM

The algorithm for eliminating unknowns illustrated in Chap. 2 dates from at least 250 B.C. even though Gauss' name is attached to it. The objective is to manipulate the equations (combine rows of the matrix A) so as to have an equivalent problem (one with the same solution) where back substitution can be used (the matrix A is transformed to a triangular matrix). That this process can always be carried out is established by the following:

Theorem 5.1 *Let* A *be a square matrix. Then there are matrices* U (*upper triangular*), M (*lower triangular and nonsingular*), *and* P (*a permutation matrix*) *so that*

$$U = MPA$$

Let L *be the inverse of* M; *then we also have* LU = PA *with* L *lower triangular.*

Gauss elimination is an algorithm to determine U, M, and P. Recall that P just interchanges the rows of A. The *principal submatrices* of $\{a_{ij}\}$ i, j = 1, 2, ..., n are the matrices $\{a_{ij}\}$ i, j = 1, 2, ..., k where k = 1, 2, ..., n. The previous result can be expressed in a more common form as

Theorem 5.2 *If the principal submatrices of* A *are all nonsingular, then one may choose* P *as the identity in Theorem 5.1, and we obtain*

$$LU = A$$

With the normalization $\ell_{ii} = 1$, *this factorization of* A *is unique.*

Note how Theorem 5.1 applies to the linear equation problem $\mathbf{Ax} = \mathbf{b}$. If we have computed U, M, and P, then we multiply both sides by MP to obtain

$$\mathrm{MP}\mathbf{Ax} = \mathrm{MP}\mathbf{b}$$

which is equivalent to

$$\mathrm{U}\mathbf{x} = \mathrm{MP}\mathbf{b}$$

These equations can be solved by *back substitution.* Note that computing $\mathrm{MP}\mathbf{b}$ is exactly forward substitution.

Example 5.1: Solution of a singular but consistent system The formulation of Theorem 5.1 allows us to attempt to solve a system which is singular such as

$$\begin{aligned} x + y + z + w &= 4 \\ 2x + 3y + z + w &= 7 \qquad \text{or} \quad \mathbf{Ax} = \mathbf{b} \\ x + y + z + w &= 4 \\ x + 2y + 2z + 2w &= 7 \end{aligned}$$

After the first Gauss elimination step we have

$$\begin{aligned} x + y + z + w &= 4 & &\text{multipliers of row 1} \\ y - z - w &= -1 & &-2 \\ 0 &= 0 & &-1 \\ y + z + w &= 3 & &-1 \end{aligned}$$

After the next step we have

$$\begin{aligned} x + y + z + w &= 4 & &\text{multipliers of row 2} \\ y - z - w &= -1 & & \\ 0 &= 0 & &0 \\ 2z + 2w &= 4 & &-1 \end{aligned}$$

We now interchange the third and fourth equations to obtain

$$\begin{aligned} x + y + z + w &= 4 \\ y - z - w &= -1 \\ 2z + 2w &= 4 \\ 0 &= 0 \end{aligned}$$

The permutation matrix that accomplishes this is

$$\mathrm{P}_3 = \begin{pmatrix} 1 & 0 & 0 & 0 \\ 0 & 1 & 0 & 0 \\ 0 & 0 & 0 & 1 \\ 0 & 0 & 1 & 0 \end{pmatrix}$$

In this particular example, no action is taken on the last step. Now the matrix **M** is the product of the effect of the multipliers. Recall that a basic Gauss elimination step like "multiply row 1 by m_4 and add to row 4" is accomplished by multiplying on the left by

$$\begin{pmatrix} 1 & 0 & 0 & 0 \\ 0 & 1 & 0 & 0 \\ 0 & 0 & 1 & 0 \\ m_4 & 0 & 0 & 1 \end{pmatrix}$$

which is the identity with one more element m_4 in column 1 (the row 4 position). One may easily verify that such matrices have a simple multiplication rule:

$$\begin{pmatrix} 1 & 0 & 0 & 0 \\ 0 & 1 & 0 & 0 \\ 0 & 0 & 1 & 0 \\ m_4 & 0 & 0 & 1 \end{pmatrix}\begin{pmatrix} 1 & 0 & 0 & 0 \\ m_2 & 1 & 0 & 0 \\ 0 & 0 & 1 & 0 \\ 0 & 0 & 0 & 1 \end{pmatrix}\begin{pmatrix} 1 & 0 & 0 & 0 \\ 0 & 1 & 0 & 0 \\ m_3 & 0 & 1 & 0 \\ 0 & 0 & 0 & 1 \end{pmatrix} = \begin{pmatrix} 1 & 0 & 0 & 0 \\ m_2 & 1 & 0 & 0 \\ m_3 & 0 & 1 & 0 \\ m_4 & 0 & 0 & 1 \end{pmatrix}$$

Thus the effect of all the row manipulations made above can be expressed in matrix terms by the product

$$\underset{\text{Eliminate } \mathbf{z}}{\begin{pmatrix} 1 & 0 & 0 & 0 \\ 0 & 1 & 0 & 0 \\ 0 & 0 & 1 & 0 \\ 0 & 0 & 0 & 1 \end{pmatrix}}\underset{\text{Switch rows 3 and 4}}{\begin{pmatrix} 1 & 0 & 0 & 0 \\ 0 & 1 & 0 & 0 \\ 0 & 0 & 0 & 1 \\ 0 & 0 & 1 & 0 \end{pmatrix}}\underset{\text{Eliminate } \mathbf{y}}{\begin{pmatrix} 1 & 0 & 0 & 0 \\ 0 & 1 & 0 & 0 \\ 0 & 0 & 1 & 0 \\ 0 & -1 & 0 & 1 \end{pmatrix}}\underset{\text{Eliminate } \mathbf{x}}{\begin{pmatrix} 1 & 0 & 0 & 0 \\ -2 & 1 & 0 & 0 \\ -1 & 0 & 1 & 0 \\ -1 & 0 & 0 & 1 \end{pmatrix}}$$

$$= \underset{\text{Total effect}}{\begin{pmatrix} 1 & 0 & 0 & 0 \\ -2 & 1 & 0 & 0 \\ 1 & -1 & 0 & 1 \\ -1 & 0 & 1 & 0 \end{pmatrix}}$$

It is easy to check that the "total effect" matrix is

$$\begin{pmatrix} 1 & 0 & 0 & 0 \\ -2 & 1 & 0 & 0 \\ -1 & -1 & 1 & 0 \\ 1 & 0 & 0 & 1 \end{pmatrix}\begin{pmatrix} 1 & 0 & 0 & 0 \\ 0 & 1 & 0 & 0 \\ 0 & 0 & 0 & 1 \\ 0 & 0 & 1 & 0 \end{pmatrix}$$

This shows what is intuitively clear: We could make all the row interchanges in advance (if we knew them) and then apply Gauss elimination (the multiplier matrices). The final result for this example is

$$\begin{pmatrix} 1 & 0 & 0 & 0 \\ -2 & 1 & 0 & 0 \\ -1 & -1 & 1 & 0 \\ 1 & 0 & 0 & 1 \end{pmatrix} \begin{pmatrix} 1 & 0 & 0 & 0 \\ 0 & 1 & 0 & 0 \\ 0 & 0 & 0 & 1 \\ 0 & 0 & 1 & 0 \end{pmatrix} \begin{pmatrix} 1 & 1 & 1 & 1 \\ 2 & 3 & 1 & 1 \\ 1 & 1 & 1 & 1 \\ 1 & 2 & 2 & 2 \end{pmatrix} = \begin{pmatrix} 1 & 1 & 1 & 1 \\ 0 & 1 & -1 & -1 \\ 0 & 0 & 2 & 2 \\ 0 & 0 & 0 & 0 \end{pmatrix}$$

M	P	A	=	U
Total effect of multipliers	Total effect of row switches	Original matrix		Upper triangular matrix

To continue the solution we compute **MPb**, which is the column vector $(4, -1, 4, 0)^T$. Note that in practice we do *not* compute M, we just keep the multipliers because we can compute **Mb** from them just as fast as we can from M itself.

We now attempt to back-substitute to find the solution. We cannot solve the last equation for anything, but it is automatically satisfied for any value of w. Thus we can pick w arbitrarily. We show the back substitution for three cases:

$w = 0$ *Case*		$w = 1$ *Case*		$w = 6.7$ *Case*	
$2z = 4$	so $z = 2$	$2z = 4 - 2$	so $z = 1$	$2z = 4 - 13.4$	so $z = -4.7$
$y = -1 + 2 = 1$		$y = -1 + 2 = 1$		$y = -1 + 2 = 1$	
$x = 4 - 3 = 1$		$x = 4 - 3 = 1$		$x = 4 - 3 = 1$	

This, of course, illustrates the fact that a singular system $A\mathbf{x} = \mathbf{b}$ which is consistent (i.e., has one solution) has infinitely many solutions.

Note that if the fourth component of **b** is *not* equal to 7, then the final equation becomes "zero = something not zero," which is impossible to solve, and thus the singular system $A\mathbf{x} = \mathbf{b}$ would have no solution at all. A little reflection shows that:

1. *A is singular if* U *has a zero on the diagonal.*
2. For singular A, $A\mathbf{x} = \mathbf{b}$ *is consistent if back substitution with diagonal zeros occurs only in equations of the form* $0 = 0$. *The unknowns associated with the diagonal zeros in these equations can be assigned arbitrarily.*

PROOF OF THEOREM 5-1 The simple example above actually illustrates the mechanism of the proof, but a formal mathematical argument is still required. The proof is by induction on the columns k of A. Visualize the matrix at an intermediate step partitioned as shown in Fig. 5.1. Thus $A_{k-1} = M_{k-1} P_{k-1} A$ is the induction assumption, and we now proceed to show that $k - 1$ can be increased to k. There are two cases (we denote the elements of A_{k-1} by a_{ij} to simplify the notation):

CASE 1: Suppose $a_{ik} = 0$ for all $i \geq k$. Then we are done.

CASE 2: Suppose $a_{jk} \neq 0$ for some $j \geq k$. Apply a permutation matrix P'_k which interchanges the k and j rows. Thus we may now assume that $a_{kk} \neq 0$. Compute the elements in rows $k + 1$ to n by the rule

$$a_{\ell m} \leftarrow a_{\ell m} - \frac{a_{\ell k}}{a_{kk}} a_{km} \qquad \begin{array}{l} \ell = k+1, \ldots, n \\ m = k, \ldots, n \end{array}$$

It is clear that this makes $a_{\ell k} = 0$ for $\ell \geq k$. This rule is multiplying row k by the multipliers $-a_{\ell k}/a_{kk} = m_\ell$ and thus its effect is the same as multiplying by the matrix

$$M'_k = \begin{pmatrix} I_{k-1} & 0 \\ 0 & M''_k \end{pmatrix} \qquad M''_k = \begin{pmatrix} 1 & & & & 0 \\ m_{k+1} & 1 & & & \\ m_{k+2} & 0 & 1 & & \\ \vdots & \vdots & \vdots & \ddots & \\ m_n & 0 & 0 & \ldots & 1 \end{pmatrix}$$

where I_{k-1} is a $k - 1$ order identity matrix. M'_k is not singular, as it is lower triangular with 1s on the diagonal. Note the following forms of the two matrices here:

$$M_{k-1} = \begin{pmatrix} L_{k-2} & 0 \\ B & I_{n-k+1} \end{pmatrix} \qquad P'_k = \begin{pmatrix} I_{k-1} & 0 \\ 0 & Q \end{pmatrix}$$

where L_{k-2} is a lower triangular matrix of order $k - 2$ and Q is a permutation matrix of order $n - k + 1$. One can check that $P'_k M_{k-1} P'_k$ is lower triangular (the effect is to apply Q to B), and thus we have

$$P'_k M_{k-1} = P'_k M_{k-1} P'_k P'_k = M^*_{k-1} P'_k$$

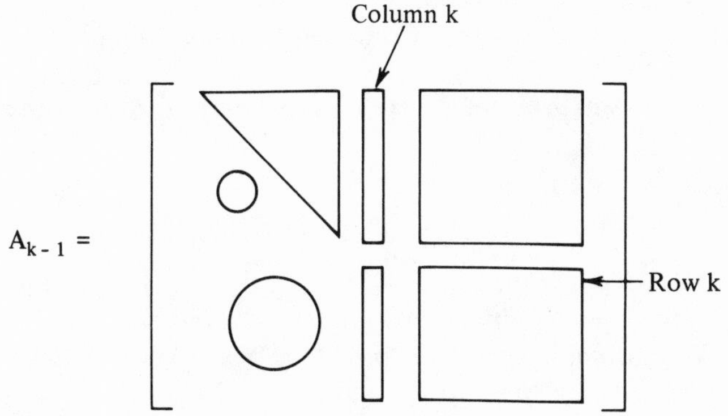

Figure 5.1

where M^*_{k-1} is lower triangular. This gives then that

$$\begin{aligned} A_k &= M'_k P'_k M_{k-1} P_{k-1} A = M'_k M^*_{k-1} P'_k P_{k-1} A \\ &= M_k P_k A \end{aligned}$$

is of the required form where $P_k = P'_k P_{k-1}$. The induction hypothesis is verified for k = 1 by the same reasoning and the proof is complete.

PROOF OF THEOREM 5.2 We first need to show that the nonsingularity of the principal submatrices implies that no row interchanges are required. This argument is also by induction on k. Clearly $a_{11} \neq 0$ by this hypothesis, so P_1 is not needed.

Recall that a triangular matrix is singular if and only if one of its diagonal terms is zero. Thus the upper triangular submatrix in A_{k-1} is nonsingular (by the hypothesis on the principal submatrices) and no row interchanges have been required. If $a_{kk} = 0$, then the $k \times k$ principal submatrix is singular, which is a contradiction. Thus $a_{kk} \neq 0$ and the induction proceeds with no row interchanges.

The construction in the proof of Theorem 5.1 produces a uniquely determined factorization except for the possible different choices of rows to interchange. Furthermore, M has 1s on the diagonal and thus so does its inverse L, i.e., $\ell_{ii} = 1$ for all i. Since no permutations are needed or allowed in Theorem 5.2, the factorization obtained is unique and the proof is complete.

5.B PIVOTING IN GAUSS ELIMINATION

The process of interchanging rows in Gauss elimination so that one has a nonzero diagonal is called *pivoting* and the matrix elements used for the elimination are the *pivots*. The use of nonzero pivots is sufficient for the theoretical correctness of Gauss elimination, but more care must be taken if one is to obtain reliable results. This is seen from the following example.

Example 5.2: The effect of small pivots in gauss elimination. Consider the simple system

$$\begin{aligned} 0.000100\,x + y &= 1 \\ x + y &= 2 \end{aligned} \qquad \text{solution:} \quad \begin{aligned} x &= 1.00010 \\ y &= 0.99990 \end{aligned}$$

to be solved using *three-digit arithmetic*. That is, only the three most significant decimal digits of any number are retained as the result of an arithmetic operation. We assume the result is rounded. With Gauss elimination we multiply the first equation by $-10{,}000$ and add to obtain

$$\begin{aligned} 0.000100\,x + y &= 1 \\ -10{,}000\,y &= -10{,}000 \end{aligned} \qquad \text{solution:} \quad \begin{aligned} x &= 0.000 \\ y &= 1.000 \end{aligned}$$

Thus a computational disaster has occurred.

If we switch the equations (that is, we *pivot*) to obtain

$$x + y = 2$$
$$0.000100\, x + y = 1$$

then Gauss elimination produces the system (again with three-digit arithmetic)

$$\begin{aligned} x + y &= 2 \\ y &= 1 \end{aligned} \qquad \text{solution:} \quad \begin{aligned} x &= 1.00 \\ y &= 1.00 \end{aligned}$$

This solution is as good as one would hope for using three-digit arithmetic.

The lesson of this example is: *It is not enough just to avoid zero pivots, you must also avoid relatively small ones.*

There are two standard pivoting strategies. The first is *partial pivoting:* At the kth step, interchange the rows of the matrix so the largest remaining element in the kth column is used as pivot. That is, after the pivoting

$$|a_{kk}| = \max\, |a_{ik}| \qquad \text{for } i = k, k + 1, \ldots, n$$

The second is *complete pivoting:* At the kth step, interchange both the rows and columns of the matrix so that the largest number in the remaining matrix is used as pivot. That is, after the pivoting

$$|a_{kk}| = \max\, |a_{ij}| \qquad \text{for } i = k, k + 1, \ldots, n;\ j = k, k + 1, \ldots, n$$

As we discuss later in some detail, round-off affects numerical computations in two ways: Some problems are inherently sensitive to round-off or other uncertainties and some algorithms enormously magnify any round-off or other uncertainties. There is little one can do about the first difficulty besides hoping to identify such problems. Pivoting is an example of a technique to control the second difficulty with the magnification of round-off effects. Certainly pivoting cured the difficulty in Example 5.2.

It has not been easy to answer the general question: How well does pivoting control error magnification? In one of the most famous papers in computer science, by J. von Neumann and H. H. Goldstein in 1947, it was shown that one might expect uncertainty to be magnified by a factor of 10^{12} or more in solving a modest, say 20×20, system using Gauss elimination. This would mean that one could not expect to solve many linear systems of that size or larger. However, some people ignored this and tried to solve large systems of equations anyway, and found that they could accurately solve systems of 100, 200, even 400 equations (if they could afford the computer costs). This discovery led to an effort to understand Gauss elimination better and, by the late 1960s, the following four facts had emerged.

FACT 1 (PROVED) Complete pivoting is safe; errors are never magnified unreasonably. The *magnification factor* is no more than

$$f_n = (n * 2 * 3^{1/2} * 4^{1/3} * 5^{1/4} * \cdots * n^{1/(n-1)})^{1/2}$$

for an n × n system of equations. A small table shows that f_n grows rather slowly:

n	5	10	15	20	30	50	80	100
f_n	5.73	18.30	39.09	69.77	155.5	536.17	1915.51	3552.41

and any error (either in the system at the start or made during the calculation) is transmitted into the solution multiplied by at most the magnification factor.

FACT 2 (EXPERIMENTALLY OBSERVED) The probability that trouble occurs using partial pivoting is *very* small. In fact, it is very unusual for the error magnification with partial pivoting to be more than two to four times greater than that with complete pivoting. The growth factor f_n seen in practice is rarely more than 8 and is frequently close to 1, especially for ill-conditioned problems.

FACT 3 (BY EXAMPLE) A special n × n matrix has been found where errors are magnified by 2^n using partial pivoting. This magnification factor grows rather rapidly as seen from the following table:

n	5	10	15	20	30	50	80	100
2^n	32	1024	32768	10^6	10^9	10^{15}	10^{24}	10^{30}

If the costs of partial and complete pivoting were nearly the same, then one would always use complete pivoting. However, the cost of complete pivoting is comparable to the rest of the whole solution process. A subtraction and test must be made for each matrix element where Gauss elimination uses an add and multiply, and one intuitively concludes that complete pivoting approximately doubles the cost of Gauss elimination. On the other hand, the cost of partial pivoting is almost negligible.

FACT 4 Thus the price of complete safety is very high and one can reasonably ask: "Why should I pay twice the cost just to protect myself from a situation so rare that it took numerical analysts years to find an example of it?" The result is that complete pivoting is rarely used. This is not simply a calculated risk, but, as we discuss later, there are other things one can do for protection from excessive error magnification.

Problems for Secs. 5.A and 5.B

1 Use Gauss elimination to show that the following system does not have a solution:

$$\begin{aligned} 3x_1 + x_2 \quad\quad &= 1.5 \\ 2x_1 - x_2 - x_3 &= 2 \\ 4x_1 + 3x_2 + x_3 &= 0 \end{aligned}$$

2 Solve the following system with a hand calculator using only three decimal digits at each step. Check the answers by substituting back into the equations, and estimate their accuracy. The exact solution is $(1, 1, 1, 1)^T$.

$$\begin{aligned} 0.31x_1 + 0.14x_2 + 0.30x_3 + 0.27x_4 &= 1.02 \\ 0.26x_1 + 0.32x_2 + 0.18x_3 + 0.24x_4 &= 1.00 \\ 0.61x_1 + 0.22x_2 + 0.20x_3 + 0.31x_4 &= 1.34 \\ 0.40x_1 + 0.34x_2 + 0.36x_3 + 0.17x_4 &= 1.27 \end{aligned}$$

3 Solve the following system with a hand calculator using only four correctly rounded digits at each step. Check the answers by substituting back into the equations, and estimate their accuracy. The exact solution is $(10, 1)^T$.

$$\begin{aligned} 0.0003x_1 + 1.566x_2 &= 1.569 \\ 0.3454x_1 - 2.436x_2 &= 1.018 \end{aligned}$$

4 Solve the following system with a hand calculator using only four correctly rounded digits at each step. Do this three times—once with a_{11} as the pivot element, once with a_{21} as the pivot element, and once with complete pivoting. Compare the answers with the exact solution $(1.000, 0.5000)^T$.

$$\begin{aligned} 0.002110x_1 + 0.08204x_2 &= 0.08415 \\ 0.3370x_1 + \quad 12.84x_2 &= 6.757 \end{aligned}$$

5 Show the following matrix A is nonsingular, but that it cannot be written as the LU product of lower and upper triangular matrices. Explain why.

$$A = \begin{pmatrix} 1 & 2 & 3 \\ 2 & 4 & 1 \\ -1 & 0 & 2 \end{pmatrix}$$

6 Consider Theorem 5.1 and explain (*a*) what its connection is with ordinary Gauss elimination, (*b*) where pivoting enters, and (*c*) why it is useful in solving the linear system $\mathbf{Ax} = \mathbf{b}$.

7 Give an example of a linear system $\mathbf{Ax} = \mathbf{b}$ where det (A) is much less than round-off (compared to the size of the elements of A) and yet where there is no numerical difficulty encountered in solving $\mathbf{Ax} = \mathbf{b}$.

8 Carry out Gauss elimination to solve the system

$$\begin{aligned} 2x + 3y - z + w &= 5 \\ x + 2y + 3z - w &= -6 \\ 4x + 5y - 9z + 6w &= 28 \\ x + y - 4z - 2w &= 7 \end{aligned}$$

and obtain *all* its solutions.

9 The matrix A is *diagonally dominant* if $|a_{ii}| > \sum_{j \neq i} |a_{ij}|$ for all i. Let A be a symmetric, diagonally dominant matrix. After one step of Gauss elimination the resulting matrix is of the form

$$\begin{pmatrix} a & y \\ 0 & A_1 \end{pmatrix}$$

(*a*) Show that A_1 is diagonally dominant.

(*b*) Show that Gauss elimination is the same thing for symmetric, diagonally dominant matrices with or without partial pivoting.

10 Show that (*a*) Gauss elimination without pivoting cannot fail for a diagonally dominant matrix. (*b*) If A is diagonally dominant, then A is nonsingular. *Hint:* Use Prob. 9.

11 Assume A is a symmetric *positive-definite* matrix (i.e., $\mathbf{x}^T A \mathbf{x} > 0$ for all $\mathbf{x} \neq 0$). Show that (*a*) A^{-1} is positive-definite. (*b*) A can be written as LL^T where L is a lower triangular matrix with positive diagonal elements. (*c*) Gauss elimination without pivoting cannot fail for A. *Hint:* Use Prob. 9.

12 The *magnification factor* for the growth of round-off error can be shown to be small for certain special matrices. Establish the indicated limit for the following cases:

(*a*) Tridiagonal—magnification factor ≤ 2.

(*b*) A^T is diagonally dominant—magnification factor ≤ 2.

(*c*) Positive-definite—magnification factor ≤ 1.

13 Solve the system

$$x_1 + 1.001\, x_2 = 2.001$$

$$x_1 + \quad x_2 = 2$$

Compute the residual $(A\mathbf{y} - \mathbf{b})$ for $\mathbf{y} = (2, 0)^T$ and compare the relative size of the error in the solution with the size of the residual relative to the right-hand side. Next solve

$$x_1 + 1.001\, x_2 = 1$$

$$x_1 + \quad x_2 = 0$$

Compute the residual for $\mathbf{z} = (-1001, 1000)^T$ and compare the relative size of the error in the solution with the size of the residual relative to the right-hand side. What do you conclude about the size of the residual as an indicator of the accuracy of a computed solution?

5.C THE ALGORITHM, SOME VARIATIONS, AND SOME PROPERTIES

5.C.1 Gauss Elimination with Partial Pivoting

We now express the algorithm described above in a compact, natural programming language form. We consider a square $n \times n$ matrix $A = (a_{ij})$ and wish to solve $A\mathbf{x} = \mathbf{b}$. This algorithm writes the upper triangular factor U and matrix of multipliers over the matrix A, thereby destroying it.

Algorithm 5.1: Gauss elimination with partial pivoting for Ax = b

```
                                        LOOP OVER COLUMNS OF A
For k = 1 to n - 1 do
    FIND MAXIMUM ELEMENT IN COLUMN
  imax = row index so that |a_imax,k| = max|a_i,k|,i ≥ k
    TEST FOR ZERO PIVOT (SINGULARITY). BUFFER IS A SMALL
    MACHINE DEPENDENT NUMBER TO GAUGE ROUND-OFF
  If |a_imax,k| ≤ buffer then go to end of k-loop
    INTERCHANGE ROWS K AND IMAX
  For j = 1 to n interchange a_kj and a_imax,j
    INTERCHANGE CORRESPONDING RIGHT SIDES
  interchange b_k and b_imax
                                        LOOP OVER ROWS
  For i = k + 1 to n do
      COMPUTE MULTIPLIER, SAVE IN K-TH COLUMN
    m = a_ik = a_ik/a_kk
                                        LOOP OVER ELEMENT OF ROW I
    For j = k + 1 to n do
     a_ij = a_ij - m * a_kj
      DO RIGHT SIDE OF ROW I
    b_i = b_i - m * b_k
  end of i-loop
end of k-loop
  BACK SUBSTITUTION
                                        LOOP OVER ROWS (REVERSE ORDER)
For i = n to 1 do
    SUBSTITUTE KNOWN VALUES INTO RIGHT SIDE
              n
  r = b_i -   Σ   a_ij x_j
            j=i+1
    TEST FOR ZERO PIVOT
  If (|a_ii| > buffer) then x_i = r/a_ii
    TEST FOR RIGHT SIDE ALSO EQUAL TO ZERO,
    ASSIGN ZERO TO SOLUTION AND PRINT MESSAGE
  else if (|r| ≤ buffer) then x_i = 0
      OR PRINT ERROR MESSAGE
    else print "inconsistent system, A is singular
end of i-loop
```

Note how the two factors M and U are both kept in the matrix A. Each multiplier is written in the spot where an element of A has just been zeroed. The diagonal elements of M are 1, so they need not be saved explicitly. While this strategy is irrelevant when just solving $A\mathbf{x} = \mathbf{b}$, there are other situations where it is very helpful to save both the matrices M and U.

5.C.2 Scaling and Testing for Floating Point Zero

The explicit algorithm forces us to consider the question of exactly when a computed number is "zero." We would be mathematically correct to set *buffer* = 0 in the algorithm, but this does not make sense in practice. Numbers which would be zero in exact arithmetic are almost sure to be nonzero in floating point arithmetic because of round-off errors. To decide whether a number is zero we must consider the *scale of two things:* the scale of the numbers in the problem and the scale of the machine.

The machine scale comes from the precision (number of digits carried) in the computer. Thus in a machine which carries 10 decimal digits, we might consider a pivot of $1.2 * 10^{-10}$ to be just residual round-off error and properly taken to be zero. *But*, this would be terribly wrong if all the numbers in the matrix A are of size 10^{-8}. So, we would like to *scale the problem* so that all the numbers are about of size 1 and then we can legitimately say that a small number like $1.2 * 10^{-10}$ is just round-off noise.

There are two natural ways to scale the problem $Ax = \mathbf{b}$. We can multiply the equations by a factor (e.g., by 10^8 if all the a_{ij} are of size 10^{-8}) to adjust the size of the numbers. We can also multiply the columns of A; this corresponds to a change in units (inches to miles) in measuring the size of the unknowns. Alas, there are some problems where scaling is not so easy and no satisfactory, completely automatic scaling method has been found. Two examples of troublesome matrices are given below. Neither one of these simple techniques or their combination properly scales these matrices.

$$\begin{pmatrix} 1 & 10^{10} & 10^{20} \\ 10^{10} & 10^{30} & 10^{50} \\ 10^{20} & 10^{40} & 10^{80} \end{pmatrix} \qquad \begin{pmatrix} 1 & 10^{20} & 10^{10} & 1 \\ 10^{20} & 10^{20} & 1 & 10^{40} \\ 10^{10} & 1 & 10^{40} & 10^{50} \\ 1 & 10^{40} & 10^{50} & 1 \end{pmatrix}$$

Fortunately, most problems can be scaled without difficulty. The crucial point is to choose units (which is what scaling amounts to) that are natural to the problem and that do not distort the relationships between the sizes of things. The examples above show that this cannot always be done, but it usually can be done easily for real problems. It is also prudent to have ordinary sized numbers, and the most common technique is to multiply each row (equation) so that the largest number in that row is 1. Assuming this is done, we then turn to the choice of a value for *buffer*. If the machine has t digits in base b, then buffer $= c * b^{-t}$ is appropriate for some small value of c. The coefficient c should be 3 or 4 and should grow gradually as the matrix size increases. There are at most $2n^2$ arithmetic operations performed on any one a_{ij}, so $c = n^2$ is the largest value one would consider. However, one expects there to be considerable cancellations in the round-off, so $c = n$ should be safe. Most numerical computation is done with relatively high precision (10 to 15 decimal digits), and one can be generous with the choice of c in these cases.

We summarize by listing the following facts:

FACT 1 The computations are more robust (less sensitive to changes) if all the elements of A are about the same size.

FACT 2 There is no known way to accomplish this in general, and matrices exist which cannot be scaled well.

FACT 3 The usual practice is to scale the rows (by dividing each equation by the largest coefficient in it). This is rather reliable for the problems that usually occur and one hopes that the *a posteriori* tests discussed in Chap. 8 give a warning if trouble occurs.

5.C.3 Algorithm Variations

There are a large number of variations of the basic algorithm for Gauss elimination. The selection of a particular variation is one of the design considerations for software and is discussed in more detail in Chap. 6. Here we list some of the more obvious variations:

1. The matrix A is not destroyed; auxiliary workspace is provided instead of using parts of A as workspace.
2. The rows of A are not explicitly exchanged in pivoting; pointers are used instead to keep track of the order of elimination.
3. The matrix A is factored into LU; the factors are to be used later for solving problems.
4. An option is available to solve for many different right sides, i.e., for solving the matrix equation $AX = B$.
5. Compute A^{-1} by solving the matrix equation $AX = I$. The right-hand sides are successively the columns of the identity and the solutions are the columns of A^{-1}. See Prob. 19 at the end of this chapter, where it is shown that this can be done with work of about $n^3/3 + 2n^3/3 = n^3$ instead of the $n^3/3 + n^3 = 4n^3/3$ one would expect.

A less obvious and more interesting variation, Crout reduction, results from observing that the order of the arithmetic can be changed. Note that, in the basic Gauss algorithm, each a_{ij} is modified numerous times during the calculation. A little reflection shows that we do not have to do these as we go. All the information is kept anyway, and we can wait and do all the operations on a_{ij} at once. The algorithm is given without pivoting, back substitution, or testing for zero pivots.

Algorithm 5.2: Crout reduction for the factorization of A

```
        LOOP OVER PARTIAL ROWS AND COLUMNS
For k = 1 to n do
        COMPUTE AND SAVE MULTIPLIERS IN THE REST OF COLUMN K
        THE PIVOTS (DIAGONALS OF U) ARE ALL ONES
  For i = k to n do
```

$$a_{ik} = a_{ik} - \sum_{j=1}^{k-1} a_{ij} a_{jk}$$

```
  end i-loop
        COMPUTE THE ELEMENTS IN THE REST OF ROW K
  For j = k + 1 to n do
```

$$a_{kj} = \left(a_{kj} - \sum_{i=1}^{k-1} a_{ki} a_{ij}\right) / a_{kk}$$

```
  end j-loop
end k-loop
```

Note that this algorithm does not produce the same numbers as the basic Gauss algorithm given earlier. The difference is in the normalization of the factorization MA = U; the Gauss algorithm is normalized by the diagonal elements of M set to 1, while this Crout algorithm has the diagonal elements of U equal to 1. A minor change can be made in either algorithm to produce the same factorization as the other (modulo the differences in how round-off errors enter). Again the two factors are stored on top of A, destroying it.

Even though the Crout variant seems to be just another way to do the same thing as Gauss elimination, there are two distinct situations where it can be advantageous. The first is where intermediate results are "expensive" to record, such as with a hand-held calculator. One can carry out the summations in the inner loops without writing down the intermediate partial sums. This results in a large savings in time. This is also a great improvement in reliability since recording numbers by hand is quite error-prone.

The second advantageous situation is for computers with comparatively fast higher-precision arithmetic or with an especially fast dot product operation. Specifically, suppose that using double-precision arithmetic to compute the sums

$$\sum_{i=1}^{k-1} a_{ij} a_{ik} \qquad \sum_{i=1}^{k-1} a_{ki} a_{ij}$$

takes only 5 percent more time than using single-precision arithmetic. It is plausible that this would eliminate most of the round-off error effects in the computation, and a lengthy analysis (not presented here) proves this to be the case. There used to be a number of computers where such higher-precision, fast arithmetic was available for these kinds of sums and the Crout algorithm was very attractive for them. There is a good chance that this feature will again become widely available. Some current computers allow the above sums to be calculated especially efficiently in single-precision arithmetic, and Crout is advantageous for them.

Finally, we note that there exist special versions of Gauss elimination for symmetric matrices. If A is symmetric, then it seems plausible that half the work could be avoided in solving $A\mathbf{x} = \mathbf{b}$. The *Cholesky factorization* $L^{-1}A = L^T$ accomplishes this, and the matrix L can be computed using half the work required for an LU factorization.

The operation of the method is seen from an induction argument on the size of the matrix. First consider the 2×2 case

$$A = \begin{pmatrix} a_{11} & a_{12} \\ a_{21} & a_{22} \end{pmatrix} \qquad L = \begin{pmatrix} \ell_{11} & 0 \\ \ell_{21} & \ell_{22} \end{pmatrix}$$

We require that $A = LL^T$, or

$$a_{11} = \ell_{11}^2 \qquad a_{12} = \ell_{11}\ell_{21}$$

$$a_{21} = \ell_{21}\ell_{11} \qquad a_{22} = \ell_{21}^2 + \ell_{22}^2$$

It is easy to see that A being positive-definite implies that $a_{11} > 0$, so that $\ell_{11} = \sqrt{a_{11}}$ is possible. The second element ℓ_{21} is determined from the equation for a_{21} (which is equal to a_{12} because A is symmetric). Finally, ℓ_{22} is determined by

$$\ell_{22} = \sqrt{a_{22} - \ell_{21}^2} = \sqrt{a_{22} - a_{12}^2/a_{11}}$$

and we need to show that this is possible. In the relation $\mathbf{x}^T A\mathbf{x} > 0$, we take $\mathbf{x} = (a_{12}, -a_{11})^T$ and find that $\mathbf{x}^T A\mathbf{x} = a_{11}^2 a_{22} - a_{12}^2/a_{11} > 0$, which is equivalent to $a_{22} - a_{12}^2/a_{11}^2 > 0$, so the square root in the formula for ℓ_{22} produces a positive number.

For the general case suppose that we can factor the $(m-1) \times (m-1)$ matrix A into LL^T. Then let A′ be an $m \times m$ matrix in the form

$$A' = \begin{pmatrix} A & \mathbf{y} \\ \mathbf{y}^T & a_{mm} \end{pmatrix} \qquad L' = \begin{pmatrix} L & 0 \\ \mathbf{w} & \ell_{mm} \end{pmatrix}$$

where y and **w** are $(m-1)$-vectors. We require that

$$A = LL^T \qquad \mathbf{y} = L\mathbf{w}$$

$$\mathbf{y}^T = \mathbf{w}^T L^T \qquad a_{mm} = \ell_{mm}^2 + \mathbf{w}^T\mathbf{w}$$

By hypothesis we can find L so that $LL^T = A$ and the equation $\mathbf{y} = L\mathbf{w}$ allows us to solve for the $m - 1$ components of **w**. Thus we have

$$\ell_{mm} = \sqrt{a_{mm} - \mathbf{w}^T\mathbf{w}}$$

and we show that the quantity in the square root is positive by imitating the argument for the 2×2 case. We take $\mathbf{x} = (A^{-1}\mathbf{y}, -1)^T$ and compute that (with $\mathbf{z} = A^{-1}\mathbf{y}$ for convenience)

$$\begin{aligned} \mathbf{x}^T A'\mathbf{x} &= \mathbf{z}^T A\mathbf{z} - 2\mathbf{z}^T\mathbf{y} + a_{mm} \\ &= -\mathbf{z}^T\mathbf{y} + a_{mm} = a_{mm} - \mathbf{y}^T A^{-1}\mathbf{y} \\ &= a_{mm} - \mathbf{y}^T(LL^T)^{-1}\mathbf{y} = a_{mm} - (L^{-1}\mathbf{y})^T(L^{-1}\mathbf{y}) \\ &= a_{mm} - \mathbf{w}^T\mathbf{w} \end{aligned}$$

Since $\mathbf{x}^T A'\mathbf{x} > 0$, we have $a_{mm} - \mathbf{w}^T\mathbf{w} > 0$, and the induction step is complete.

This argument actually proves that a symmetric factorization is possible; the computation follows the argument exactly and is given in Algorithm 5.3.

Algorithm 5.3: The Cholesky factorization of a symmetric matrix

```
        LOOP OVER COLUMNS OF A
For k = 1 to n do
        COMPUTE THE NEXT ROW VECTOR
        EXCEPT FOR THE DIAGONAL ELEMENT
  For i = 1 to k - 1 do
```

$$a_{ki} = \left(a_{ki} - \sum_{j=1}^{i-1} a_{ij} a_{kj}\right) \Big/ a_{ii}$$

```
  end of i-loop
        COMPUTE THE DIAGONAL ELEMENT
```

$$a_{kk} = \sqrt{a_{kk} - \sum_{j=1}^{k-1} a_{kj}^2}$$

```
end of k-loop
  THE FACTOR L IS NOW THE LOWER TRIANGULAR PART OF A
```

Algorithm 5.3 can be made more robust by replacing the statement with the square root by

$$t = a_{kk} - \sum_{j=1}^{k-1} a_{kj}^2$$

$$\text{If } t > 0 \text{ then } a_{kk} = \sqrt{t}$$

$$\text{else } a_{kk} = 0$$

This avoids a program stop when a_{kk} is nearly or exactly zero and round-off accidentally makes t negative.

5.C.4 Operations Counts

The work of solving $\mathbf{Ax} = \mathbf{b}$ by Gauss elimination can be estimated directly by counting the arithmetic operations. This counting goes as follows: The matrix at the kth stage appears as

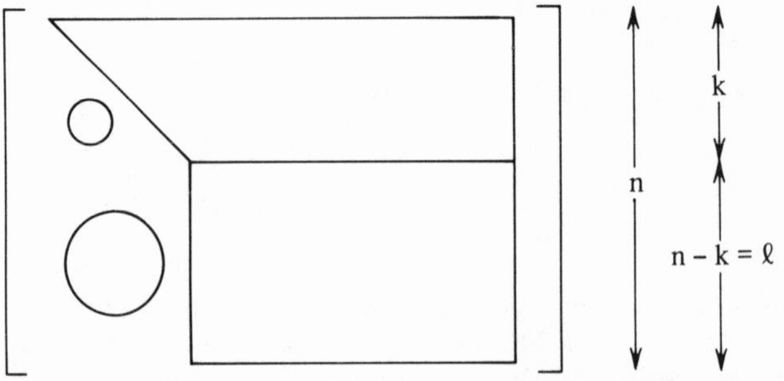

Figure 5.2

The work for the next elimination is

1. Multipliers $\quad m_i = a_{ik}/a_{kk}, \qquad i = k + 1 \text{ to } n$
2. Elimination $\quad a_{ij} = a_{ij} - m_i * a_{kj}, \; i = k + 1 \text{ to } n, \; j = k + 1 \text{ to } n$
3. Right-hand side $\quad b_i = b_i - m_i * b_k, \quad i = k + 1 \text{ to } n$

Operations for step 1 are ℓ divides (or 1 divide and ℓ multiplies); operations for step 2 are $\ell * [\ell$ adds + ℓ multiplies]; operations for step 3 are $\ell * [1$ and $+1$ multiply].

We introduce the abbreviations A = add, M = multiply, D = divide. Now we sum these expressions for all values of k so

$$\sum_{k=1}^{n-1} (\text{operations for step 1}) = \left(\sum_{k=1}^{n-1} \ell\right) D = \left(\sum_{k=1}^{n-1} n - k\right) D$$

$$= \left(\sum_{i=1}^{n-1} i\right) D = \frac{(n-1)(n-2)}{2} D$$

By replacing the divisions by multiplies, this is also

$$(n-1)D + \frac{(n-1)(n-2)}{2} M$$

$$\sum_{k-1}^{n-1} (\text{operations for step 2}) = (A + M) \sum_{k=1}^{n-1} \ell^2 = (A + M) \sum_{i=1}^{n-1} i^2$$

$$= \frac{n(n-1)(2n-1)}{6} (A + M)$$

The work for the factorization is the sum of these two counts:

$$\left(\frac{n^3}{3} + \text{lower-order terms}\right)(A + M)$$

The operations count for the right-hand side is

$$(A + M) \sum_{k=1}^{n-1} \ell = \frac{(n-1)(n-2)}{2} (A + M)$$

and the work for back substitution is seen to be

$$\sum_{1=n}^{1} [\ell(A + M) + 1D] = \frac{n(n+1)}{2} (A + M) + nD$$

The total for processing the right-hand side (forward substitution) and back substitution is thus

$$(n^2 + \text{lower-order terms})(A + M)$$

The primary work of Gauss elimination is the $n^3/3$ operations (A + M) to obtain the factorization.

This operation counting procedure is a form of *computational complexity* analysis. One estimates the work to compute something (the solution of $A\mathbf{x} = \mathbf{b}$ in this case) in terms of basic machine operations (arithmetic in this case). An obvious and important question is whether this is the fastest way to solve $A\mathbf{x} = \mathbf{b}$. For large enough values of n, the Strassen algorithm for matrix multiplication leads to a method with a smaller arithmetic count. It requires the order of $n^{2.7}$ multiplications and additions. Study and experimentation is currently under way to see just how advantageous this new algorithm is in practice. Preliminary results suggest that it becomes more efficient in practice for n above 250.

Problems for Sec. 5.C

1 Implement Algorithm 5.1 as a Fortran subroutine. Explain the objectives in designing the calling sequence. Explain the source of the value for the machine-dependent constant "buffer."

2 Implement Algorithm 5.1 as a set of three Fortran subroutines. FACTOR forms the LU factorization without pivoting, replacing A with it. FSUB is to apply the appropriate result from FACTOR to the right-hand side of the system. BSUB is to do the back substitution. Give a complete description of the calling sequence variables. Rough out the Fortran program that would use these three subroutines to solve the following problem:

The matrices A and B have dimensions 10 × 10 and 20 × 20.

There are seven systems $A\mathbf{x}_i = \mathbf{b}_i$ to be solved with right-hand side vectors in the Fortran array B(10,7).

There are 16 systems $D\mathbf{y}_i = \mathbf{e}_i$ to be solved with right-hand side vectors in the Fortran array E(20,16).

3 Consider two library routines FACTOR (A) and SOLVE (A,X,B) where, for simplicity, various arguments about the size of A or the problem are omitted. FACTOR (A) replaces the matrix A by its two triangular factors. SOLVE (A,X,B) assumes A is *already* factored and actually solves $A\mathbf{x} = \mathbf{b}$.

Suppose you are to compute the vector **y** from the formula

$$\mathbf{y} = B(2C + D^{-1})\mathbf{x} + (I - D^{-1}L)\mathbf{z}$$

Rough out a Fortran program to compute **y** using FACTOR and SOLVE, but one which does not compute any matrix inverses. For brevity you may use statements like "add vector V to S" or "multiply vector V by matrix M" in the description to indicate the standard vector/matrix arithmetic operations. Make it clear how you use variables and retain information.

4 Give an efficient algorithm based on Algorithm 5.1 for reducing a tridiagonal matrix to upper triangular form. Assume no pivoting is needed.

5 Rough out a Fortran subroutine to implement the algorithm in Prob. 4 so that it is efficient in storage. Describe in detail the data structures used and the calling sequence.

6 Extend the algorithm and programs of Probs. 4 and 5 to band matrices with bandwidth K. Assume no pivoting is needed.

7 Incorporate partial pivoting in Prob. 6. How much more storage does this require?

8 Give an efficient algorithm without pivoting based on Algorithm 5.1 for solving a linear system $A\mathbf{x} = \mathbf{b}$ where A is symmetric and only the upper half of A is actually given.

9 Make a diagram that shows the sequence in which Algorithm 5.2 processes the elements of the matrix A.

10 Give an efficient algorithm based on Algorithm 5.2 for reducing a tridiagonal matrix to upper triangular form. Assume no pivoting is needed.

11 Rough out a Fortran subroutine to implement the algorithm in Prob. 10 so that it is efficient in storage. Describe in detail the data structures used and the calling sequence.

12 Extend the algorithm and programs of Probs. 10 and 11 to band matrices with bandwidth K. Assume no pivoting is needed.

13 Incorporate partial pivoting in Prob. 12. How much more storage does this require?

14 Give an efficient algorithm based on Algorithm 5.3 for reducing a symmetric band matrix to upper triangular form.

15 Rough out a Fortran subroutine to implement the algorithm of Prob. 14 so that it is efficient in storage. Describe in detail the data structures and calling sequence.

16 Modify Algorithm 5.1 for four variations: (*a*) The matrix A is not destroyed; (*b*) pointers are used for pivoting rather than explicit interchanges of rows (this is an example of indirect addressing or subscripted subscripts); (*c*) solve the matrix equation AX = B where B is an n × m matrix; (*d*) compute A^{-1}.

17 Explain the relationship between the following three methods for solving $A\mathbf{x} = \mathbf{b}$: Gauss elimination (LU factorization), Crout reduction, and Cholesky decomposition.

18 An "x-matrix" has a pattern of nonzero elements that forms an "x" as in the following 5 × 5 and 6 × 6 examples:

$$\begin{pmatrix} x & x & x & x & x \\ 0 & x & x & x & 0 \\ 0 & 0 & x & 0 & 0 \\ 0 & x & x & x & 0 \\ x & x & x & x & x \end{pmatrix} \qquad \begin{pmatrix} x & x & x & x & x & x \\ 0 & x & x & x & x & 0 \\ 0 & 0 & x & x & 0 & 0 \\ 0 & 0 & x & x & 0 & 0 \\ 0 & x & x & x & x & 0 \\ x & x & x & x & x & x \end{pmatrix}$$

(*a*) In the spirit of Gauss elimination, describe an algorithm to transform a general matrix into this form by solving a sequence of 2 × 2 problems.

(*b*) Show how one can "back-substitute" in an x-matrix by solving a sequence of 2 × 2 problems.

(*c*) Make operations counts for parts (*a*) and (*b*) and compare the work of this scheme with ordinary Gauss elimination. Ignore pivoting.

19 Let $\mathbf{e}_i = (0, 0, \ldots, 0, 1, 0, \ldots, 0)^T$ with the 1 in the ith position so $\mathbf{e}_i$ is the ith column of the identity. The columns $\mathbf{x}_i$ of A^{-1} may be calculated by solving $A\mathbf{x}_i = \mathbf{e}_i$ for i = 1, 2, ..., N. Assume that A has been factored using the first part of Algorithm 5.1. Give an efficient algorithm (based on the back-substitution part of Algorithm 5.1) to compute the $\mathbf{x}_i$. The algorithm is to take into account the special nature of the right-hand sides $\mathbf{e}_i$.

20 Make an operations count for the algorithm of Prob. 19. How much effort is saved compared to the work to solve $A\mathbf{x}_i = \mathbf{b}_i$ for i = 1, 2, ..., N where the $\mathbf{b}_i$ are arbitrary right-hand sides?

CHAPTER

SIX

MATHEMATICAL SOFTWARE OBJECTIVES

Before discussing specific software for linear algebra, we review the philosophy, objectives, and conflicts for mathematical software in general.

6.A SOFTWARE PHILOSOPHY

The underlying philosophy used here is summarized by four statements:

1. *General goals:* We want to provide more powerful computational tools, to ease the burden on the user, and to raise the "level of the language" that is used.
2. *Mechanism = powerful operators:* The primary weakness of current languages (Fortran and friends) is the lack of powerful operators.
3. *Operators needed:* In each area of computation there are certain standard, useful tasks to be performed and these should be represented by language operators.
4. *Expert knowhow should be embodied in the software:* Each of these standard tasks has been extensively studied and there are people who have a deep understanding of how to perform them best. These experts should write the software and embed their expertise in it for the rest of the world to use as standard operators in the languages.

6.A.1 The Two Alternatives for Implementing this Philosophy

The obvious approach is to develop a new programming language which has many of these operators built in. For example, a general-purpose mathematical language should be at least at the calculus/matrix algebra level. This would allow the practicing scientist and engineer to program using his standard professional language, mathematics. Programs should allow statements like

```
FUNCTION ARRAY: F(X,I,J)
POLYNOMIAL: F(X,I,J) FOR I,J≤10
A(I,J) = INTEGRAL (F(X,I,J), X = 1.2 TO 5.) FOR I,J = 1 TO 6
SOLVE A*X=B FOR X
FMIN(I) = MIN(MIN(F(X,I,J),X = 1.2 TO 3), J = 1 TO 6)
```

Such languages have been implemented since the early 1960s using either numerical or symbolic methods to implement the operators. These efforts have shown such languages to be feasible, although they naturally require considerably more computer resources than Fortran, Algol, Pascal, etc.

The prospects for a modern mathematical system are not good. The advantages of better control structures, more flexible data types, and more powerful operators do not seem likely to offset the opposing forces. One of these is the great difficulty in introducing any new, general-purpose language. The prospects for the lasting use of newer languages are not bright in spite of their advantages. Another problem is the lack of interest shown in operators in general and mathematical operators in particular by those active in language development. They hope that better control structures and data types together with programming discipline are sufficient to undo the programming logjam. But powerful operators shorten programs and that is a big step in increasing programming ease and productivity.

While the prospects for general-purpose languages with powerful operators are dim, special-purpose languages (or problem-oriented languages) are appearing in many different user communities. These languages and systems are generally implemented by people outside computer science and they often lack some of the niceties that appeal to computer scientists. However, the developers do attack the central problem, which is to allow the user to "program" in his or her own terms. The language the user wants to use must contain both the relevant nouns (data structures) *and* verbs (operators) as well as lots of adjectives. This approach is most developed in statistics, where there are several good systems. Some of these allow users who know practically nothing about programming (in the computer science sense) to do large-scale and meaningful computations. Often these users also know little about statistical computation methods.

We can expect each specialty to have its own systems, and eventually the bulk of computing may be done this way rather than by direct use of general languages. While the statistical systems have a broad audience primarily external to statistics, most of these systems will be used inside the specialty where they originated. Structural engineering is an example of a large consumer community of computer power where problem-oriented systems play a large role. An early and large example of these is NASTRAN. It has about 300,000 Fortran statements, a 2000-page reference manual, a 1200-page primer, and cost over $10,000,000 to develop. Some features of it look "horrible," but it has been widely used because it partially succeeds in doing the right thing: getting engineers out of Fortran coding and giving them more powerful tools developed by people who are expert in structural engineering calculations.

The second approach is to make powerful operators available through *program libraries.* If a good problem-oriented language is not available (and most of the time one is not), then the next best way to use an expert's knowhow is through library procedures which interface to general-purpose languages. Thus, even though problem-oriented languages may be the "wave of the future," the concentration here is on libraries as the approach that is possible now. The Appendix presents material from several libraries with matrix computation facilities. The reader may want to look there to see typical examples of library contents and documentation.

6.B ALGORITHMIC OBJECTIVES

The kernel of a library routine is a basic algorithm. By this we mean computational procedures based on textbook descriptions: Gauss elimination, Simpson's rule, Newton's method, etc. The details of the algorithm can have a large influence on its usefulness and the objectives of an algorithm design are (1) speed, (2) storage efficiency, (3) reliability, (4) accuracy, (5) simplicity, and (6) robustness. These terms are self-explanatory except possibly for "reliability" and "robustness." For some tasks there are algorithms which always work or, perhaps, the circumstances for failure are so improbable that they can be ignored. However, many mathematical problems are algorithmically unsolvable. That is, for each algorithm there is a problem where it fails completely. Solving nonlinear equations and differential equations and evaluating integrals are examples of such problems. Thus *reliability* refers to probability of failure; either by producing no result (which is not so bad) or by producing an erroneous result (which is very bad). One usually measures reliability with some combination of the probability of getting correct results and the probability of getting a wrong result without recognizing it.

Robustness is closely related to reliability but has further implications about where and how failures occur. One might say that an algorithm is robust if its failures occur gracefully and without surprises. Thus the behavior of a robust algorithm depends continuously on the problem; one should not find two similar problems, one where the algorithm fails completely and one where it works easily. A graceful failure occurs, for example, if the execution time steadily increases or the estimated accuracy steadily decreases as the problems become more difficult. A robust algorithm does not generate an illegal situation (e.g., $\sqrt{-0.01}$ in real arithmetic) which aborts the calculation at some intermediate point. See the remark after Algorithm 5.3 indicating one of the things that must be done to make it robust.

6.C LIBRARY SOFTWARE OBJECTIVES

We list the qualities that a library program should have:

Powerful	Portable
Flexible	Easy to modify
Easy to use	Safe to use
Good algorithms	

We view a good library program as a good algorithm (with all its nice properties) embedded in a program so as to achieve these other objectives. These qualities are somewhat self-explanatory, but a few words of amplification are appropriate. *Power* is the primary objective of the whole operation; we want a program that can solve a lot of difficult problems. The main, but not the only, determinant of this quality is the power of the underlying algorithm. *Flexibility* is needed because even standard problems come in variations. For example, the linear equations problem might be:

Solve $A\mathbf{x} = \mathbf{b}$	
Solve $AX = B$	(multiple right-hand sides and solutions)
Solve $AX = I$	(X is the inverse of A)
Solve $A\mathbf{x} = \mathbf{b}$	where A is a band matrix
Solve $A\mathbf{x} = \mathbf{b}$	where a_{ij} is given by a formula

Flexibility adds to the power of a program but also detracts from other qualities. *Ease of use* is both essential and difficult to achieve. There are examples of programs that have been widely used because they were easy to use even though they were unreliable or inefficient. A program is *portable* if it can run on different machines with little or no modifications. See Probs. 1 and 11 below for programs with portability difficulties. It is obvious that we want to avoid the duplication of expensive software. Costs of \$15 to \$20 per statement are minimal for good software, and poor software may cost just as much. This cost figure assumes there are no technical difficulties in the algorithm design. Some people use the term "transportable" for software that requires a small amount of modification and reserve the word "portable" for programs that run on different machines with no change at all. *Ease of modification* is needed for maintenance and because any library program, no matter how flexible, will fail to meet some users' needs. *Maintenance* refers to the processes of keeping the program compatible with language changes, compilers, operating systems, documentation standards, etc., and of adding convenience or safety features, removing minor bugs, or making changes to enhance efficiency. *Safety* means not only the reliability and robustness of a good algorithm, but also general protection from failures. Many library procedures become deeply embedded in a larger program or system and are invisible to the end user. You do not want a message like CPU ABORT AT LOCATION 094637 that turns out to be in SUBROUTINE MYSTRY which the user has never heard of.

6.C.1 Conflicts in Software Objectives

The objectives for good library software and algorithms are not very compatible, and we mention five conflicts that occur:

1. Flexibility versus ease of use
2. Portability versus efficiency
3. Safety (robustness) versus efficiency
4. Human nature versus subroutine write-ups
5. Language constraints versus ease of use

Actually, almost everything conflicts with efficiency as measured by computer time used. One background assumption here is that we want to consider the efficiency of the entire problem-solving process. Thus execution time efficiency is sacrificed to increase this overall efficiency.

More flexibility means more complexity, and the user wants something simple. Flexibility usually manifests itself through option switches and more arguments for the various parameters. The user must assign values to these even if they are irrelevant to the particular problem involved. Note that arguments (*lists*) may also include items unrelated to flexibility or the problem. These items are usually algorithm parameters which the software designer chose not to set, thus placing the burden on the user instead. The user sometimes has little or no idea about how to choose appropriate values for these parameters. A useful tactic to resolve this conflict is to have one program of maximum flexibility (and length of calling sequence) and to then have a number of simpler interface programs which merely set various arguments to default values and perform other services for the user.

That efficiency conflicts with portability, safety, and other things is easy to see. A program tailored to one particular problem on one particular machine can leave out all safety checks because those troubles that *do not* occur can be ignored and some remedial action can be inserted for those that *do* occur. Likewise, particular features of the machine, compiler, operating systems, and problem can be exploited to increase efficiency. The question is not whether to sacrifice efficiency, but how much efficiency should be sacrificed to enhance the other qualities of the program.

One quickly learns that most library subroutine write-ups are misleading, confusing, ambiguous, and generally inscrutable. This is true even for write-ups where great effort has been spent to make them clear, complete, and easy to understand. Error after error after error is made because the user misses various fine—or not so fine—points about the use of a library program. Some people would rather spend four days writing their own program for a problem than spend half a day figuring out how to use a library routine properly.

The reason for this difficulty is not completely clear. The ideal write-up puts everything one needs to know into a short, clean, and clear presentation. This write-up has a high density of information, much of which is unfamiliar, and people just seem to be unable to absorb it on the first (or second or third) reading. The reader gets the general idea and then jumps to conclusions, usually wrong, about specific details. The process of getting all the details correct usually involves several runs and considerable frustration. Care should be taken in write-ups to word things, choose names, etc., so as to increase the probabilities of the reader jumping to the right conclusions.

The conflicts discussed above are intrinsic, but there are others that merely reflect the realities of computing. One of these is that language limitations force added complexity and confusion. Fortran often requires arguments which are relevant only to getting the programs to work. These are unnatural for a user and thus more liable to error than other types of library program arguments. The library examples in the Appendix should be studied to see how the designers of these libraries choose to compromise these conflicting objectives.

Problems for Secs. 6.B and 6.C

1 What are the objectives of an algorithm for solving linear equations?

2 What are the objectives of a library software routine for solving linear equations?

3 Give the calling statement (in Fortran with symbolic arguments) of a good library routine for solving $\mathbf{A}\mathbf{x} = \mathbf{b}$. Explicitly state the objectives of your design. Describe an application where your design has a weakness compared to some alternative.

4 *Briefly* state the strengths and weaknesses of teaching people (*a*) how to solve problems or algorithms for solving problems and (*b*) how to use software to solve problems.

5 Choose two library subroutine write-ups from your local computing center and make a critique of them. Points to consider include:

(*a*) Are all the variables defined clearly and given good names?
(*b*) Does the program require arguments whose values are obscure?
(*c*) Is an example given?
(*d*) Is a reference to the algorithm source given?
(*e*) Are there common situations where the user must modify the program before using it?
(*f*) Does the program waste storage for a small problem?
(*g*) Can the source code be obtained easily? If so, is it well documented?
(*h*) Does the input data have to be in an unnatural form?

6 Discuss the conflicts between the library software objectives of efficiency and ease of modification.

7 Give three specific instances where maintenance would be needed for a library program due to external factors. Explain each situation briefly.

8 There are four approaches to handling errors in deeply embedded library procedures:

(*a*) Abort the computation and print a good explanation.

(*b*) Abort the library program (but not the job) and return a flag indicating that an error has occurred.

(*c*) Fix the error as best you can and print a message explaining what happened.

(*d*) Fix the error as best you can and return a flag indicating that an error has occurred.

Discuss the strengths and weaknesses of each of the alternatives. Consider the context of a user with a high-level problem-oriented language for statistics where, somehow, a linear equation has been generated to be solved which (1) is singular, (2) has coefficient matrix identically 0 and right-hand side 1, and (3) has order n = −2.

9 Locate an example in your local library that has a lengthy calling sequence and define a "front-end" routine that handles a simpler class of problems by setting some default values and then calling the library program.

10 Locate a linear equation solver in your local library and test it for robustness in the presence of illegal and nonsense arguments. Examples of input to try are

- (*a*) Matrix order is 1, 0, −1 or a real number.
- (*b*) Matrix argument is, in fact, a simple variable.
- (*c*) Too few arguments are given.
- (*d*) Matrix is declared INTEGER in main program.
- (*e*) Matrix is identically zero.
- (*f*) Right-hand side vector has errors like those in (*a*), (*b*), and (*d*).
- (*g*) Various incompatibilities in declared dimensions are present.

11 The following Fortran program has at least 18 items which prevent it from being portable. Identify them and see how many of them cause errors or diagnostics on your local Fortran system.

```
      INTEGER CLUE, CHARACT(7), POINT, BLANK
      REAL DIGITS (10)
      DATA (DIGITS(I), I = 1,10)/0,1,2,3,4,5,6,7,8,9/
      DATA MORE, BLANK/4HMORE, 1H /
      POINT = 1H.
 1    READ 5, CLUE, N, (CHARACT(I),I = 1,N)
 5    FORMAT (7A1)
      PI = 3.141592654
      DO 10 I = 1,N
10    IF(CHARACT(I) .NE. BLANK)                  GO TO 20
12    PRINT 15, CHARACT, POINT
                                                 GO TO 50
15    FORMAT('0 ERROR***' 7A2,A3)
20    VAL = 0
      K = 1
      DO 30 J = 1,N+1-I
        DO 25 L = 1,10
          IF (CHARACT(N+1-J) .NE. DIGIT(L))      GO TO 25
                                                 GO TO 26
25      CONTINUE
                                                 GO TO 12
26      VAL = L * 10.**K+VAL
30      K = K+1
      ANS = VAL*PI
      PRINT 40, ANS
40    FORMAT(20X9HANSWER  =  E40.11)
50    IF(CLUE .EQ. MORE)                         GO TO 1
      STOP
      END
```

6.D CASE STUDY: DESIGN OF THE INTERFACE FOR A LINEAR EQUATIONS SOLVER

We consider in some detail the design of a library program to solve systems of linear equations. Even in this relatively simple and very standard problem we see some of the compromises that must be made in the software design.

We want to solve $\mathbf{Ax} = \mathbf{b}$ so we might hope to have a Fortran subroutine call:

```
CALL SOLVE (A,X,B)
```

This cannot work because the number N of equations is missing, so we might hope for:

```
CALL SOLVE (A,X,B,N)
```

Some of the shortcomings of this design are

1. The matrix A must be destroyed; otherwise there is no working space for the subroutine SOLVE to use, for the triangular factors generated.
2. The user is not warned if A is singular or if the subroutine SOLVE failed.
3. The dimensions of the Fortran arrays for A, X, and B are not given.
4. If you have two systems of equations $\mathbf{Ax}_1 = \mathbf{b}_1$ and $\mathbf{Ax}_2 = \mathbf{b}_2$ with the same matrix, then A is factored twice.
5. The computation of A^{-1} is not efficient.

So, while this is a simple design, it lacks flexibility, power, and safety features and it has Fortran language problems.

The following two designs have fewer shortcomings:

Linear Equation Solver—Design 1

```
C           NO WORKSPACE, A IS DESTROYED
      CALL SOLVE (A,X,B,N,I,J,K,L,M,M1)
      ----
      SUBROUTINE SOLVE (A,X,B,N,I,J,K,L,M,M1)
      DIMENSION A(I,J), X(I,K), B(I,K)
      ----
C     I = NUMBER OF ROWS DECLARED IN DIMENSIONS OF A,X,B
C     J = NUMBER OF COLUMNS DECLARED IN DIMENSIONS OF A
C     K = NUMBER OF COLUMNS DECLARED IN DIMENSIONS OF X,B
C     L = NUMBER OF RIGHT SIDES
C     M = SWITCH TO COMPUTE A^-1
C     M1 = FLAG FOR SINGULARITY OF A
```

Linear Equation Solver—Design 2

```
C     WORKSPACE W PROVIDED, A IS NOT DESTROYED
      CALL SOLVE (A,X,B,N,I,J,K,L,M,M1,W)
      ----
      SUBROUTINE SOLVE (A,X,B,N,I,J,K,L,M,M1,W)
      DIMENSION A(I,J), X(I,K), B(I,K), W(I,J)
```

Now we have flexibility, but we also have users who will say: "Good grief, I'll never figure out all this mess! All I want is to solve my little 5 × 5 system. I'll write my own program."

The situation can be improved somewhat by using better mnemonics for the names.

Design 1—With Good Variable Names

```
SUBROUTINE SOLVE (A,X,B, NEQS, KDIMA, KDIMB, NSOLS, INVERS, ISING)
DIMENSION A(KDIMA, KDIMA), X(KDIMA, KDIMB), B(KDIMA, KDIMB)
```

Note that we forced A to be square with this change. The two arguments KDIMA, KDIMB are artifacts of Fortran, while the others are really needed by the problem. Keep in mind that in Fortran (and most other languages) the matrix A is *not* passed to a subroutine as some sort of object or collection of numbers. Only its address (location in memory) is passed and a subroutine like SOLVE uses A where it is stored by the calling program and SOLVE itself does not have memory allocated for the matrix.

One might decide to avoid the INVERS switch and require the user to program something like

```
    B = IDENTITY MATRIX
    CALL SOLVE( A,X,B,NEQS,KDIMA,KDIMB,NEQS,ISING)
    IF( ISING .EQ. 0) GO TO ERROR MESSAGE
```

For the user who wants the original simple routine we can include in the library

```
    SUBROUTINE LINSYS (A,X,B,NEQS)
    REAL A(NEQS, NEQS), X(NEQS), B(NEQS)
    CALL SOLVE( A,X,B,NEQS,NEQS,NEQS, 1, ISING)
    IF ( ISING .EQ. 0) PRINT 10
10  FORMAT( 20X,20(1H*), 19HMATRIX IS SINGULAR)
    RETURN
    END
```

Thus we see that even in this standard problem there are nontrivial design questions—and we have ignored the question of how to let the user tell the program SOLVE that A is symmetric, a band matrix, etc.

6.D.1 Storage Allocation and Variable Dimensions

Many people using matrix software become confused by the difference between the size of A in the linear equations problem $\mathbf{Ax} = \mathbf{b}$ and the size of A as a Fortran array. We first note that a library program *cannot* assume these two sizes are the same. The routine LINSYS given above is, in fact, not very useful because of the need for flexibility in the number of equations. We illustrate this by two skeleton Fortran programs which are typical of common applications:

```
      REAL A(50,50),R(50),B(50)
    5 READ 10, NEQS, ((A(I,J),I=1,NEQS),J=1,NEQS)
   10 FORMAT( I10/ (8F10.5))
      IF( NEQS .LE. 0) STOP
C           DO SOME THINGS HERE
      CALL SOLVE(A,X,B,NEQS, 50, 1, 1, ISING)
      IF( ISING .EQ. 0) PRINT 20
C           DO MORE THINGS, THEN DO ANOTHER CASE
      GO TO 5
      END

      REAL A(50,50), X(50,10), B(50,10)
C           GENERATE FIRST PROBLEM
      CALL SOLVE(A,X,B,5,50,10,1,ISING)
C           GENERATE NEXT PROBLEM 2 RIGHT SIDES
      CALL SOLVE(A,X,B,NPROB2,50,10,2,ISING)
C           GENERATE LAST PROBLEM, 10 CASES
      CALL SOLVE(A,X,B,50,50,10,10,ISING)
      STOP
      END
```

Fortran has very limited capabilities to handle arrays of different sizes, and the most obvious and common approach is to choose a size of A for SOLVE which is always big enough, say 100. With this design, the library subroutine instructions say A must be declared 100 × 100 and SOLVE looks like:

```
      SUBROUTINE SOLVE( A,X,B, NEQS, ISING )
      REAL A(100, 100), X(100), B(100)
```

This approach is grossly wasteful of memory for the person who has four equations in four unknowns. The person who has 102 equations must either write his own program or get the library program and modify it.

The variable dimension facility of Fortran used earlier overcomes both of these difficulties at the price of including the sizes of the array in the calling sequence. While using variable dimensions is clearly the choice for a library routine, we can hope that someday Fortran—or whatever our standard language is—will eliminate this redundant and confusing feature.

CHAPTER

SEVEN

MATHEMATICAL SOFTWARE PERFORMANCE EVALUATION

7.A COMPILER EFFECTS ON PORTABILITY AND EFFICIENCY

Achieving high-quality, portable software is difficult, and here we show that substantial losses in efficiency *cannot be avoided* in using one program in several different environments. The data presented here are taken from the work of Parlett and Wang (see References at end of book).

We examine two fundamental linear equation calculations and show that, no matter how they are coded in Fortran, there is a large loss of efficiency in some computing environment. That is, what is good in one is bad in another and vice versa; further, every way of doing these calculations is bad in some environment.

Five different environments are considered, involving only two different computers:

CDC 6400 with RUN, FUN, and FTN compilers
IBM 360/50 with G and H compilers

Two calculations are examined which occur in solving $\mathbf{Ax} = \mathbf{b}$:

1. *Implementation of pivoting.* One can accomplish pivoting in two ways: direct switching of the rows in memory or using pointers (indirect addressing) to keep track of the order of elimination.
2. *Inner loop in Crout.* Mathematically, the inner loop of the Crout version of Gauss elimination is

$$a_{ij} \leftarrow a_{ij} - \sum_k a_{ik} * a_{kj}$$

This assignment can be coded in several ways. (The paper of Parlett and Wang uses $j + 1$ instead of j in this loop.)

7.A.1 Environment Effects on Pivoting Implementation

The two different ways to implement pivoting were put into programs just to do the pivoting.These two programs were timed on each computer with each compiler. Table 7.1 presents the results on execution time for the 75 × 75 case. Each choice gets a score of 100 times its execution time divided by the best execution time. This means that 100 is the lowest possible score, and it is given to the fastest code. Thus in column 1 (IBM 360/50, G compiler) we see that explicit switching is the fastest and using pointers takes 13 percent longer. All of the differences are substantial, up to 40 percent. Note, however, that this is a small part of Gauss elimination, and even the 40 percent difference here would not be obvious in the complete solution process.

Table 7.1 Execution time comparisons for two pivoting implementations in five environments

Times are normalized in each column so that the fastest is 100

	IBM 360/50		CDC 6400		
	G compiler	H compiler	RUN compiler	FUN compiler	FTN compiler
Explicit switch:	100	143	100	125	140
Using pointers:	113	100	119	100	100

7.A.2 Environment Effects on the Inner Loop of Crout

Three different Fortran codings are considered:

Code 1—Maximum Use of Indexes

```
      DO 1 K=1,M
1         A(I,J) = A(I,J) - A(I,K) * A(K,J)
```

Code 2—Remove Fixed Index Term from Loop

```
      SUM=A(I,J)
      DO 1 K=1,M
1         SUM = SUM - A(I,K) * A(K,J)
      A(I,J)     = SUM
```

Code 3—Case 2 with a Temporary Variable T Added

```
      SUM = A(I,J)
      DO 1 K=1,M
            T = A(I,J) * A(K,J)
1           SUM = SUM - T
      A(I,J)      = SUM
```

Programs for solving linear equations were written which were identical except for this segment of code. These three programs were timed for linear systems of order 25, 50, and 75 on each computer with each compiler. Table 7.2 presents the results for the 75 × 75 case; the others were similar. As in Table 7.1, the fastest code gets a score of 100 and the slower ones are proportionally higher. Note that the time is based on the entire linear equation solving time, not just the time for the inner loop. Of course, the inner loop accounts for the bulk (probably over 98 percent) of the time for the whole program.

We see that CODE 3, which is surely unnatural, is never best. However, the penalty for this "minor" variation varies from 2 to 90 percent. CODE 1 directly expresses the desired calculation. Our hope for "optimizing" compilers (as all of these are to some extent) is that they can produce the best code for a particular calculation—at least if it is a two-line DO loop. Only the FTN compiler achieves this, and all the others produce code which is substantially less efficient, with a 15 to 49 percent loss in efficiency.

Not only do these examples show that there is no one best way to code a calculation, they also show that seemingly trivial differences in code can produce very large differences in execution time.

7.A.3 Compiler Effects on Code Efficiency

The data in this study allow us to examine the value of different levels of optimization in compilers.

The same data that give Table 7.2 can be normalized so that the fastest time for each code on each computer is 100; the results are shown in Table 7.3. There we see that the IBM H compiler produces object code which is

Table 7.2 Execution time comparisons for three ways to code the inner loop of the Crout algorithm

Times are normalized in each column so that the fastest is 100

	IBM 360/50		CDC 6400		
	G compiler	H compiler	RUN compiler	FUN compiler	FTN compiler
CODE 1:	149	117	115	119	100
CODE 2:	100	100	100	100	104
CODE 3:	102	105	190	190	107

Table 7.3 Execution time comparisons of compilers for three programs on two machines

Times are normalized so that the fastest execution time for a program and machine is 100

	IBM 360/50		CDC 6400		
	G compiler	H compiler	RUN compiler	FUN compiler	FTN compiler
CODE 1:	395	100	165	170	100
CODE 2:	311	100	139	137	100
CODE 3:	304	100	257	255	100

three to four times faster than that produced by the G compiler. Similarly, the CDC FTN compiler produces code that is 40 to 150 percent faster than the RUN or FUN compilers (which are quite similar). One may interpret this by saying that, even though small code changes can produce large differences in efficiency, the choice of compiler can produce much larger differences yet.

7.B TESTING AND EVALUATION OF MATRIX COMPUTATION SOFTWARE

We now look at the fundamental question: *Which program is the best?* We limit ourselves here to programs that solve $\mathbf{Ax} = \mathbf{b}$.

7.B.1 Preliminary Screening

There are certain general properties that a program must have before it can be taken as a serious candidate for evaluation as mathematical software. These are

1. *Good construction and design.* The program must have a logical, systematic organization. This usually means a modular design. Good programming practices have been followed, e.g., structured programming principles and thorough comments.
2. *Portability.* There is usually little point in expending effort on mathematical software that cannot be widely used. Even proprietary programs to be used only within one organization should be protected from changes in computing equipment or systems. Evidence of portability includes actual use on several machines or the results of a program checker such as PFORT (which checks a Fortran program for portability) (Ryder, 1974; see References at end of book). Good software may have machine or

system dependencies; the crucial thing is that they are well identified so that it is straightforward to take care of these dependencies.

Adhering to language standards is necessary (but not sufficient) for portability. Transition periods (such as going from Fortran IV to Fortran 77) may create extra difficulties with language processors.

3. *Good user instructions.* It seems so obvious to require this, yet the instructions are often confusing. One cause of this is that the programmer frequently has considerable difficulty in anticipating how someone else will see his program.

A program which fails to have these properties should simply be returned to the author. Their lack surfaces, of course, when one attempts to incorporate the program into a test procedure.

7.B.2 The Performance Evaluation Framework for $Ax = b$

The first few paragraphs of this section outline a framework that is presented in considerably more detail and generality at the end of this chapter.

Let us assume that we have one or more programs for solving $\mathbf{Ax} = \mathbf{b}$ and we wish to evaluate or compare their performance. The first, and perhaps most critical, question is: What problems are to be considered? Thus we must define the *problem space* for the evaluation. This might be done by picking a sample of 5, 50, or 500 problems which are believed to represent the problems of interest. This may be the best (or even the only) way if we are concerned only with a very specialized set of problems (e.g., those problems that arise in the course of some other computations such as a particular kind of bridge or network analysis). More often we are interested in a general class of problems which we describe in terms of *problem space features* or attributes. Typical features for $\mathbf{Ax} = \mathbf{b}$ are

Matrix size	Sparsity
Number of right-hand sides	Conditioning
Symmetry	Noise level in matrix
Bandwidth	Scale of matrix

These features define numerical coordinates in the *feature space* and we choose a range for these coordinates which we consider in the evaluation. Note that the feature space is of much lower dimension than the original problem space. We indicated eight dimensions above; the set of 10×10 matrices has 100 dimensions, one for each element.

There are three reasons for looking at the feature space: (1) When a new problem arises, we can usually only determine (guess at) a few of its features and cannot possibly place it accurately with respect to all other problems that might arise. (2) We expect programs to work similarly on problems with similar features. Indeed, features where this is not true are "irrelevant" and should not be considered. (3) We must reduce the complexity of the framework and the original problem set in order to get anywhere at all.

Once the problem and feature spaces are defined, then we have to choose *performance criteria.* Four common ones for solving $\mathbf{Ax} = \mathbf{b}$ are

p_1 = execution time used p_3 = accuracy obtained

p_2 = memory used p_4 = reliability

The concept of "best" requires a linear ordering, so some way must be chosen to combine these basically independent performance criteria. We might quantify and normalize them so that each varies from 0 to 1. Then we could choose weights w_i, $i = 1, 2, 3, 4$ with $\sum w_i = 1$ and define the overall performance to be

$$\sum_{i=1}^{4} w_i p_i$$

In fact, we can view the choice of the weights w_i as a "user option." In an ideal world the user could specify these weights and then the same person (or someone else) could select the program that maximizes performance as measured with this criterion. This is not always possible, such as when choosing the routine to put into the computing center's library.

We are now ready to measure the performance of the programs. Ideally, one would do this for the entire problem space; then one would really "know" how the programs perform. This is almost always impractical because it requires too much computation, so we must sample the problems somehow. The next most satisfactory thing is to choose a set of problems whose features fill out the feature space well. Even this is often impractical. Note that with eight features and ten values for each we have 10^8 problems to solve. Even five features with five values for each leads to 3125 problems, which might still be many more than we can afford to solve. We should then use statistical techniques of sampling and experimental design or, at least, very carefully select the most important cases to be run.

The evaluation can be further complicated by the uncertainty in picking a "representative" problem. Thus, in the context of solving $\mathbf{Ax} = \mathbf{b}$, it is easy to measure execution time and memory use. These two criteria often depend directly on the matrix order (which is easy to get) and little else. On the other hand, accuracy is not so easy to measure. As we will see in Chap. 8, the "right answer" is not as well defined as we would like. Reliability is even more difficult to measure. Among other things, its value depends on the entire problem space, so the sampling used to measure it must be controlled very carefully.

In any performance evaluation it is necessary to quantify various conclusions and to reduce the experimental results to some easily understood form.

One might say things like

1. The expected round-off error effect is $3 * 10^{-8}$.
2. The maximum round-off error effect is $5 * 10^{-7}$.
3. The requested accuracy is achieved 98.6 percent of the time.
4. The execution time grows like $0.073N^3$ for $N \times N$ matrices.

Single numbers, as in the first three examples, are the simplest and to be preferred. However, one number sometimes fails to convey enough information and *performance profiles* are useful devices to display the results.

A performance profile is simply a graph of one performance criterion versus one problem feature (or a one parameter family of problems). Plots of execution time versus matrix order, memory versus matrix order, accuracy versus condition number, and memory versus sparsity are useful for the problem $\mathbf{Ax} = \mathbf{b}$. Two examples are shown in Fig. 7.1 for matrix computation. Figure 7.2 shows two performance profiles from numerical integration (where this technique was first introduced).

We close by noting that systematic performance evaluation has been very fruitful in producing new ideas and techniques for better algorithms. It has also shown that the opinions of "experts" have not been very reliable indicators of which methods will work best in practice.

7.B.3 The Use of Program Proofs in Numerical Software

Even though mathematical software was the first software to receive intensive evaluation, there has been little use of "program proofs." That is, attempts have not been made to prove mathematical software correct in some mathematical sense. Some reasons for this are: (1) It is difficult to incorporate the uncertainties of round-off into proofs. Of course, one can hypothesize that round-off does not occur and the results would still be very nice. (2) The software tends to be too long for current proof methods (either automatic or manual). For example, a program of 661 lines (368 comments, 39 declarations, and 254 executable statements) required 20 pages of manual proof after a more abstract version was proved correct in about 15 pages. See the work of Rice (1976), listed in the References at the end of the book. (3) Most mathematical software has heuristic segments whose performance cannot be specified in terms of input-output relationships. That is to say, the question is not whether these segments are right or wrong, but rather how well they perform. One can make the analogy with a program for playing chess. Even though there may exist a right move in all situations, no one knows what it is, and the program's choices for moves must be judged on how well the program fares in chess competition.

The most common situation of this type in numerical computation is testing for the convergence of some process. In many cases it can be *proved*

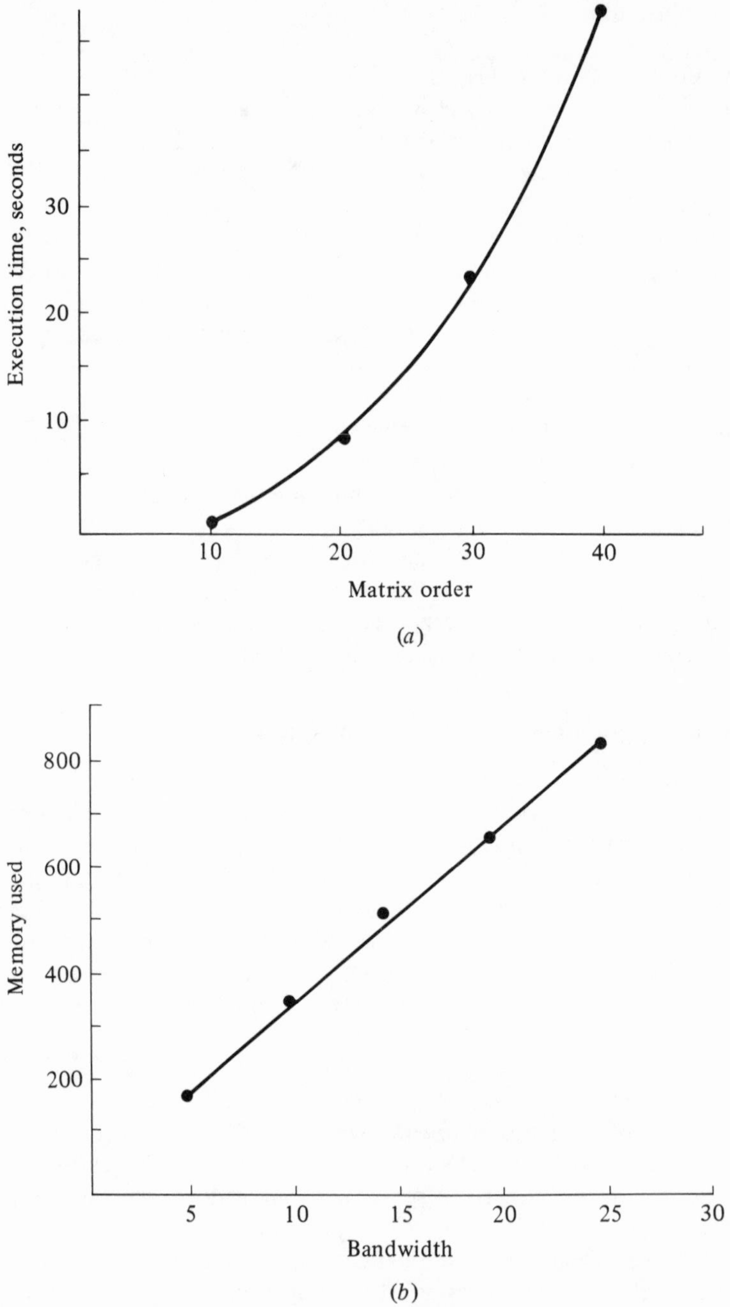

Figure 7.1 Two performance profiles for a program to solve $\mathbf{Ax} = \mathbf{b}$. (*a*) Execution time versus matrix order for a standard Gauss elimination program. (*b*) Memory versus bandwidth for a band matrix routine and 25 × 25 matrices.

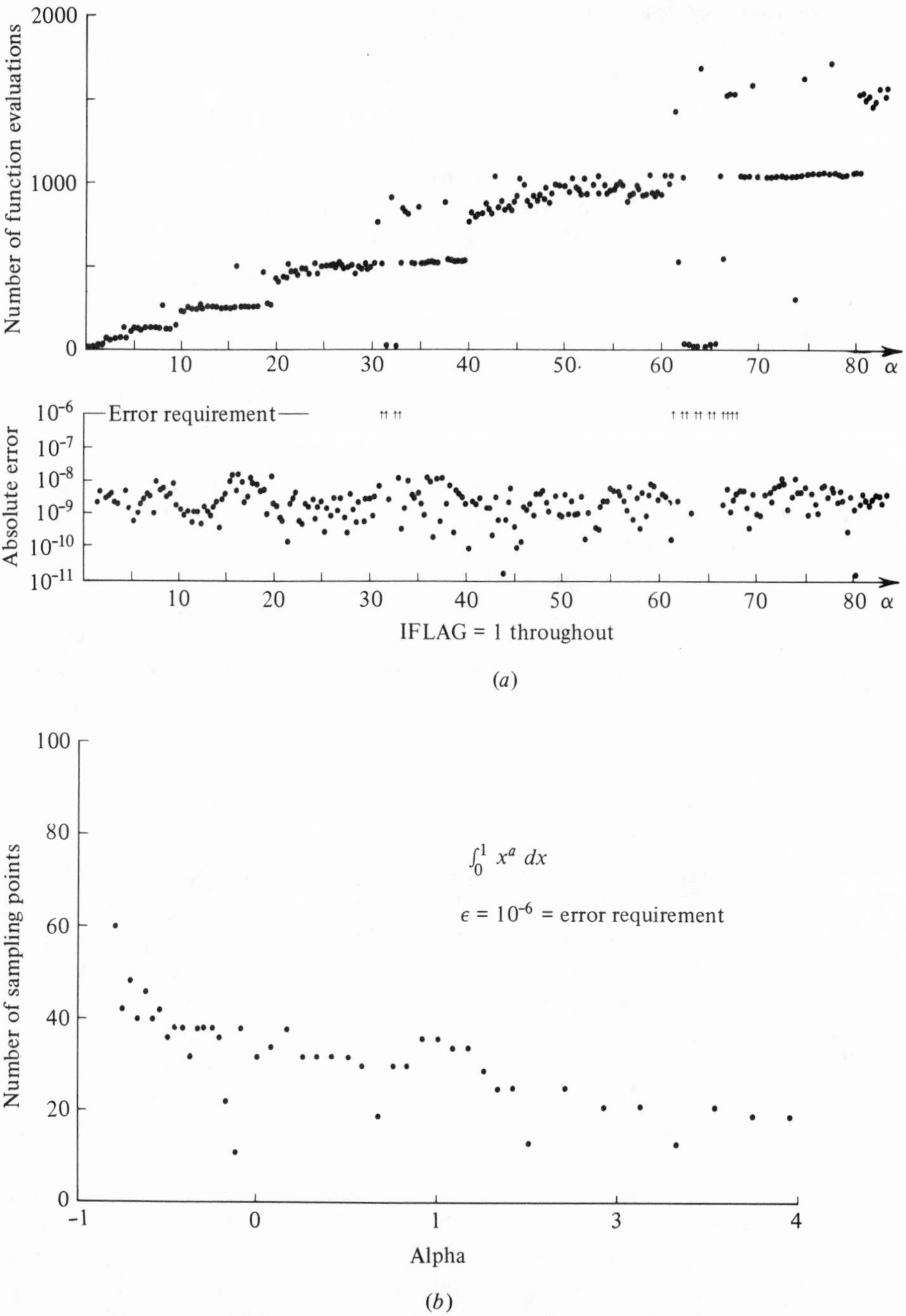

Figure 7.2 Two performance profiles from numerical integration. (*a*) CADRE [de Boor, 1971] applied to $\int_0^1[\cos(\alpha\pi x) + 1]$ dx. This profile shows the work increasing as the oscillation increases, but in an unexpected way. The large errors near $\alpha = 32$ and 64 are due to an interaction between the algorithm and the frequency. (*b*) DQUAD [Blue, 1975] applied to $\int_0^1 x^\alpha$ dx. This profile shows that the work is unaffected by the singularity strength; it decreases slowly as α increases.

that *no* convergence test is completely reliable, no matter how many lines of code it may involve. Thus the objective of any code actually used is to be "hard to fool" or "highly reliable for real applications." These objectives are vague, and heuristic tests are used to attempt to meet them. The values of these tests usually can be judged by how well they fare in use; there is no way to mathematically state what they are to accomplish.

One can modify the idea of program proof in a useful way in some such situations. For example, one could prove the following assertion about a subprogram:

> "This code finds a value of x so that ABS(F(x)) < EPS or it returns a value of 1 for the argument IFAIL."

Such an assertion may be critical information for establishing the reliability of a program, but it does not give any clue as to when the subprogram might produce correct results [assuming that $|F(x)|$ less than EPS is required for correct results]. One might attempt to find a hypothesis on F(x) so as to ensure that the case of ABS(F(x)) < EPS holds. Such hypotheses tend to involve mathematical properties of F(x) which cannot be verified in practice or which restrict the applicability of the proof to a trivial or degenerate set of input. Only *verifiable hypotheses* are of value in program correctness proofs.

7.C REPORTING COMPUTATIONAL EXPERIMENTS

The performance evaluation of software is primarily an experimental science. The analysis of algorithms and related techniques can give a good indication of what to expect from many programs, but actual measurements must be taken to be certain of the performance. For example, the execution time of a program using Gauss elimination should increase like N^3 for solving N equations. However, it makes a big difference whether it is $0.05N^3$ or $500N^3$ (see Table 7.2). For small N (say $N \leq 6$), the execution time is almost surely better represented by $a + bN + cN^2$ (with appropriate coefficients a, b, and c), and there is always the chance that a programming error has completely changed the expected behavior.

There are certain standard procedures that have been adopted in the experimental sciences in order to achieve confidence in the validity of experimentally based conclusions. At the highest level these procedures are required to "be systematic, organized, objective, consider all relevant influences and report exactly what was done and what the results were." Each experimental science develops its own techniques, and the material in this chapter has been an exposition of some of these techniques for mathematical software. In addition, there are the general techniques of the design of experiments from the statistical point of view. While these statistical

Table 7.4 Checklist for reporting computational evaluations

	Algorithm information
Required:	Complete description of algorithm plus the class of problems it is supposed to handle
Nice:	Information on computational complexity, convergence rates, error estimates, work per step, etc.
	Computer program and computational environment
Required:	Programming language and compiler Computer, operating system, and options used Input formats, tolerances, and other program "settings" Special techniques or tactics used
Nice:	Information on the availability of the programs, user's manual, etc.
	Experimental design and results
Required:	A clear statement of the experimental objectives Documentation of procedures used, preprocessing of problems or postprocessing of data Description of data to be obtained, including units of measurement and accuracy Problem population considered and sampling method used
Nice:	Use of standard problems, preprocessing, units of measurements etc. Availability of problems, programs, and procedures for others to use
	Reporting the results
Required:	Complete description of the experimental design and procedures Justification of experimental design and performance measures used How measurements were made with detailed breakdowns (if appropriate) Failures that occurred, with explanation, if possible Program parameters used (e.g., tolerances, initial states, options, switches)
Nice:	Effects of varying components of the experiment such as termination criteria, tolerances, or measurement techniques
	Conclusions stated
Required:	Clear distinction between objective results and speculation Description of hypotheses and assumptions made
Nice:	Directions for future study or algorithm improvement Identification of special problems classes where interesting things were observed

procedures are not discussed in this book, they are an essential part of many software performance evaluations.

The algorithm and software community does not have a tradition of high-quality performance evaluations. This section is based on a paper by Crowder, Dembo, and Mulvey (1979), where they report on a survey of over 50 papers to evaluate algorithms and software for a certain class of problems. None of the 50 papers was found to have used consistently good experimental techniques; most were found to be poor in many respects. A particularly common failing is to report conclusions without describing the experiments adequately or reporting the data obtained. They cite one paper which contains the statement:

> Since the methods were coded for different machines in different languages by different programmers, there is little point in giving a detailed assessment of the results, particularly as so many of the problems were degenerate. However, the results show that . . .

Such an experiment cannot show anything, but it is often hard to argue against the conclusions stated because the data which lead to them are not given.

In Table 7.4 of this section a checklist is presented for reporting computational experiments. Some of these items are not needed for all experiments and, conversely, some experiments need other items. Nevertheless, this checklist is a good guide as to the amount and kind of information that is required to instill confidence in the conclusions drawn from experiments with software.

7.D THE ALGORITHM SELECTION PROBLEM

The problem of selecting an effective or good or best algorithm arises in a wide variety of situations. The context of these situations often obscures the common features of this selection problem, and the purpose of this section is to formulate an abstract model appropriate for considering it.

It should be made clear that these models will not lead directly (by simple specialization) to superior selection procedures. One must always exploit the specific nature of the situation at hand. Even so, these models do clarify the consideration of this problem.

A selection procedure is often obtained by assigning values to parameters in general "form." More precisely, the selection procedure itself is an algorithm, and a specific class of algorithms is chosen with free parameters, which are then, in turn, determined to satisfy (as well as they can) the objectives of the selection problem. Classical forms include polynomials (with coefficients as parameters) and linear formulas (with matrix coefficients or weights as parameters). Other relevant forms are decision trees (with size, shape, and individual decision elements as parameters) and programs (with various program elements as parameters). The assignment of parameters is not common for matrix computation software where one is to choose among a small collection of programs.

The models presented here are primarily aimed at algorithm selection problems with one or more of the following three characteristics:

Problem space. The set of problems involved is very large and quite diverse. This set is of high dimension in the sense that there are many independent characteristics of the problems that are important for the algorithm selection and performance. There is usually considerable uncertainty about these characteristics and their influences.

Algorithm space. The set of algorithms that needs to be considered is large and diverse. Ideally there might be millions of algorithms, and practically there might be dozens of them. In counting algorithms we do not distinguish between two that are identical except for the value of some numeric parameter. Again, this set is of high dimension and there is uncertainty about the influence of algorithm characteristics.

Performance measure. The criteria to measure the performance of a particular algorithm for a particular problem are complex and hard to compare (e.g., one wants fast execution, high accuracy, and simplicity). Again, there is considerable uncertainty in assigning and interpreting these measures.

The basic abstract model is illustrated by Fig. 7.3. The items in this model are defined here:

Problem space = collection of problems to be solved (program data)

Algorithm space = collection of algorithms (programs) that could be used

S = mapping that gives an algorithm for a particular problem

p = vector of performance measures of algorithm A applied to problem x

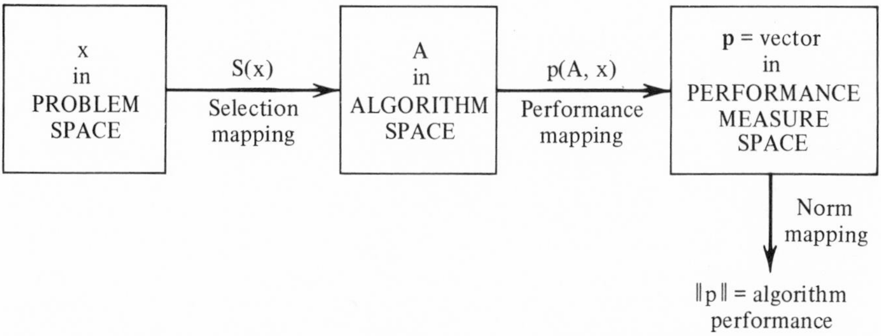

Figure 7.3 Schematic diagram of the basic model for the algorithm selection problem. The objective is to determine S(x) so as to have high algorithm performance.

The norm provides *one number* to evaluate an algorithm's performance on a particular problem.

For completeness we now state the *algorithm selection problem:* Given all the other items in the above model, determine the selection mapping S(x).

There must, of course, be some criteria for this selection and we present three primary ones:

1. *Best selection.* Choose that selection mapping B(x) which gives maximum performance for each problem; that is $\|\mathbf{p}(B(x), x)\| \geq \|\mathbf{p}(A, x)\|$ for all possible algorithms A.
2. *Best selection for a subclass of problems.* One is to choose just one algorithm to apply to every member of a subclass of problems. Choose that algorithm A_0 which minimizes the performance degradation for members of the subclass [compared to choosing B(x)]. That is, A_0 gives performance as close as possible to the best B(x).
3. *Best selection from a subclass of mappings.* One is to restrict the mapping S(x) to be of a certain form or from a certain subclass of algorithms. Choose that selection mapping S*(x) which minimizes the performance degradation for all problems.

Example 7.1: A game-playing problem We are to find an algorithm for playing tic-tac-toe. The problem space is the set of partial games of tic-tac-toe. While this number is large, there are in fact only 28 distinct reasonable games if one eliminates blunders, symmetries, and board rotations. The algorithm space may be represented as a space of large tables of responses for each situation. However, we restrict our selection to a subclass of algorithms by making the algorithm a decision tree that involves only the existence of immediate winning positions and vacant position types. The algorithm form is represented as in Fig. 7.4. There are 16 parameters a_i, which take on one of the following five values:

1. Play the winning move
2. Block the opponent's win
3. Play in the center square
4. Play in a corner (first free one clockwise from upper right)
5. Play in a side (first free one clockwise from right)

This example is so simple that one can make immediate assignments of certain of the values of the a_i. Experiments have shown that a variety of crude schemes for computing values of the a_i (selecting the best algorithm) work very quickly. Nevertheless, it is still of interest to reflect upon how one would compute them if one had no experience with the game.

In practice, algorithm selection is usually based on *features* of the problem instead of on the problem itself. The extension of the abstract model to include this is shown by the diagram in Fig. 7.5.

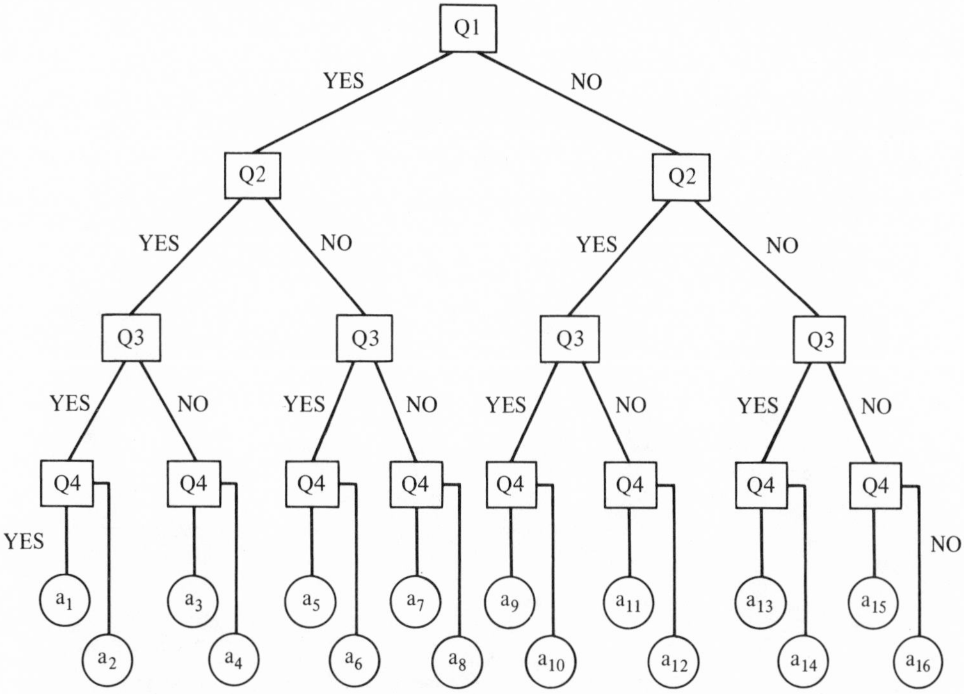

Figure 7.4 The form of the selection mapping for the tic-tac-toe example. Each a_i is one of five moves. The Q's are questions.

Q1: Do I have a winning position?
Q2: Does opponent have a winning position?
Q3: Is the center free?
Q4: Is a corner free?

The additional definitions for this model are the feature space of vectors of feature values and F, the feature extraction mapping that associates features with problems. Note that the selection mapping now depends only on the features f(x), yet the performance mapping still depends on the problem x. The introduction of features can be viewed as a way to systematize the introduction of problem subclasses in the basic model.

The previous statement of the algorithm selection problem and the criteria for selection are still valid for this expanded model. The determination of the features to be used is part of the selection process, often one of the most important parts. One can view the features as an attempt to introduce an approximate coordinate system into the problem space. Ideally, those problems with the same features would have the same performance for any algorithm being considered. This ideal is rarely achieved.

The determination of the best (or even good) features is one of the most important, yet nebulous, aspects of the algorithm selection problem. Many

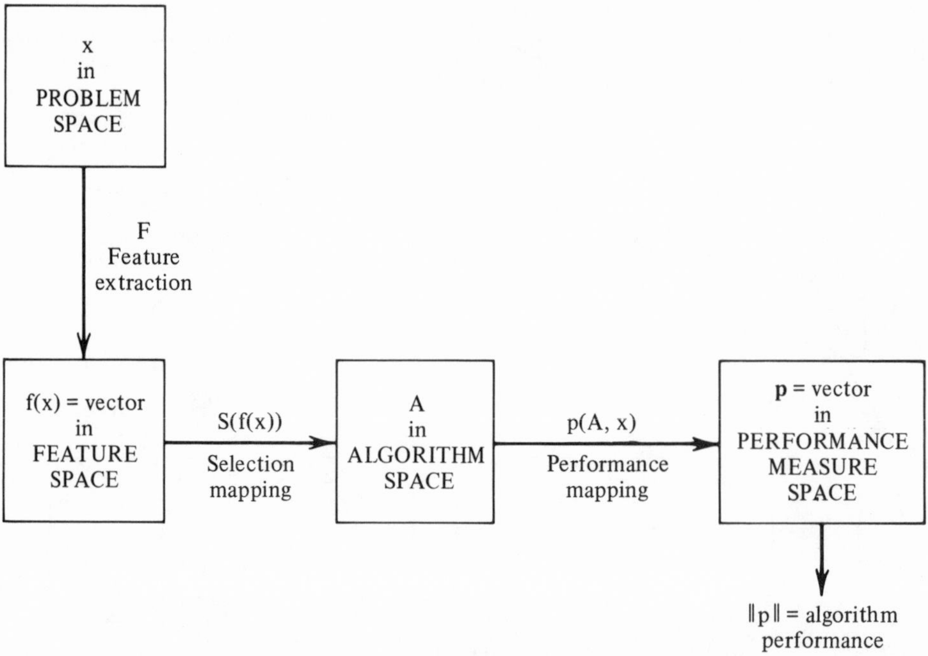

Figure 7.5 Schematic diagram of the model with selection based on features of the problem. The selection mapping depends only on the features f(x), yet the performance still depends on the problem x.

problem spaces are known only in vague terms, and hence an experimental approach is often used to evaluate the performance of algorithms over P. That is, one chooses a sample of problems and studies this sample. An appropriate sample is obviously crucial to this approach and, if one has a good set of problem features, then one can at least force the sample to be representative with respect to these features. Note that good features are the items of information most relevant to the performance of algorithms.

In some well-understood areas of computation there is a generally agreed upon set of features. For example, in matrix computations the features include items like small order, sparse, band, diagonally dominant, positive-definite, and ill conditioned. Given values for these features, an experienced person can select an appropriate algorithm for this problem with considerable confidence. The selection problem for numerical integration is already much more difficult, and the solution of simultaneous systems of nonlinear equations is very poorly understood. If this situation exists for problems that have been studied for one or two centuries, then one should not be surprised by the difficulties and uncertainties for problems that have just appeared in the past one or two decades.

So far we have assumed that there is a fixed way to measure the performance of a particular algorithm for a particular problem. There are some situations where it is reasonable to view the performance criteria as input to

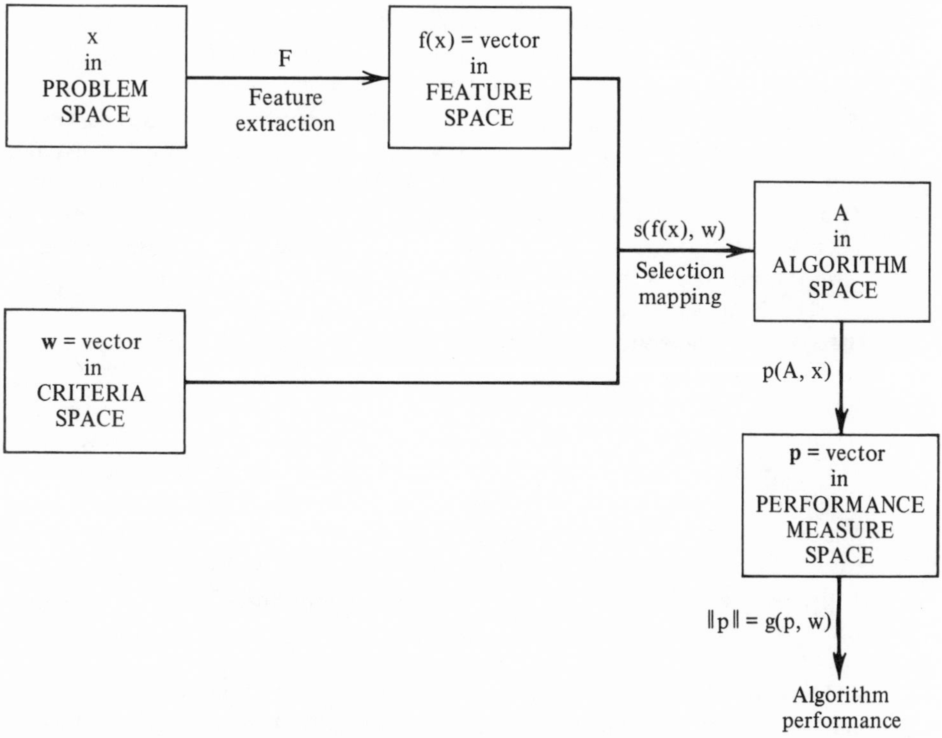

Figure 7.6 Schematic diagram of the model with selection based on problem features and variable performance criteria.

the selection problem. Consider, for example, the selection of a program to solve ordinary differential equations and the criteria of speed, accuracy, reliability, and ease of use. In different situations the weight given to each of these might vary from almost 0 to almost 100 percent. A model for this version of the selection problem is shown in Fig. 7.6.

The additional ingredient for this model is g, a new norm function that depends on performance measures and criteria values, which measures the algorithm performance **p**(A, x) with the criterion weight **w**.

We could formulate new versions of the algorithm selection problem involving the criteria space. The variables of these formulations are

Problem subclasses:	P_0
Algorithm subclasses:	A_0
Selection mapping subclasses:	S_0
Feature space:	F
Norm mapping:	g

The number of interesting combinations is now quite large, but we refrain from formulating them.

Example 7.2: The selection of operating system schedulers The general case of this selection problem is expressed as follows: Consider a computing installation with a fixed configuration and a work load with reasonably well-known properties. How should jobs be scheduled in order to give the best service?

A thorough analysis of this problem requires many hundreds of pages and is beyond the scope of this section. We formulate a simple, but not trivial, case of this problem within the framework provided by the abstract models. Then we describe a simplified version of a real scheduling algorithm and, in turn, formulate a much more specific algorithm selection problem.

The abstract model involves spaces for the problems, the features, the criteria, the algorithms, and the performance measures. These spaces are described as follows:

1. PROBLEM SPACE This space consists of configurations of computer runs, which are mixtures of batch, remote batch, time-shared, and interactive jobs. These configurations are very dynamic in nature and normally only average values are known for the population characteristics (and most of these values are not known accurately). In addition to very rapid and substantial changes in the problem characteristics, there are often well-identified long-term variations in the average values of the problem characteristics.

2. FEATURE SPACE The features of a configuration of computer runs are a combination of the features of the individual jobs. The features of individual jobs that might be considered are indicated by a key word plus a short explanation:

Priority: value given by user and computing center
CPU time: value estimated for job by user less time already run
Memory: value estimated for job by user and observed by operating system (both core and auxiliary memory values might be considered)
I/O requirements: values estimated by user for use of standard devices (printers, punches, disk channels, etc.)
Special facilities: indications of use of less common facilities (e.g., tape units, plotters, graphics consoles)
Program locality and stability: indication of the likelihood of page requests or job roll-outs

In addition, features of the total problem configuration that might be considered are:

Batch load: length of the input queue plus average values for some of the job features
On-line load: number of terminal users plus average values of features for the stream of jobs they create

Interactive load: number of users and nature of system being used
I/O load: length of queues at the various I/O devices

3. Algorithm Space A fair variety of simple scheduling algorithms have been proposed and analyzed (e.g., round-robin, first-come first-served, simple priority). An essential characteristic of successful algorithms is that they are fast to execute (otherwise the system devotes an excessive amount of its resources to scheduling instead of production). This favors some very simple schemes, but one must realize that rather complex algorithms can be fast to execute.

4. Performance Measures The performance of an operating system depends on one's viewpoint—each user wants instant service and the computing center director wants zero dissatisfied customers. Neither of these desires is very realistic, but efforts to measure the progress made toward satisfying them usually involve throughput and response time. These measures are applied to different classes of jobs as follows:

Batch: small job response; median and maximum turnabout for jobs with small resource requirements
Batch: large job response; median and maximum turnabout for all batch jobs other than small ones (or special runs)
On-line response: median and maximum response time for common service functions (e.g., fetching a file, editing a line, submitting a batch job)
Interactive response: median and maximum response times for standard short requests
Throughput: total number of jobs processed per unit time, number of central processing unit (CPU) hours billed per day, etc.

5. Criteria Space This consists of numbers to weigh the relative importance of the performance measures. Values of some of these measures can be improved only by making others worse, and it is difficult to compare them. Scaling the measures to a standard interval (say 0 to 1) and then applying weights (which sum to unity) is simple, but often satisfactory.

We consider a simplified version of a real scheduling algorithm used on the system at Purdue University. Jobs are scheduled according to priority; i.e., if a waiting job has queue priority QP_1 larger than an executing job with queue priority QP_2 and if the central memory CM_2 used by the executing job is large enough for the waiting job (which requires CM_1 in memory), then the executing job is terminated and rolled out and the waiting job is rolled in and placed into execution. In summary, if $QP_1 > QP_2$ and $CM_1 < CM_2$, then job 2 is rolled out and replaced by job 1.

The queue priority QP is a function of four priority parameters $\mathbf{r} = (r_1, r_2, r_3, r_4)^T$ as follows:

r_1 = job card priority parameter

r_2 = central memory (current requirement)

r_3 = time remaining on CPU time estimate

r_4 = I/O units remaining on I/O transfer unit estimate

The value of QP is then a linear combination

$$QP = \sum_{i=1}^{4} R_i(r_i)$$

where

$$R_1(r_1) = a_1 * r_1$$
$$R_2(r_2) = a_2 * (150{,}100 - r_2)$$
$$R_3(r_3) = a_3 * (a_4 - r_3)_+^0 + a_5 * (a_6 - r_3)_+^0 + a_7 * (a_8 - r_3)_+^0$$
$$R_4(r_4) = a_9 * (a_{10} - r_4)_+^0 + a_{11} * (a_{12} - r_4)_+^0 + a_{13} * (a_{14} - r_4)_+^0$$

Recall the notation

$$(x - c)_+^n = \begin{cases} (x - c)^n & \text{if } x \geq c \\ 0 & \text{if } x \leq c \end{cases}$$

R_3 and R_4 are shown in Fig. 7.7. This function QP involves 14 coefficients or parameters.

We now consider algorithms that involve three features of the configuration of computer runs:

f_1 = number of short jobs (with 30 seconds or less CPU time estimate)

f_2 = remaining number of jobs

f_3 = number of active terminals (which may be used in a variety of modes)

We choose a three-dimensional performance measure space with

$$\mathbf{p} = (p_1, p_2, p_3)^T$$

where p_1 = (mean internal processing time for short batch jobs)/1000

p_2 = (mean internal processing time for other batch jobs)/4000

p_3 = (mean response time for standard short on-line tasks)/10

The scaling implies that $\mathbf{p} = (1, 1, 1)^T$ corresponds to approximately a 15-minute average processing time for short batch jobs, a 1-hour average processing time for other jobs, and a 10-second response time on-line. The algorithm performance is then measured by

$$\|\mathbf{p}\| = w_1 p_1 + w_2 p_2 + w_3 p_3$$

where the w_i are from the three-dimensional criteria space with $w_i \geq 0$ and $w_1 + w_2 + w_3 = 1$.

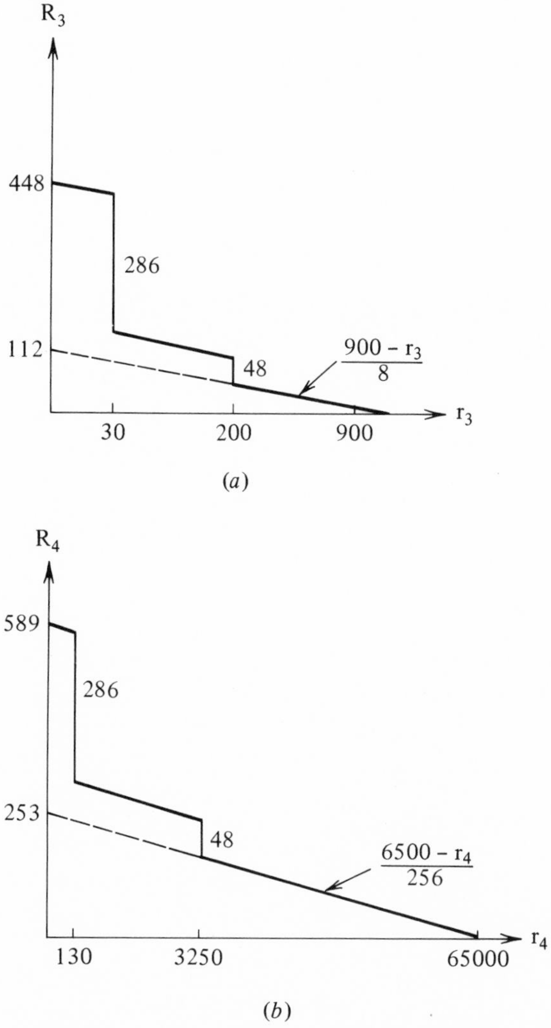

Figure 7.7 Graphs of the function $R_3(r_3)$ and $R_4(r_4)$. The horizontal axes are not drawn to scale. Each function is piecewise linear. (*a*) Priority contribution for CPU time. (*b*) Priority contribution for I/0 units.

The situation for determining the coefficients of the scheduling algorithm is as follows:

1. The computer operator selects a criteria vector **w**.
2. The operating system measures the configuration features f_1, f_2, f_3.
3. The appropriate best coefficients **a** are used for these values of w_i and f_i.

Thus we see that the 14 coefficients are, in fact, functions of six other independent variables, the w_i and f_i.

We now consider how to find the best scheduler of this form. To set the context, let us outline how the computation might go in an ideal world. The basic building block would be the computation of best a_i for given w_i and f_i. This block is designated by the function OPT, i.e., OPT(**w, f**) is the set of 14 best coefficients for given vectors **w** and **f**. We would then select an appropriate set of values for the variables w_i and f_i, say $w_{i\ell}$, $\ell = 1$ to m_w, and f_{ik}, $k = 1$ to m_f, and execute the algorithm

For $\ell = 1$ to m_w, $k = 1$ to m_f do $a_i(\ell, k) = \text{OPT}(w_\ell, f_k)$

At this point we now have a tabulation of the coefficients a_i as a function of the w_i and f_i. One could just interpolate in this table or, perhaps, one would obtain a linear least-squares fit of the form

$$a_i = \alpha_{i0} + \sum_{i=1}^{3} (\alpha_{ij} f_j + \alpha_{i,\, j+3} w_j)$$

Let us consider ways that this simple-minded computational approach can go wrong. We list some obvious ways (no doubt there are others waiting if one actually tries the approach):

1. The function OPT is too difficult to compute. We would say that 50 to 200 evaluations of functions (that is, **p** as a function of **a**) should be considered reasonable. More than 500 or 1000 indicates real difficulties, and less than 50 real luck.
2. The form chosen for QP as a function of **a** is inadequate. This is not likely since the form is based on one in current use.
3. The linear form for the **a** as a function of the w_i and f_i is inadequate.
4. One is unable to vary f_1, f_2, and f_3 over the range of values as indicated in the system, and thus they are continually varying and uncontrollable. To create configurations with known features is probably a very substantial task.
5. The measurement of $\|\mathbf{p}\|$ is uncertain due to the dynamic nature of the process. That is, in the 15 minutes that it takes for a batch job to go through the system, there may have been wide variations in the values of **f** (due to the changing job configuration) and the values of **a** (due to changes made by OPT).

We note that difficulties 2 and 3 are from the problem formulation and not the computation, so we ignore them here. The difficulty with OPT might be very real, but one can be optimistic that a good minimization algorithm will handle this part of the computation—especially after some experience is obtained so that good initial guesses are available. This leaves difficulties 4 and 5, which are very interesting and somewhat unusual in standard optimization problems. They can be handled, but how it is done is outside the scope of this book. See Sec. 4 of Rice (1976) (see References at back of book) for further details.

PROBLEMS FOR CHAP. 7

1 Consider the Fortran program given below.

(*a*) Indicate what changes need to be made to make this program easily portable and indicate what local changes (i.e., changes for a local computing environment) would still be needed.

(*b*) Indicate the changes required to make this program double precision.

```
      PROGRAM PROB1(INPUT,OUTPUT)
C
C       PROBLEM 1, CHAPTER 7 CONCERNING FORTRAN PORTABILITY
C
C            SECANT METHOD FOR SOLVING AN EQUATION
      DATA PI / 3.1415 92653 58979 /
      F(T) = .3*T*EXP(T) + COS(PI*T) - 3.
C
C               GUESS TO START
      XSECOND = 1.4
      XFIRST = 1.2
      DO 10 J = 1,100
          BOTTOM = (F(XFIRST)-F(XSECOND))/(XFIRST-XSECOND)
C                  DONT DIVIDE BY ZERO
          IF( ABS(BOTTOM) .LE. 1.E-14 )   GO TO 99
          XCHANGE = F(XFIRST)/BOTTOM
          XNEXT = XFIRST - XCHANGE
C                  TEST FOR CONVERGENCE TO FULL ACCURACY
          IF( ABS(XCHANGE) .LE. 5.E-14 )      GO TO 30
          XSECOND= XFIRST
          XFIRST = XNEXT
   10 CONTINUE
C                    NO CONVERGENCE
      PRINT 20, XFIRST,XCHANGE
   20 FORMAT(10(3H **),18H NO CONVERGENCE AT,F20.15,11HLAST STEP = ,E15.5)
      STOP
C
C                  CONVERGENCE
   30 PRINT 40, XFIRST,J
   40 FORMAT(20X,13HCONVERGED TO ,F20.15,3H IN,I3,10HITERATIONS )
      STOP
C
C                  TRIED TO DIVIDE BY ZERO
   99 PRINT 100, XFIRST
  100 FORMAT(10(3H **),5X≠ TRIED TO DIVIDE BY ZERO AT≠F25.15/
     A       10(3H **),5X≠ ITERATION ABORTED≠)
      STOP
      END
```

2 Identify some local "enhancements" of Fortran in your local compiler which are not portable.

3 Why is it generally impossible to write an algorithm in a high-level language (Fortran, Algol, PL/1, Pascal, etc.) which is both portable and has top efficiency?

4 Sketch the performance profile that you would expect for execution time versus number of right-hand sides for a good linear equation solver. Show some reasonable numerical values on the scales.

5 Consider a new, fast linear equation solver MYLIN. Describe in detail an evaluation of MYLIN reliability and robustness compared to some other routine.

6 Write a set of Fortran matrix utility programs that does the following:

(*a*) Computes the dot product of two n-vectors: ANS = DOT(X, Y, N).

(*b*) Computes a linear combination $\mathbf{ax} + \mathbf{y}$ of n-vectors and writes the result on top of $\mathbf{y}$: CALL AXY(A, X, Y, N).

(*c*) Computes the 1, 2, or ∞ norm of a vector: ANS = XNORM(X, K) when K = 1, 2, or 3 (use 3 for ∞) indicates the desired norm.

(*d*) Computes the product AB of two $n \times n$ matrices and writes it on top of A: CALL PROD(A, B, N).

(*e*) Computes the product AT of two $n \times n$ matrices where T is upper triangular. The result replaces A: CALL PRODT(A, T, N).

(*f*) Computes the product AR of two $n \times n$ matrices where R is of the form

$$\begin{pmatrix} I & 0 \\ 0 & B \end{pmatrix}$$

and B is an $m \times m$ matrix. The result replaces A: CALL PRODR(A, R, N, M).

7 Suppose you are to prepare a library subroutine to solve the differential equation

$$y'' + a(x)y' + b(x)y = f(x), \quad x\varepsilon[\alpha, \beta] \qquad y(\alpha) = y_0 \qquad y(\beta) = y_1$$

with input data a(x), b(x), f(x), α and β, and y_0 and y_1. Further input data are the accuracy desired in solving the problem. You have two candidates for methods to use: (*a*) Use finite difference linearization and systematically increase the number of points used until the accuracy is obtained. (Assume you can measure the accuracy well.) (*b*) Use Taylor's series expansion and increase the number of terms used until the accuracy is obtained. Describe a computational experiment that you would perform to comparatively evaluate two programs, one using (*a*) and the other (*b*). Identify the independent variables in this experiment, the quantities that you would measure, and the criteria for comparison that you would use. Describe the selection of actual cases you would run and make a ball-park estimate of how much effort (both human and machine time) this experiment might take. Do not consider the effort in preparing the programs to be tested.

8 Investigate the effects of compilers on the execution time of Fortran programs as follows:

(*a*) Obtain two programs. One, which you will probably write yourself, is to have simple code everywhere, i.e. simple assignments, loops, or tests. The second should be a library program for matrix computations, e.g., solution of systems of linear equations.

(*b*) Compile each program with two (or more) different compilers.

(*c*) Time the execution of the programs as accurately as your local system permits. Note that it is usually not possible to obtain accurate timings for very short runs. You might have to put the program in a loop and run it many times.

(*d*) Prepare a table like Table 7.3.

9 Describe in considerable detail the design of an experiment to evaluate and compare two subroutines for solving $A\mathbf{x} = \mathbf{b}$ where A is small or of moderate size (say of order less than 40) and A is a band matrix. Specifically, describe the problem space, the feature space, the performance criteria, the actual problem population used, and the computational experiments to be run.

10 What measures can be taken to eliminate bias in the performance evaluation of matrix computation software? Describe various ways that someone might make an evaluation go the way desired without actually falsifying the experimental data.

11 Choose a linear equation solver from your local library and prepare the following performance profiles:

(*a*) Execution time versus matrix order.

(*b*) Memory used versus matrix order.

(*c*) Execution time versus number of right-hand sides.

(*d*) Execution time versus percent of zeros (use band matrices). Some programs do not take advantage of zeros in the matrix.

CHAPTER

EIGHT

HOW DO YOU KNOW YOU HAVE THE RIGHT ANSWERS?

The ideal situation for a program to solve $\mathbf{Ax} = \mathbf{b}$ would be for it to either (1) return the correct answer (modulo modest round-off effects) or (2) say that A is singular. The Gauss elimination algorithm (or variants) is not able to provide such results. Furthermore, matrices are not simply singular or nonsingular; there is a continuous variation from nonsingular to singular. In this chapter we consider mechanisms for a program to solve $\mathbf{Ax} = \mathbf{b}$ to judge whether it has obtained the correct answer.

Unfortunately, it is quite common for practical problems to lead to very difficult matrix computation problems. We begin by examining an example from Sec. 3.A.2 and the present three approaches to estimating the accuracy of computed solutions of $\mathbf{Ax} = \mathbf{b}$.

8.A POLYNOMIAL REGRESSION AND THE HILBERT MATRIX

Example 8.1 Suppose we have 101 observations (data points) for equally spaced x's between 0 and 1:

$$(x_i, d_i) \qquad \text{for } i = 1 \text{ to } 101 \text{ where } x_i = (i-1)/100$$

We believe that the data d_i varies with the x_i as a polynomial of degree k; that is,

$$d_i \sim \sum_{j=0}^{k} c_j(x_i)^j = P_k(x_i)$$

Recall the least-squares regression (or approximation) method of choosing the c_j so that

$$\text{Error} = \sum_i [d_i - P(x_i)]^2 = \text{minimum}$$

As shown earlier (and as will be discussed again in Chap. 11), this results in a system of k + 1 linear equations (the normal equations) for the best c_j^* with matrix elements

$$a_{mn} = \sum_i x_i^{m-1} x_i^{n-1} \sim 100 \int_0^1 x^{m+n-2}\,dx = \frac{100}{m+n-1}$$

We have interpreted the sum $\sum_i$ as a rough approximation to the integral shown. Thus the equations for the c_j^* are something close to

$$\begin{aligned}
c_0^* + \tfrac{1}{2}c_1^* + \tfrac{1}{3}c_2^* + \tfrac{1}{4}c_3^* + \cdots + \frac{1}{k+1}c_k^* &= \Big(\sum_i d_i\Big)\Big/100\\
\tfrac{1}{2}c_0^* + \tfrac{1}{3}c_1^* + \tfrac{1}{4}c_2^* + \tfrac{1}{5}c_3^* + \cdots + \frac{1}{k+2}c_k^* &= \Big(\sum_i x_i d_i\Big)\Big/100\\
\tfrac{1}{3}c_0^* + \tfrac{1}{4}c_1^* + \tfrac{1}{5}c_2^* + \tfrac{1}{6}c_3^* + \cdots + \frac{1}{k+3}c_k^* &= \Big(\sum_i x_i^2 d_i\Big)\Big/100\\
\vdots \qquad \vdots \qquad \vdots \qquad \vdots \qquad &\\
\frac{1}{k+1}c_0^* + \frac{1}{k+2}c_1^* + \frac{1}{k+3}c_2^* + \frac{1}{k+4}c_3^* + \cdots + \frac{1}{2k+1}c_k^* &= \Big(\sum_i x_i^k d_i\Big)\Big/100
\end{aligned}$$

The matrix

$$H_k = \left\{ a_{mn} = \frac{1}{m+n-1} \right\}_{m,\,n=1}^{k}$$

is called the *Hilbert matrix* of order k. It is famous because it (or small variations of it) arise in many situations and it is so difficult to use in actual conputations. For the Hilbert matrix of order 10 (9th degree polynomials), the process of solving this system may (and almost always does) magnify the uncertainty in the data d_i by a factor larger than $3 * 10^{12}$. Thus even if the calculation is made using 10 digits, one has an uncertainty of at least 300 in the coefficients c_j^* of the polynomial approximation just due to round-off errors. Furthermore, the accuracy of measured data is rarely so good that it can allow for such a large magnification of uncertainty. In other words, this regression procedure is useless in almost all situations.

The uselessness of the computed results is sometimes obscured by the fact that the residual might be reasonably small. We have already noted that one can have large errors and small residuals, and this is seen again in the examples at the end of this chapter. Nevertheless, many users are misled by seeing that the residuals are small, say 10^{-5}. This suggests, assuming 14-digit arithmetic, that 9 digits have been lost in the calculation and the results are unlikely to be meaningful for the user's problem.

There are some applications where obtaining small residuals is sufficient. For example, if one merely wants a formula to nearly reproduce the data values d_i, then one does not care what happens between the x_i values and does not attempt to interpret the c_j as parameters for some model. Only a small fraction of the regression applications are of this nature.

8.B CONDITION NUMBERS

The condition number of a matrix was originally introduced as a means of making an *a priori* (advance) estimate of how bad errors can be in solving $A\mathbf{x} = \mathbf{b}$. As we will see, the original condition number idea is not very reliable, but later improvements have made it more useful. The improvements have primarily come from using the condition number as an *a posteriori* (after the fact) estimate; that is, we wait until we have "solved" the problem before trying to assess the correctness of the solution. Various kinds of information developed while solving $A\mathbf{x} = \mathbf{b}$ are useful in this assessment.

8.B.1 Derivation of Three Condition Numbers

We derive three different ways to estimate the effect on the solution of errors in the original problem. The situation is as follows: We have an original problem $A\mathbf{x} = \mathbf{b}$ and a perturbed problem $A\bar{\mathbf{x}} = \mathbf{b} + \mathbf{r}$ where $\mathbf{r}$ represents the perturbation in both the right-hand side and A. That is, if A is perturbed to $A + \delta A$, then we simply move $\delta A\mathbf{x}$ to the right-hand side and incorporate it into $\mathbf{r}$. This is technically not quite correct since δA is multiplied by $\mathbf{x}$, but keep in mind that we are now just making rough estimates. The objective is to estimate $\delta\mathbf{x} = \mathbf{x} - \bar{\mathbf{x}}$ in terms of $\mathbf{r}$ and the problem data and, more precisely, to estimate how the uncertainty $\mathbf{r}$ in $\mathbf{b}$ is transmitted to $\delta\mathbf{x}$.

We first define the *natural condition number*. We have

$$A\mathbf{x} = \mathbf{b} \qquad A\bar{\mathbf{x}} = \mathbf{b} + \mathbf{r}$$

so, by subtraction

$$A(\bar{\mathbf{x}} - \mathbf{x}) = \mathbf{r}$$

or

$$\bar{\mathbf{x}} - \mathbf{x} = \delta\mathbf{x} = A^{-1}\mathbf{r}$$

We take the norm of each side to obtain

$$\|\delta\mathbf{x}\| = \|A^{-1}\mathbf{r}\| \le \|A^{-1}\|\,\|\mathbf{r}\|$$

and we see, as no surprise, that the size of A^{-1} estimates how much the uncertainty represented by **r** may be magnified. It is more meaningful to use relative errors, and we have from the above that

$$\frac{\|\delta\mathbf{x}\|}{\|\mathbf{x}\|} \leq \frac{\|A^{-1}\| \, \|\mathbf{r}\|}{\|\mathbf{x}\| \, \|\mathbf{b}\|} * \|\mathbf{b}\| = \frac{\|A^{-1}\| \, \|\mathbf{b}\|}{\|\mathbf{x}\|} * \frac{\|\mathbf{r}\|}{\|\mathbf{b}\|}$$

which shows the natural condition number $\|A^{-1}\| \, \|\mathbf{b}\|/\|\mathbf{x}\|$.

This is called the "natural" condition number because, if you specialize the general theory of conditioning to the particular case of linear equations, then you get this condition number. However, it has not been widely used in linear algebra, probably because of the desire to have-an *a priori* estimate, and this condition number depends on $\|\mathbf{x}\|$, which is not known *a priori*. One can eliminate the dependence on **x** to obtain the *standard condition number* as follows. We have

$$A\mathbf{x} = \mathbf{b}$$

which implies that

$$\|\mathbf{b}\| = \|A\mathbf{x}\| \leq \|A\| \, \|\mathbf{x}\|$$

or

$$\frac{1}{\|\mathbf{x}\|} \leq \frac{\|A\|}{\|\mathbf{b}\|}$$

If we substitute this into the previous estimate of $\|\delta\mathbf{x}\|/\|\mathbf{x}\|$, we get

$$\frac{\|\delta\mathbf{x}\|}{\|\mathbf{x}\|} \leq \frac{\|A^{-1}\| \, \|\mathbf{b}\|}{\|\mathbf{x}\|} * \frac{\|\mathbf{r}\|}{\|\mathbf{b}\|} \leq \frac{\|A^{-1}\| \, \|\mathbf{b}\| \, \|A\|}{\|\mathbf{b}\|} * \frac{\|\mathbf{r}\|}{\|\mathbf{b}\|}$$

$$= \|A^{-1}\| \, \|A\| * \frac{\|\mathbf{r}\|}{\|\mathbf{b}\|}$$

which defines the standard condition number $\|A^{-1}\| \, \|A\|$. Note that both these condition numbers are only estimates of how much the uncertainty in **b** may be magnified. They always overestimate the magnification, sometimes by a tremendous amount, but in special cases they give the magnification exactly.

The Aird-Lynch estimates are more precise and take a little longer to derive. They give both upper and lower bounds on the error magnification. Let C be an approximate inverse of A (C will be a by-product of the Gauss elimination process in practice) and we have

$$C\mathbf{r} = C(\mathbf{b} - A\bar{\mathbf{x}}) = CA(\mathbf{x} - \bar{\mathbf{x}})$$

or

$$\|\mathbf{x} - \bar{\mathbf{x}}\| = \|(CA)^{-1}C\mathbf{r}\| \leq \|(CA)^{-1}\| \, \|C\mathbf{r}\|$$

We use the matrix inequality

$$\|B^{-1}\| \leq \frac{1}{1 - \|B - I\|} \qquad \text{if } \|B - I\| < 1$$

to obtain (with $B = CA$)

$$\|\delta \mathbf{x}\| \leq \frac{\|C\mathbf{r}\|}{1 - \|CA - I\|}$$

or, setting $T = \|CA - I\|$,

$$\frac{\|\delta \mathbf{x}\|}{\|\mathbf{x}\|} \leq \frac{\|C\mathbf{r}\|}{\|\mathbf{x}\|(1 - T)}$$

In practice T is usually a small number because C is taken to be a reasonably good approximation to A^{-1}. It is crucial that $\|C\mathbf{r}\|$ not be replaced by $\|C\| \, \|\mathbf{r}\|$, both for reasons of accuracy and of computational effort. We leave it as an excercise for the reader to derive the lower-bound estimate

$$\frac{\|C\mathbf{r}\|}{\|\mathbf{x}\|(1 + T)} \leq \frac{\|\delta \mathbf{x}\|}{\|\mathbf{x}\|}$$

Note that this last estimate provides a lower bound on the error in the approximate solution $\bar{\mathbf{x}}$ in terms of the residual $\mathbf{r}$.

8.B.2 Computation of Condition Numbers

The difficulty with each of these error estimates is that they involve A^{-1}. There are a few times where $\|A^{-1}\|$ can be found without finding A^{-1} (one can look up the norms for Hilbert matrices), but these are so rare that we ignore them. We specifically consider the following common situation: The system $A\mathbf{x} = \mathbf{b}$ has been solved by Gauss elimination; we have an approximate solution $\bar{\mathbf{x}}$ and its residual $\mathbf{r}$, and the factors M and U so that $MA = U$. We now want to estimate the error $\delta\mathbf{x}$ by these three methods. We assume A is $n \times n$ in this section.

For the natural and standard condition numbers, the only difficulty is with $\|A^{-1}\|$. We have three alternatives:

1. *Compute* A^{-1} *and its norm.* This requires about $n^3 + 2n^2$ extra operations and approximately quadruples the work of solving $A\mathbf{x} = \mathbf{b}$.
2. *Estimate* $\|A^{-1}\|$ *roughly*. Note that, if $\mathbf{w} = A^{-1}\mathbf{y}$, then $\|\mathbf{w}\| \leq \|A^{-1}\| \, \|\mathbf{y}\|$, so $\|A^{-1}\| \geq \|\mathbf{w}\|/\|\mathbf{y}\|$. We can choose k vectors $\mathbf{y}_i$, $i = 1, 2, \ldots, k$ and solve $A\mathbf{w}_i = \mathbf{y}_i$ and take

$$\|A^{-1}\| \sim \max_i \|\mathbf{w}_i\|/\|\mathbf{y}_i\|$$

   If k is small this requires about kn^2 operations, which is small compared to the work invested in solving $A\mathbf{x} = \mathbf{b}$. There is a heuristic argument which says that, if $\mathbf{y}$ is picked at random, then the expected value of $\|\mathbf{w}\|/\|\mathbf{y}\|$ is about $\frac{1}{2}\|A^{-1}\|$. Thus it seems fairly safe to use a small value of k.

   We can get the estimate $\|A^{-1}\| \geq \|\bar{\mathbf{x}}\|/\|\mathbf{b}\|$ practically free.

3. *Use the LINPACK estimate of* $\|A^{-1}\|$. The previous idea has been refined so that a special vector $\mathbf{v} = \mathbf{y}$ with components ± 1 is chosen so as to improve the reliability of the estimate (Dongarra et al., 1979; see References at end of book). Further once $\mathbf{w}$ is found then $\mathbf{v}$ is computed from

$$A^T\mathbf{v} = \mathbf{w}$$

and $\|A^{-1}\|$ is then estimated by $\|\mathbf{v}\|/\|\mathbf{w}\|$. The computational effort of this approach is about the same as the previous one with $k = 3$.

The matrix C for the Aird-Lynch estimate is $U^{-1}M$ of the factorization. To compute $C\mathbf{r}$ requires only solving with another right-hand side, about n^2 operations. There are various ways to estimate $T = \|CA - I\|$:

a. *Compute* $CA - I$ *and its norm.* Let $S = CA - I = U^{-1}MA - I$. Then $US = MA - U$, where MA is very close to U. Thus the columns $\mathbf{s}_i$ of S can be calculated by solving n systems of equations

$$U\mathbf{s}_i = \mathbf{d}_i \qquad i = 1, 2, \ldots, n$$

where $\mathbf{d}_i$ is the ith column of $D = MA - U$. The computation to do this is the $n^3/2$ to form MA, $n^2/2$ to subtract U, and $n^3/2$ to solve the n upper triangular systems of equations. To compute the row sum or column sum norm of $CA - I$ requires another n^2 operations. The net result is that this requires about n^3 extra operations and approximately quadruples the work of solving $A\mathbf{x} = \mathbf{b}$.

b. *Estimate* $\|CA - I\|$ *roughly.* The matrix $D = MA - U$ should be exactly zero and will differ from zero only by normal round-off effects. Thus it should be a random matrix with entries proportional to the round-off error level ε of the machine. This implies $\|S\| = \|U^{-1}D\|$ becomes larger only by $\|U^{-1}\|$ being large. Thus

$$T = \|S\| \leq \|U^{-1}\| * c\varepsilon$$

where c is a "small" function of n (say $\sqrt{n}$). We can then estimate $\|U^{-1}\|$ by either of the techniques described in steps 2 and 3 above. There will be a savings of a factor of 2 because U is upper triangular. Furthermore, T has a much less sensitive role in this error estimate than $\|A^{-1}\|$ does in the natural or standard condition numbers. The work involved here is thus proportional to n^2

c. *Take* $T = \frac{1}{2}$. This, of course, is extremely crude and is based on the idea that the $1/(1 - T)$ factor is of secondary importance. If T is larger than $\frac{1}{2}$, in which case A is very nearly singular, then $\|C\mathbf{r}\|$ is large and the inaccuracy in the solution should already be known. This alternative is, of course, very cheap and easy to program.

In summary, there is a trade-off in reliability with work for each of these three methods. Further, the amount of work for each alternative is comparable for a given level of crudeness in the calculation of the estimates.

8.C SENSITIVITY ANALYSIS

The idea behind sensitivity analysis is very simple and quite general: *Resolve the problem with slighly different data to see how sensitive the solution is to changes in the data.* For programs to solve $A\mathbf{x} = \mathbf{b}$ there are two natural ways to proceed:

1. Perturb the right-hand side. Here one computes $\bar{\mathbf{x}}$ in trying to solve $A\mathbf{x} = \mathbf{b}$, and then one chooses $\mathbf{r}_i$ and solves

$$A\mathbf{x}_i = \mathbf{b} + \mathbf{r}_i \qquad i = 1, 2, \ldots, k$$

Call the solutions produced $\bar{\mathbf{x}}_i$, and then

$$\max_i \|\bar{\mathbf{x}} - \bar{\mathbf{x}}_i\|$$

estimates the sensitivity of the computed solution $\bar{\mathbf{x}}$ to the perturbations $\mathbf{r}_i$. The $\mathbf{r}_i$ should be chosen small compared to $\mathbf{b}$—of the order of round-off errors if one is concerned about them or the order of original data uncertainties if they are present.

This analysis is not expensive for a few perturbations because the additional solutions are done with the factorization of A found for the first solution.

2. Perturb A **and b.** One chooses E_i and $\mathbf{r}_i$, small compared to A and $\mathbf{b}$, respectively, and solves

$$(A + E_i)\bar{\mathbf{x}}_i = \mathbf{b} + \mathbf{r}_i$$

Again,

$$\max_i \|\bar{\mathbf{x}} - \bar{\mathbf{x}}_i\|$$

estimates the sensitivity of $\bar{\mathbf{x}}$. This way is more expensive since no use can be made of the previous solution effort. Also note that solving for $\bar{\mathbf{x}}_i$ from

$$A\bar{\mathbf{x}}_i = b + \mathbf{r}_i - E_i\mathbf{y}_i$$

gives the same result, and thus this way makes sense only if $E_i\bar{\mathbf{x}}_i$ is thought to be comparable in size to $\mathbf{b} + \mathbf{r}_i$. Of course, $\mathbf{y}_i$ is not known in advance, so the full perturbations give one more confidence in the results.

There is a very easy way to perform an analysis of sensitivity to round-off errors. One simply runs the same problem with another compiler. Different compilers are almost certain to produce code which does the arithmetic in a different order, and hence they produce different round-off errors.

8.D ITERATIVE IMPROVEMENT

Iterative improvement is a method to "improve" a solution that is already computed. Suppose $\bar{\mathbf{x}}$ has been computed in solving $A\mathbf{x} = \mathbf{b}$, and let $\mathbf{r} = \mathbf{b} - A\bar{\mathbf{x}}$ be the residual. Then we have

$$A\mathbf{x} = \mathbf{b} \qquad A\bar{\mathbf{x}} = \mathbf{b} - \mathbf{r}$$

so, with $\mathbf{y} = \mathbf{x} - \bar{\mathbf{x}}$,

$$A(\mathbf{x} - \bar{\mathbf{x}}) = A\mathbf{y} = \mathbf{r}$$

and we can solve for the correction $\mathbf{y} = \mathbf{x} - \bar{\mathbf{x}}$ for $\bar{\mathbf{x}}$. It is easy to solve for $\mathbf{y}$ since A is already factored. The idea is that the matrix A is such that one only gets, say, three digits of the solutions correct. So $\bar{\mathbf{x}} + \bar{\mathbf{y}}$ will have six correct digits, three from the original solution, and three more from the correction. But this reasoning is erroneous and such a calculation gives no improvement at all. $\bar{\mathbf{x}} + \bar{\mathbf{y}}$ is usually no more accurate than $\bar{\mathbf{x}}$. To see why this is so, we analyze a particular case where we assume

1. All numbers in A, $\mathbf{x}$, and $\mathbf{b}$ are about 1.0.
2. Eight decimal digit arithmetic is used.
3. Five digits are lost in solving $A\mathbf{x} = \mathbf{b}$, and $\bar{\mathbf{x}}$ has three correct digits.

We examine the digits in the computed numbers and let x denote a correct digit and z denote a garbage digit. We put blanks in the digit strings to indicate where things happen. The form of the numbers after computing $\bar{\mathbf{x}}$ and $\mathbf{r}$ is

A, **b**	numbers:	.xxx xxxxx
$\bar{\mathbf{x}}$	numbers:	.xxx zzzzz
r	numbers:	.000 xxxxx zzz

Thus the first five digits of **r** are the correct values of the residual for the incorrect digits of $\bar{\mathbf{x}}$, but the last three digits of **r** are garbage digits generated by the arithmetic. These last three digits cannot contain information because the corresponding digits of $\bar{\mathbf{x}}$ are missing. When we compute $\bar{\mathbf{y}}$, we lose five digits; that is, the uncertainty in the $\bar{\mathbf{y}}$ digits is moved five places to the left so the $\bar{\mathbf{y}}$ numbers have the following form: .000 zzzzz zzz. They are all garbage digits, and thus we gain nothing by adding $\bar{\mathbf{y}}$.

This approach can be made to work *if the residual* **r** *is computed more accurately*. We redo the above example except that 10-digit arithmetic is used to evaluate **r**. The form of the numbers is then

A, **b** numbers:	.xxx xxxxx
$\bar{\mathbf{x}}$ numbers:	.xxx zzzzz
r numbers:	.000 xxxxx xxzzz
$\bar{\mathbf{y}}$ numbers:	.000 xxzzz zzz
$\bar{\mathbf{x}} + \bar{\mathbf{y}}$ numbers:	.xxx xxzzz

We can interpret the use of 10 digits as changing the A, **b** number to .xxx xxxxx 00 and $\bar{\mathbf{x}}$ numbers to .xxx zzzzz 00 before calculating **r**. The 10-digit **r** numbers would be rounded (or truncated) to eight digits before going ahead to solve for $\bar{\mathbf{y}}$.

In practice, higher precision almost always means double precision, as in the examples given later in this chapter. A second fact is that, *if* the correction $\bar{\mathbf{y}}$ does not change $\bar{\mathbf{x}}$ (i.e., $\bar{\mathbf{y}}$ is comparable to round-off in $\bar{\mathbf{x}}$), *then* $\bar{\mathbf{x}}$ is the "right" answer. Note, however, that the final residual (computed in single precision) actually may be larger than the first one. Gauss elimination is very good at achieving a small residual error even if it does not produce a very accurate solution.

Algorithm 8.1: Iterative improvement of the solution of A$\mathbf{x}$ = $\mathbf{b}$

1. Factor A to obtain M and U so MA = U.
2. Solve for **x** from **v** = M**b**, U**x** = **v**.
3. For k = 1, 2, ..., maxk do the following:
   3.1. Compute **r** = **b** − A**x** in double precision.
   3.2. Solve for **y** from **v** = M**r**, U**y** = **v**.
   3.3. If $\|\mathbf{y}\|/\|\mathbf{x}\|$ is satisfactory go to END.
   3.4. **x** = **x** + **y**.
   If you fall out of the loop, there is no convergence and the algorithm has failed.
4. Print "Iterative Improvement Failure, last solution estimate = **x**."
5. END

The usual test for $\|\mathbf{y}\|/\|\mathbf{x}\|$ to be satisfactory is that it be the size of round-off. Thus we can test

$$\frac{\|\mathbf{y}\|}{\|\mathbf{x}\|} \leq 10^{-1}$$

for a t-digit arithmetic calculation. A machine-independent form of this test is

$$\|\mathbf{x}\| + \|\mathbf{y}\| = \|\mathbf{x}\|$$

The condition number of the problem $A\mathbf{x} = \mathbf{b}$ can be estimated crudely by counting the number of iterations required for iterative improvement to converge. Let t be the number of digits used in the arithmetic and s be the number of correct digits obtained in solving $A\mathbf{x} = \mathbf{b}$. Then, if $s \geq t/2$, only one iteration is required to get the correct answer plus one more to verify that the correct result has been obtained. Only if $s = t$ does the iteration terminate the first time. If $t/2 > 2 \geq t/3$, then the correct result is obtained in two iterations and one more is required to verify the result. In general we have

Number of iterations	1	2	3	...	k
Range of values for s	$s = t$	$s \geq t/2$	$t/2 > s \geq t/3$	...	$t/(k-1) > s \geq t/k$

and thus the condition number is roughly given by $10^{t(1-1/k)}$.

8.E COMPARISON OF ERROR ESTIMATION PROCEDURES

The art of designing software for $A\mathbf{x} = \mathbf{b}$ involves choosing a combination of these error estimation methods (with their many variations) so that one has both efficiency and reliability. In this section we make a comparison of these methods in a few examples in order to see some of their characteristics. First we present a list of matrices for which one can expect to have difficulty when solving $A\mathbf{x} = \mathbf{b}$.

8.E.1 Some Matrices with Computational Sensitivity

We list 13 matrices A with varying levels of sensitivity: The elements of A are denoted by a_{ij} and the order of A by n. Note that randomly generated matrices do not form a suitable set for testing sensitivity; almost all such matrices are very well behaved.

1. *Hilbert matrix:* $a_{ij} = 1/(i + j - 1)$.
2. $a_{ii} = i$ for $i = 1$ to 20, $a_{i,\,i+1} = 20$ for $i = 1$ to 19, $a_{ij} = 0$ otherwise. This matrix is especially difficult for eigenvalue calculations.
3. $a_{ij} = \min\,[i, j]$.
4. *Pei matrix* (with parameter α): $a_{ii} = \alpha$, $a_{ij} = 1$ for $i \neq j$. Difficulty occurs for α near 1 or α near $n - 1$
5.

$$\begin{pmatrix} 5 & 4 & 7 & 5 & 6 & 7 & 5 \\ 4 & 12 & 8 & 7 & 8 & 8 & 6 \\ 7 & 8 & 10 & 9 & 8 & 7 & 7 \\ 5 & 7 & 9 & 11 & 9 & 7 & 5 \\ 6 & 8 & 8 & 9 & 10 & 8 & 9 \\ 7 & 8 & 7 & 7 & 8 & 10 & 10 \\ 5 & 6 & 7 & 5 & 9 & 10 & 10 \end{pmatrix}$$

6. Involves a parameter θ:

$$R = \begin{pmatrix} \cot\theta & \csc\theta \\ -\csc\theta & \cot\theta \end{pmatrix} \qquad S = \begin{pmatrix} 1-\cot\theta & \csc\theta \\ -\csc\theta & 1+\cot\theta \end{pmatrix}$$

The eigenvalues of R are $\pm i$, those of S are $1 \pm i$.

7. $a_{ii} = 0.01/[(n - i + 1)(i + 1)]$, $a_{ij} = 0$ for $i < j$, $a_{ij} = i(n - j)$ for $i > j$.
8. Same as matrix No. 7, except $a_{ij} = j(n - i)$ for $i < j$.
9. Use R and S from matrix No. 6, plus

$$T = \begin{pmatrix} 1 & 1 \\ 1 & 1 \end{pmatrix}$$

to form

$$\begin{pmatrix} R & S & T & T \\ S & R & S & T \\ T & S & R & S \\ T & T & S & R \end{pmatrix}$$

Difficulty occurs for θ near zero or π.

10. Involves a parameter α:

$$a_{ii} = \alpha^{|n-2i|/2} \qquad a_{1j} = a_{11}/\alpha^{j} \qquad a_{nj} = a_{nn}/\alpha^{j}$$

$$a_{j1} = a_{1j} \qquad a_{jn} = a_{nj} \qquad a_{ij} = 0 \text{ otherwise}$$

11. $a_{ij} = e^{i*j*h}$. Difficulty occurs for h near zero or h large (negative or positive).
12. $a_{ij} = c + \log_2 (i * j)$. Difficulty for all values of c, but especially so for large c.
13.

$$\begin{pmatrix} 0.9143 \times 10^{-4} & 0 & 0 & 0 \\ 0.8762 & 0.7156 \times 10^{-4} & 0 & 0 \\ 0.7943 & 0.8143 & 0.9504 \times 10^{-4} & 0 \\ 0.8017 & 0.6123 & 0.7165 & 0.7123 \times 10^{-4} \end{pmatrix}$$

8.E.2 Comparison of Error Estimates by Condition Numbers

We show 10 different error estimates based on condition numbers for four examples. The first example is the 10×10 Hilbert matrix, and the second is a small triangular system. Both examples are badly conditioned, and one should expect difficulty with them. The third example is the following relatively well-behaved 14×14 matrix:

$$\begin{pmatrix} A & B \\ C & A \end{pmatrix}$$

where A is the 7 × 7 matrix No. 5 of Sec. 8.E.1 and

$$b_{ij} = a_{8-ij}$$

$$C = \begin{pmatrix} \frac{1}{8} & \frac{1}{9} & \frac{1}{10} & \frac{1}{11} & \frac{1}{12} & \frac{1}{13} & 5 \\ \frac{1}{9} & \frac{1}{10} & \frac{1}{11} & \frac{1}{12} & \frac{1}{13} & 6 & \frac{1}{15} \\ \frac{1}{10} & \frac{1}{11} & \frac{1}{12} & \frac{1}{13} & 7 & \frac{1}{15} & \frac{1}{16} \\ 0 & 0 & 0 & 5 & 0 & 0 & 0 \\ 0 & 0 & 6 & 0 & 0 & 0 & 0 \\ 0 & 7 & 0 & 0 & 0 & 0 & 0 \\ 6 & 0 & 0 & 0 & 0 & 0 & 0 \end{pmatrix}$$

The final example is a 40 × 40 random matrix generated so as to have a condition number of about 10^8. Its first 36 rows are random vectors and the last four rows are a random linear combination of the first 36 plus 10^{-5} times another random vector. Specifically, the matrix A is generated by the following code [we assume that RAND(0) produces a random number between zero and one]:

```
      INDEP  = 36
      DEPEND=4
      EPS     = .00001
      NEQS   = INDEP + DEPEND
      DO 10 I = 1, INDEP
          DO 10 J = 1,NEQS
              A(I,J) = 2.*(RAND(0)-.5)
10    CONTINUE
      DO 20 K = 1, INDEP
20        COEF(K) = RAND(0)
      DO 40 I = INDEP+1,NEQS
          DO 40 J = 1,NEQS
              SUM = 0.0
              DO 30 K = 1,INDEP
30                SUM = SUM + COEF(K) * A(K,J)
              A(I,J) = SUM + EPS*(RAND(0)-.5)
40    CONTINUE
```

For each matrix we give a right-hand side **b**, the true solution **x** of A**x** = **b** as calculated by a double-precision program (LINEQ2 of the Appendix), and a computed or trial solution $\bar{\mathbf{x}}$. The objective is to estimate the error $\|\mathbf{x} - \bar{\mathbf{x}}\|$. We also give a number of basic numerical values associated with each problem; all the norms used are infinity or row-sum norms. The time needed to solve A**x** = **b** is given. All computations were made on the CDC 6500 at Purdue University, which carries 48 bits (about 14.5 decimal digits) in single precision. The natural, standard, and Aird-Lynch error estimates are given, each computed in three different ways. These ways are labeled A, B, and C: A indicates a cheap way to evaluate the error estimates, C indicates an accurate calculation, and B is an intermediate method. Specifically, A indicates that $\|A^{-1}\|$ is estimated by $\|\mathbf{b}\|/\|\mathbf{x}\|$ and $T = \frac{1}{2}$ is used. B indicates that $\|A^{-1}\|$ for the natural case is estimated using two random vectors (alternative 2 of Sec. 8.B.2), $\|A^{-1}\|$ for the standard case is estimated by LINPACK algorithm (alternative 3 of Section 8.B.2), and $\|CA - I\|$ for the Aird-Lynch case is estimated using two random vectors (alternative b of Sec. 8.B.2 using alternative 2 for $\|U^{-1}\|$). C indicates that all quantities are computed normally without regard to cost.

The program BOUNDS is described briefly at the end of the Appendix. It uses interval arithmetic to obtain guaranteed bounds on the error, and its estimates are indicated by A/L BOUNDS.

In addition to the actual error estimate, we give the *cost* in seconds to compute the error estimate and the *relative cost*, which is the time for the error estimate divided by the time for solving $A\mathbf{x} = \mathbf{b}$. Finally, we give the quantity *digits off*, which is defined by

$$\log_{10}\left[\frac{\text{estimated relative error}}{\text{actual relative error}}\right]$$

This quantity is the number of decimal digits by which the error estimate misses the correct value. A value of 3 for digits off indicates that the error is $1000 = 10^3$ times too large.

Example 8.2: Hilbert matrix of order 10

$$\mathbf{b} = (1, 0, 0, 0, 0, 0, 0, 0, 0, 0)^T$$

$$\mathbf{x} = (99.9989793495089, \ -494.995439565316, \ldots, \ -923884.077853199)^T$$

by LINEQ2

$$\bar{\mathbf{x}} = (100.005711648351, \ -495.057320082578, \ldots, \ -924185.572651327)^T$$

by LINPACK

Basic numbers of problem:

$\|A\| = 2.9290$ $\quad\|\bar{\mathbf{x}}\| = 9.6129 * 10^6$ $\quad\|\mathbf{x}\| = 9.6103 * 10^6$

$\|A^{-1}\| = 1.2074 * 10^{13}$ $\quad\|\mathbf{r}\| = 5.1223 * 10^{-9}$ $\quad\dfrac{\|\mathbf{x} - \bar{\mathbf{x}}\|}{\|\mathbf{x}\|} = 2.7700 * 10^{-4}$

$\|\mathbf{b}\| = 1.0$ $\quad\|\mathbf{x} - \bar{\mathbf{x}}\| = 266.21$

Time to solve $A\mathbf{x} = \mathbf{b}$ is 0.024 second.

Summary of error estimation tests

Method used	Error estimate	Cost, seconds	Digits off	Relative cost
Natural-A	4.9240E − 02	0.002	2.2498	0.08333
Natural-B	1.9230E − 03	0.014	0.8415	0.58333
Natural-C	6.4337E − 03	0.419	1.3660	17.47917
Standard-A	1.4422E − 01	0.003	2.7165	0.14583
Standard-B	1.3730E + 05	0.020	8.6952	0.83333
Standard-C	1.8115E + 05	0.421	8.8155	17.54167
Aird-Lynch-A	5.3832E − 04	0.014	0.2886	0.58333
Aird-Lynch-B	2.8506E − 04	0.044	0.0125	1.83333
Aird-Lynch-C	2.6926E − 04	0.044	−0.0123	1.83333
A/L BOUNDS	4.3471E − 02	1.310	2.1957	54.58333

Example 8.3: Wilkinson's 4 × 4 triangular example

$$\mathbf{b} = (0.00009143,\ 0.87627156,\ 1.60869504,\ 2.13057123)^T$$

$$\mathbf{x} = (1.0,\ 0.999999999979416,\ 1.00000017635355,\ 0.998226242846176)^T$$

by LINEQ2

$$\bar{\mathbf{x}} = (1.0,\ 1.0,\ 1.0,\ 1.0)^T \qquad \text{exact}$$

Basic numbers of problem:

$\|A\| = 2.1306$ $\qquad \|\bar{\mathbf{x}}\| = 1.0000$ $\qquad \|\mathbf{x}\| = 1.0000$

$\|A^{-1}\| = 1.1541 * 10^{16}$ $\qquad \|\mathbf{r}\| = 1.4566 * 10^{-14}$ $\qquad \dfrac{\|\mathbf{x} - \bar{\mathbf{x}}\|}{\|\mathbf{x}\|} = 0.0017738$

$\|\mathbf{b}\| = 2.1306$ $\qquad \|\mathbf{x} - \bar{\mathbf{x}}\| = 0.0017738$

Time to solve $A\mathbf{x} = \mathbf{b}$ is 0.005 second.

Summary of error estimation tests

Method used	Error estimate	Cost, seconds	Digits off	Relative cost
Natural-A	6.8367E − 15	0	−11.4140	0
Natural-B	2.1110E + 02	0.004	5.0756	0.80000
Natural-C	1.6811E + 02	0.020	4.9767	3.90000
Standard-A	6.8367E − 15	0.001	−11.4140	0.10000
Standard-B	1.9505E + 02	0.007	5.0412	1.40000
Standard-C	1.6811E + 02	0.020	4.9767	4.00000
Aird-Lynch-A	3.5271E − 07	0.003	−3.7015	0.60000
Aird-Lynch-B	3.1024E + 06	0.007	9.2428	1.40000
Aird-Lynch-C	1.7814E − 07	0.007	−3.9981	1.40000
A/L BOUNDS	4.4114E − 02	0.080	1.3957	16.00000

Example 8.4: Well-behaved 14 × 14 matrix

$b_i = \text{sum of } a_{ij},\ 1 \le j \le 14$

$\mathbf{x} = (0.999999999999996, 1.00000000000000, \ldots, 0.999999999999996)^T$ by LINEQ2

$\bar{\mathbf{x}} = (0.999999999999925, 0.999999999999908, \ldots, 0.999999999998739)^T$ by LINPACK

Basic numbers of problem:

$\|A\| = 100 \qquad \|\bar{\mathbf{x}}\| = 1 \qquad \|\mathbf{x}\| = 1$

$\|A^{-1}\| = 13.983 \qquad \|\mathbf{r}\| = 2.2737 * 10^{-12} \qquad \dfrac{\|\mathbf{x} - \bar{\mathbf{x}}\|}{\|\mathbf{x}\|} = 1.4495 * 10^{-12}$

$\|\mathbf{b}\| = 100 \qquad \|\mathbf{x} - \bar{\mathbf{x}}\| = 1.4495 * 10^{-12}$

Time to solve $A\mathbf{x} = \mathbf{b}$ is 0.048 second.

Summary of error estimation tests

Method used	Error estimate	Cost, seconds	Digits off	Relative cost
Natural-A	2.2737E − 14	0.003	−1.8045	0.06250
Natural-B	1.6893E − 11	0.021	1.0665	0.43750
Natural-C	3.1794E − 11	0.581	1.3411	12.09375
Standard-A	2.2737E − 14	0.006	−1.8045	0.13542
Standard-B	9.2643E − 12	0.027	0.8056	0.56250
Standard-C	3.1794E − 11	0.584	1.3411	12.16667
Aird-Lynch-A	2.5224E − 12	0.023	0.2406	0.47917
Aird-Lynch-B	1.2612E − 12	0.092	−0.0604	1.91667
Aird-Lynch-C	1.2612E − 12	0.092	−0.0604	1.91667
A/L BOUNDS	2.8492E − 11	2.484	1.2935	51.75000

Example 8.5: Random with 36 independent rows plus 4 dependent rows perturbed by 10^{-5}

$\mathbf{b} = (1, 1, \ldots, 1)^T$

$\mathbf{x} = (-1.83181002028004 * 10^6, \ldots)^T$ by LINEQ2

$\bar{\mathbf{x}} = (-1.83181001071588 * 10^6, \ldots)^T$ by LINPACK

Basic numbers of problem:

$\|A\| = 74.049$ $\quad \|\bar{\mathbf{x}}\| = 3.4822 * 10^6$ $\quad \|\mathbf{x}\| = 3.4822 * 10^6$

$\|A^{-1}\| = 9.1857 * 10^6$ $\quad \|\mathbf{r}\| = 1.5199 * 10^{-6}$ $\quad \dfrac{\|\mathbf{x} - \bar{\mathbf{x}}\|}{\|\mathbf{x}\|} = 1.5285 * 10^{-8}$

$\|\mathbf{b}\| = 1$ $\quad \|\mathbf{x} - \bar{\mathbf{x}}\| = 0.053225$

Time to solve $A\mathbf{x} = \mathbf{b}$ is 0.549 second.

Summary of error estimation tests

Method used	Error estimate	Cost, seconds	Digits off	Relative cost
Natural-A	5.2926E + 00	0.024	8.5394	0.04372
Natural-B	1.0631E − 06	0.105	1.8423	0.19126
Natural-C	4.0094E − 06	13.189	2.4188	24.02277
Standard-A	3.9191E + 02	0.048	10.4089	0.08652
Standard-B	2.0694E + 02	0.153	10.1316	0.27869
Standard-C	1.0338E + 03	13.212	10.8302	24.06557
Aird-Lynch-A	1.8295E − 08	0.152	0.0781	0.27687
Aird-Lynch-B	9.1474E − 09	0.983	−0.2230	1.79053
Aird-Lynch-C	9.1474E − 09	0.983	−0.2230	1.79053
A/L BOUNDS	1.5030E − 06	55.929	1.9927	101.87432

Table 8.1 Use of sensitivity analysis to estimate errors for Examples 8.2 through 8.5.†

Sensitivity method	Number of perturbations	Estimate error for Example				Relative cost for Example			
		8.2	8.3	8.4	8.5	8.2	8.3	8.4	8.5
Perturbations	1	2.7E + 3	1.0E + 5	4.7E − 5	2.0E + 3	0.29	0.6	0.25	0.12
of **b** only	2	2.7E + 3	1.0E + 5	4.7E − 5	2.0E + 3	0.58	1.2	0.50	0.23
by 10^{-7}	3	2.7E + 3	1.8E + 5	4.7E − 5	2.0E + 3	0.88	1.8	0.75	0.35
	5	2.7E + 3	1.8E + 5	4.7E − 5	2.0E + 3	1.50	3.0	1.00	0.59
	10	2.7E + 3	1.8E + 5	4.7E − 5	2.0E + 3	2.90	6.0	2.00	1.17
Perturbations	1	4.6E + 3	5.4E + 4	1.3E − 5	2.9E + 3	1.25	1.2	1.1	1.0
of A and **b**	2	3.0E + 4	7.6E + 4	1.3E − 5	2.9E + 3	2.50	2.4	2.1	2.1
by 10^{-7}	3	3.0E + 4	7.6E + 4	3.1E − 5	2.9E + 3	3.75	3.6	3.2	3.1
	5	3.0E + 4	1.5E + 5	3.1E − 5	2.9E + 3	6.25	6.0	5.3	5.2
	10	3.3E + 4	1.5E + 5	3.4E − 5	2.9E + 3	12.50	12.0	10.7	10.5

Note: The error estimates for Example 8.5 are all the same because (1) perturbing **b** actually gave the same results for all perturbations, and (2) perturbing **b** and A happened to give the largest error estimate first (the 10 cases ranged rather randomly from 6.9E + 2 to 2.9E + 3).

† The cost relative to solving $A\mathbf{x} = \mathbf{b}$ is given, which grows linearly with the number of perturbations, while the gain of making additional perturbations falls off rapidly.

8.E.3 Comparison of Sensitivity Analysis and Iterative Improvement

The same four examples of the preceding comparison are used here (Table 8.1). For each we (1) perturb the right-hand side by 10^{-7}, (2) perturb the matrix and the right-hand side by 10^{-7}, and (3) apply iterative improvement. The results are used to estimate the accuracy obtained and the computation time used is given.

If we assume that perturbations of 10^{-14} instead of 10^{-7} would simply decrease the error estimates by a factor of 10^{-7}, we may compare the estimated errors given in Table 8.1 with those actually found for the four examples:

	Example			
	8.2	8.3	8.4	8.5
Actual error	2.8E − 4	1.8E − 3	1.4E − 12	1.5E − 8
Perturb **b** by 10^{-14}	2.7E − 4	1.8E − 2	4.7E − 12	2.0E − 4
Perturb A and **b** by 10^{-14}	3.3E − 3	1.5E − 2	3.4E − 12	2.9E − 4

Table 8.2 shows the effect of iterative improvement on the accuracy of the solutions of $A\mathbf{x} = \mathbf{b}$. These calculations were performed by LINEQ1 (which is described at the end of the Appendix). Some comparative data are

Table 8.2 Application of iterative improvement routine LINEQ1 to previous examples.

	Example			
	8.2	8.3	8.4	8.5
LINEQ1:				
Original error	$9.96 * 10^{1}$	$4.74 * 10^{-7}$	$4.90 * 10^{-13}$	$4.42 * 10^{-1}$
Final error	$5.96 * 10^{-8}$	$7.10 * 10^{-15}$	$7.10 * 10^{-15}$	$1.19 * 10^{-7}$
Original residual	$3.07 * 10^{-9}$	$7.22 * 10^{-15}$	$3.91 * 10^{-13}$	$4.81 * 10^{-7}$
Final residual	$1.67 * 10^{-9}$	$5.40 * 10^{-15}$	$3.26 * 10^{-13}$	$5.59 * 10^{-7}$
Iterations	3	2	2	3
Condition estimate	10^{9}	10^{7}	10^{7}	10^{9}
Relative cost	1.00	1.25	0.48	0.26
LINPACK:				
Original error	$1.17 * 10^{3}$	$4.65 * 10^{-4}$	$6.61 * 10^{-13}$	$3.81 * 10^{0}$
Original residual	$8.38 * 10^{-9}$	$4.73 * 10^{-15}$	$3.24 * 10^{-12}$	$1.34 * 10^{-5}$

Note: For comparison, some results from LINPACK are also given. These data are from programs run with a different compiler than that of the previous examples, and this has changed the round-off effects given for LINPACK, which differ slightly from the previous LINPACK data for the same examples because a different compiler was used.

The three points of interest seen from Table 8.2 are: (1) The size of the residual does not change appreciably even though great improvement is made in the accuracy of the computed solution. (2) Iterative improvement is somewhat expensive; it cost 50 percent more for a well-behaved 14×14 matrix and 25 percent more for a not badly behaved 40×40 matrix. (3) The resulting estimate of the condition number is almost useless. There is no ready explanation for why the LINEQ1 error without iterative improvement is consistently better than that of LINPACK; this situation occurred in all 10 examples tried except for three ties.

PROBLEMS FOR CHAP. 8

1 In an attempt to solve $\mathrm{A}\mathbf{x} = \mathbf{b}$ there was an error $\delta\mathbf{b}$ in $\mathbf{b}$ so that a solution $\mathbf{y}$ to $\mathrm{A}\mathbf{y} = (\mathbf{b} + \delta\mathbf{b})$ was actually found. Find an estimate of $\|\mathbf{x} - \mathbf{y}\|$ in terms of the size of $\delta\mathbf{b}$.

2 Consider

$$\mathrm{A} = \begin{pmatrix} 6 & 13 & -17 \\ 13 & 29 & -38 \\ -17 & -38 & 50 \end{pmatrix} \qquad \mathrm{A}^{-1} = \begin{pmatrix} 6 & -4 & -1 \\ -4 & 11 & 7 \\ -1 & 7 & 5 \end{pmatrix}$$

(*a*) What is the standard condition number of A?

(*b*) Suppose we attempt to solve $\mathrm{A}\mathbf{x} = \mathbf{b}$ and obtain $\bar{\mathbf{x}}$ so that $\|\mathbf{b} - \mathrm{A}\bar{\mathbf{x}}\| \le 0.01$. How small an upper bound can be given for the absolute error $\|\bar{\mathbf{x}} - \mathbf{x}\|$?

(*c*) With the same situation as part (*b*), how small an upper bound can be given for the relative error $\|\bar{\mathbf{x}} - \mathrm{A}^{-1}\mathbf{b}\|/\|\mathrm{A}^{-1}\mathbf{b}\|$?

3 Let λ_1 and λ_n be the smallest and largest in absolute value eigenvalues of the $n \times n$ matrix A.

(*a*) Show that $|\lambda_n/\lambda_1| \le \|\mathrm{A}\|\,\|\mathrm{A}^{-1}\|$.

(*b*) The eigenvalues for the matrix A in Prob. 2 are 0.05888, 0.2007, and 84.74. How well does the eigenvalue ratio estimate the standard condition number of A using $\|\mathrm{A}\|_\infty \|\mathrm{A}^{-1}\|_\infty$?

(*c*) Show that $|\lambda_n/\lambda_1| = 1$ for an orthogonal matrix.

(*d*) Give an example of a matrix with all eigenvalues of absolute value 1 and yet where the condition number is large.

4 (*a*) For any matrix P with $\|\mathrm{P}\| < 1$ show that

$$\|(\mathrm{I} - \mathrm{P})^{-1}\| \le \frac{1}{1 - \|\mathrm{P}\|}$$

(*b*) Apply part (*a*) to show that

$$\|\bar{\mathbf{x}} - \mathbf{x}\| < \frac{\|\mathrm{C}\mathbf{r}\|}{1 - \|\mathrm{CA} - \mathrm{I}\|}$$

if C is a good enough approximate inverse of A so that $\|\mathrm{CA} - \mathrm{I}\| < 1$. The vector $\mathbf{r}$ is the residual in $\mathrm{A}\mathbf{x} - \mathrm{A}\bar{\mathbf{x}}$.

(*c*) Suppose that A is factored into LU and $\bar{\mathbf{x}}$ computed by Gauss elimination and the results saved. Then what is the approximate inverse C that should be used in (*b*)? How would you compute $\|\mathrm{C}\mathbf{r}\|$ efficiently? How would you compute $\|\mathrm{CA} - \mathrm{I}\|$ efficiently?

5 For a 100 × 100 linear system, state in percentage terms an estimate of the *minimum* amount of extra computations required for iterative improvement to "verify" that the solution to $\mathbf{Ax} = \mathbf{b}$ is correct. Assume that a double-precision operation takes three times as long as the corresponding single-precision operation.

6 Solve the following system using four-digit arithmetic [the true solution is (2, 3)]:

$$7x_1 + 6.990x_2 = 34.97$$

$$4x_1 + \quad 4x_2 = 20.00$$

Save the factorization of the coefficient matrix and carry out iterative improvement until it converges. It should take four iterations.

7 Write a Fortran subprogram that computes the three condition numbers by the crudest means (alternatives 1 or *a* of Sec. 8.B.2). Apply these to compute an error estimate based on the round-off expected in your local computer. Use this program to compare the three condition numbers for the remaining example matrices of Sec. 8.E.1.

Hint: Construct problems with known solutions by choosing the solution and substituting it in to find the corresponding right-hand side.

8 Use a local linear equation solver for the problems in Prob. 7 and compare the estimated errors with the actual errors.

9 How large can the order of a Hilbert matrix H_n be before all significance is lost in solving $H_n\mathbf{x} = \mathbf{b}$ with your local computer and linear equation solver? Make a performance profile of n versus actual accuracy.

10 Compute the standard condition number of H_n and make a performance profile (using the results of Prob. 9) of standard condition number versus actual accuracy.

11 Repeat Prob. 10 with the natural condition number.

12 Repeat Prob. 10 with the Aird-Lynch condition number.

13 Study the effectiveness of sensitivity analysis by making a performance profile of (estimated error)/(true error) versus number of perturbations of the right-hand side. Use H_6 as the test matrix with $b = (1, 1, 1, 1, 1, 1)^T$ and perturbations of 10^{-6}.

14 Repeat Prob. 13 by perturbing both the right-hand side and the matrix.

15 Design and carry out a computational experiment to test the correctness that alternative 2 of Sec. 8.B.2 gives an expected value of $\frac{1}{2}\|A^{-1}\|$.

CHAPTER

NINE

CONDITIONING AND BACKWARD ERROR ANALYSIS

We have analyzed in detail how to ascertain that one has the right solution of a linear system of equations. Unfortunately, one can have the right answers to a computational problem and still have complete garbage for the solution of the original problem. This seemingly contradictory situation is a source of considerable confusion and it is not so easy to understand how it can happen. The objective of this chapter is to explain how it happens and to present a viewpoint which is very useful for considering such computational situations.

9.A THE CONDITIONING OF A PROBLEM AND OF A COMPUTATION

The difficulty of understanding the nature of computational errors was first recognized for linear systems, and this is an area where the difficulties arise frequently. However, the situation exists throughout numerical computation, and we briefly present the theory of conditioning in a general context.

Consider what it means to have a problem and its answer. The "data" of the problem-solving process include *all* the information that defines the problem. Much of this consists of numerical values, but it also includes the mathematical model with all its formulas and assumptions. Thus, for $\mathbf{A}\mathbf{x} = \mathbf{b}$, data are not only the numbers in the matrix A and the vector $\mathbf{b}$, but also the choice of variables and equations to be included in the linear system. In a simple differential equation problem

$$3.1\frac{d^2u}{dt^2} + \left(1 - \frac{t^2}{2}\right)u = \sin(4.6t) \qquad u(0) = 0.2 \qquad u(6.2) = 4.7$$

the nine numbers 3.1, 1., $\frac{1}{2}$, 1. (coefficient of sin), 4.6, 0.0, 0.2, 6.2, and 4.7 are numerical data items. Equally significant "data" are the assumption that no du/dt term is present, the possible fact that $1 - (t^2/2)$ is a simplification of cos (t), the probable assumption that the oscillating right-hand side term is exactly a sine function, and so forth. All of these numbers, assumptions, and formulas affect the solution of the original problem and all of them are lumped into the term "data."

The "answer" to a problem may be a single number, a set of numbers (for a linear system), a function (for a differential equation), or a complicated combination of such items. Figure 9.1 shows a geometrical view of the problem-solving process. We have "true data" $\mathbf{d}^*$ and "true answer" $\mathbf{x}^*$. We also have "perturbed data" $\mathbf{d}$ and corresponding "true answer for perturbed data" $\mathbf{x}$. In a numerical computation we almost never obtain the true answer, so we must also consider "computed answer for true data" $\bar{\mathbf{x}}^*$ and "computed answer for perturbed data" $\bar{\mathbf{x}}$.

In reality we end up with $\bar{\mathbf{x}}$ instead of $\mathbf{x}^*$, so we would like to estimate $\|\mathbf{x}^* - \bar{\mathbf{x}}\|$. Unfortunately, one is often completely unable to do this in a useful way, and therein lies the difficulty in understanding the nature of errors. The *theory of condition* is an attempt to systematically study this question. Something (a problem, a model, or computation) is said to be *ill conditioned* if it is

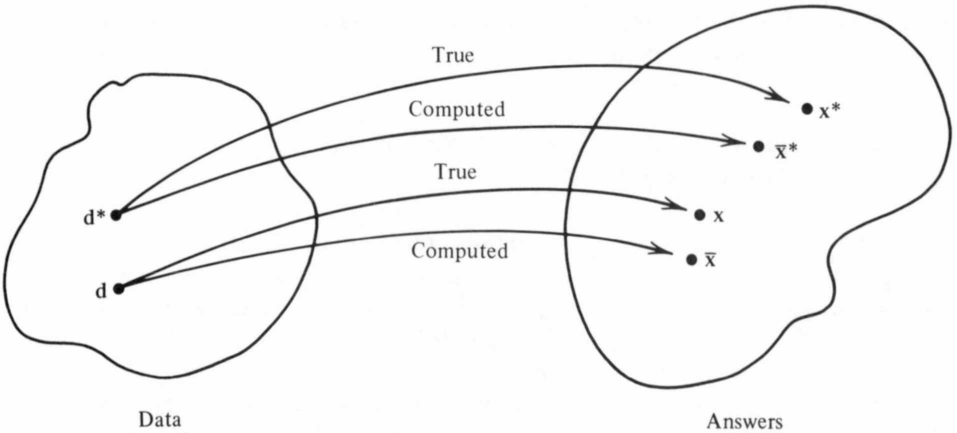

Figure 9.1 Geometric view of the effect of data uncertainty ($\mathbf{d}^*$ to $\mathbf{d}$) and computational errors ($\mathbf{x}$ to $\bar{\mathbf{x}}$, $\mathbf{x}^*$ to $\bar{\mathbf{x}}^*$) in solving a problem.

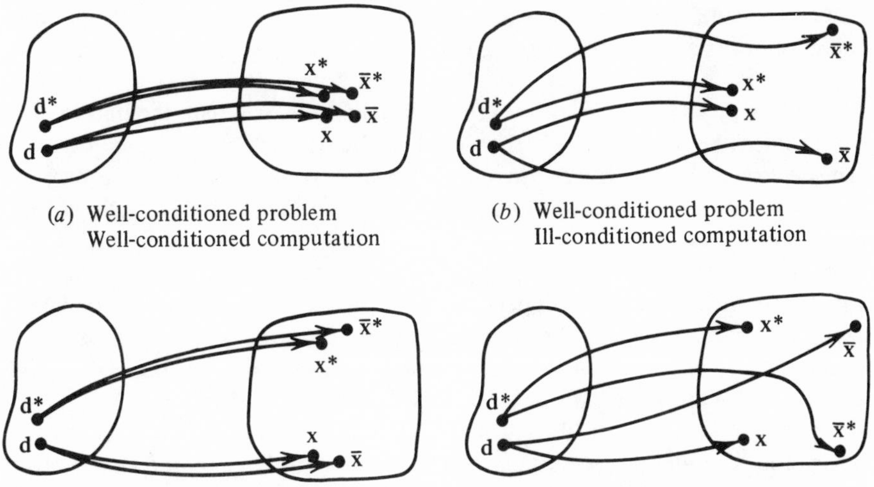

(*a*) Well-conditioned problem
Well-conditioned computation

(*b*) Well-conditioned problem
Ill-conditioned computation

(*c*) Ill-conditioned problem
Well-conditioned computation

(*d*) Ill-conditioned problem
Ill-conditioned computation

Figure 9.2 The four combinations of ill- and well-conditioning for a problem and a computation to solve the problem.

sensitive to errors or uncertainty. Conditioning is a qualitative property, although we will try to assess it quantitatively.

First, we differentiate between an *ill-conditioned problem* and an *ill-conditioned computation.* All ill-conditioned computation is usually the result of using a numerically unstable algorithm. The four possible combinations of "ill" and "well" conditioning are illustrated in Fig. 9.2. The key point to understand is the following:

> *If the problem is ill conditioned, then no amount of effort, trickery, or talent used in the computation can produce accurate answers except by chance.*

Thus in Fig. 9-2*c*, one can make $\bar{\mathbf{x}}$ closer to $\mathbf{x}$ and $\bar{\mathbf{x}}^*$ closer to $\mathbf{x}^*$, but computations cannot affect the distance from $\mathbf{x}$ to $\mathbf{x}^*$.

This situation is well illustrated by the example in Chap. 8 involving the Hilbert matrix. When an ill-conditioned model (problem) is used in statistical regression (as frequently happens), the problem solver usually recognizes that the computed results are nonsense. The first reaction is to suspect a bug in the library routine used. So the individual may write his or her own linear equation solver. This will usually produce completely different but equally nonsensical results. Then the use of double-precision arithmetic—or triple-precision arithmetic—or interval arithmetic may be tried. This produces more precisely defined garbage, but still garbage. It may then be decided the computational algorithm is the source of the trouble. An attempt can be made to solve the system with methods using elementary reflections or elementary rotations or Gauss-Seidel iteration or Jacobi iteration or SOR iteration or generalized inverses or whatever. The results will all be new sets of nonsense answers. The fact is that the *true solution* of the problem is unrelated to reality. The only way to generate meaningful results is to reformulate the mathematical problem to be solved so that neither the Hilbert matrix nor anything remotely resembling it ever enters into the model or problem-solving process.

As an aside, we mention how to do this reformulation. The culprit here is the fact that the polynomials are written in terms of the powers of x, i.e., 1, x, x^2, x^3, ... These functions are nearly linearly dependent, so their vectors of values are nearly linearly dependent and the normal equations coefficient matrix is nearly singular. If a good representation of polynomials is used, say writing them in terms of the Tchebycheff polynomials $T_0(x)$, $T_1(x)$, $T_2(x)$, $T_3(x)$, ..., or the Legendre polynomials $P_0(x)$, $P_1(x)$, $P_2(x)$, $P_3(x)$, ..., then this problem may be solved accurately. That is, provided the assumption that polynomials model the experimental data is reasonably valid and that precautions are taken during computations never to use the powers of x in any way.

Condition involves a process (problem solving) or transformation (from data to answer). It may also depend very heavily on the particular data of a problem from within a class of problems. From this we make the following definition:

> *Condition of a problem: The condition of the problem "Solve* $\mathrm{A}\mathbf{x} = \mathbf{b}$*" is the condition of the transformation* A^{-1} *(problem-solving process) at the point* **b**.

The definition is given for the special instance of linear equations, but the same idea applies in general.

Note that the cardinal sin for numerical software is to produce an ill-conditioned computation for a well-conditioned problem (see Fig. 9-2*b*). A program that uses Gauss elimination without pivoting could do this. It is acceptable for a program to produce an ill-conditioned computation for an ill-conditioned problem. After all, solving this problem is almost surely a lost cause anyway, and one set of nonsensical answers is probably just as good as another. Of course, it is highly desirable for the program to recognize that its calculations are ill conditioned and to report this fact.

9.B CONDITION NUMBERS REVISITED

In Chap. 8 we defined condition numbers to measure the condition of a problem or computation. We elaborate on this approach here. We want to find *one* number which measures the condition, even though the problem-solving process is often very complicated and it is very optimistic to hope that just one number can accurately reflect its sensitivity to all kinds of errors and uncertainty. The condition number is based on the model shown in

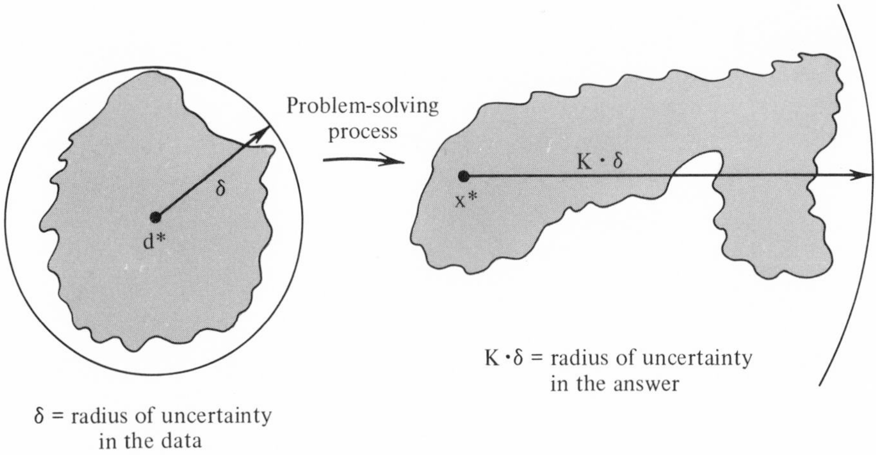

Figure 9.3 Model for the definition of the condition number K of a problem solving process.

Fig. 9.3. From that illustration we see that *the condition number* K *is the factor by which the uncertainty* δ *is multiplied during the problem-solving process.* In general this factor K depends on δ, which is undesirable for simplicity's sake. So, for this discussion, we *assume* that *as* δ *becomes small, the factor* K *approaches a constant and we take this constant as the condition number.*

The situation is further complicated by the fact that sometimes we are interested in absolute errors or uncertainty but usually we are interested in relative errors. The above definitions apply in either case, and we refer to them as *absolute condition* or *relative condition.*

These ideas can be developed in a precise, mathematical way (see Rice, 1966*a* in References at end of book), but we present a more intuitive account here.

Example 9.1: Evaluation of a function at a point Suppose that one is given a function f(x) [say $f(x) = x^2 + \cos(x^3 + 1)$] to evaluate at a point x_0. The data consist of one number x_0 from the data space of the interval $(-\infty, +\infty)$. The answer also consists of one number $f(x_0)$ from the interval $(-\infty, +\infty)$. The situation is shown in Fig. 9.4. Near x_0 we may approximate f(x) by its tangent line and use that to estimate the condition of this evaluation. The case shown has δ rather large, so there is a considerable difference between the true condition number and that obtained by using the tangent line. Recall, however, that we are restricting ourselves to the case where δ is arbitrarily small.

The range of values that f(x) may take on while x is in the interval $[x_0 - \delta, x_0 + \delta]$ is

$$[f(x_0 - \delta), f(x_0 + \delta)] \sim [f(x_0) - f'(x_0)\delta, f(x_0) + f'(x_0)\delta]$$

and thus we see that the absolute condition of f(x) at x_0 is just $|f'(x_0)|$.

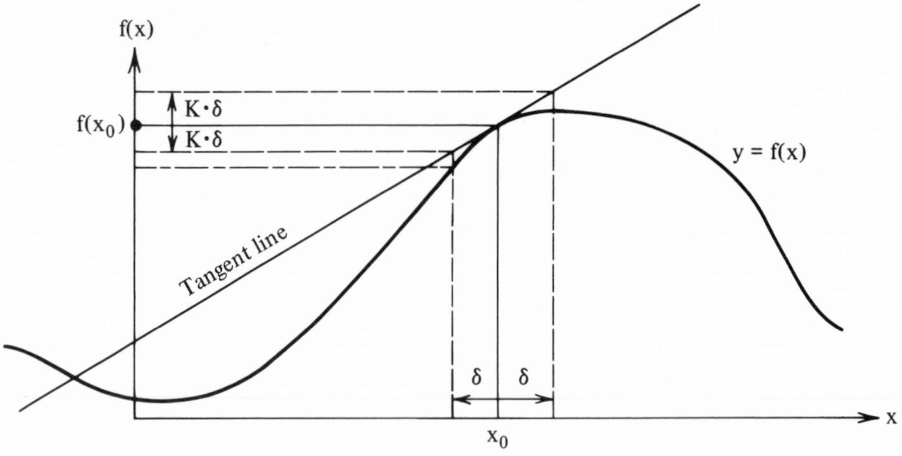

Figure 9.4 The situation for determining the condition of evaluating f(x) at the point x_0.

To find the relative condition, we need to consider what happens for $x \varepsilon [x_0(1-\delta), x_0(1+\delta)]$. The values obtained are in

$$[f(x_0(1-\delta)), f(x_0(1+\delta))] \sim [f(x_0) - f'(x_0)\delta x_0, f(x_0) + f'(x_0)\delta x_0]$$

and the size of this interval relative to $f(x_0)$ is

$$\left| \frac{f'(x_0)x_0}{f(x_0)} \right| \delta$$

so the relative condition number is

$$|x_0| \frac{|f'(x_0)|}{|f(x_0)|}$$

Example 9.2: Solution of Ax = b Even though we have already found condition numbers for this problem, we rederive them from our general framework. We will see that it is not quite as straightforward as we might hope. We want to find the result of perturbing A by a matrix δA and $\mathbf{b}$ by a vector $\delta\mathbf{b}$. We have

$$A\mathbf{x}^* = \mathbf{b}$$

$$(A + \delta A)\bar{\mathbf{x}} = \mathbf{b} + \delta\mathbf{b}$$

We see that

$$\begin{aligned} \mathbf{x}^* - \bar{\mathbf{x}} &= A^{-1}\mathbf{b} - (A + \delta A)^{-1}(\mathbf{b} + \delta\mathbf{b}) \\ &= [A^{-1} - (A + \delta A)^{-1}]\mathbf{b} - (A + \delta A)^{-1}\delta\mathbf{b} \end{aligned}$$

We now assume δA and $\delta \mathbf{b}$ are small enough so that anything involving $(\delta A)^2$ or $\delta A \delta \mathbf{b}$ may be dropped. Then a linear algebra manipulation yields

$$\mathbf{x}^* - \bar{\mathbf{x}} \sim A^{-1}\delta A A^{-1}\mathbf{b} - A^{-1}\delta\mathbf{b}$$

We are now faced with *two* different perturbations and we require *one* factor for the condition number. There is the possibility of vector-valued condition numbers, but we ignore that and instead *assume* some relationship between the sizes of δA and $\delta \mathbf{b}$. The simplest is that *the perturbations on each side of the system are of the same size* δ. This means that

$$\|\delta A \mathbf{x}^*\| \sim \|\delta \mathbf{b}\|$$

which leads to

$$\begin{aligned}
\|\mathbf{x}^* - \bar{\mathbf{x}}\| &\sim \|A^{-1}\delta A A^{-1}\mathbf{b}\| + \|A^{-1}\delta\mathbf{b}\| \\
&= \|A^{-1}\delta A \mathbf{x}^*\| + \|A^{-1}\delta\mathbf{b}\| \\
&\le \|A^{-1}\|\,\|\delta A\mathbf{x}^*\| + \|A^{-1}\delta\mathbf{b}\| \\
&\sim 2\|A^{-1}\|\,\|\delta\mathbf{b}\| = 2\|A^{-1}\|\delta
\end{aligned}$$

Since the perturbation in the data is of size 2δ (one δ for each of $\mathbf{b}$ and $A\mathbf{x}$), we see that the absolute condition is $\|A^{-1}\|$.

The relative condition is found from

$$\frac{\|\mathbf{x}^* - \bar{\mathbf{x}}\|}{\|\mathbf{x}^*\|} \le \frac{2\|A^{-1}\|\,\|\delta\mathbf{b}\|}{\|\mathbf{x}^*\|} \le \frac{\|A^{-1}\|\,\|\mathbf{b}\|}{\|\mathbf{x}^*\|} * \frac{2\|\delta\mathbf{b}\|}{\|\mathbf{b}\|}$$

which gives $\|A^{-1}\|\,\|\mathbf{b}\|/\|\mathbf{x}^*\|$, the same as the *natural condition* number found earlier. The *standard condition* number is found by substituting the estimate $1/\|\mathbf{x}\| \le \|A\|/\|\mathbf{b}\|$, which holds for all $\mathbf{x}$.

9.C COMPOSITE ERROR ESTIMATOR AND ALGORITHMS

We now make another study of the linear equations problem and identify three distinct linear systems:

Original problem:	$A\mathbf{x} = \mathbf{b}$
Machine problem:	$A(I + P)\mathbf{x}' = (I + D)\mathbf{b}$
Solved problem:	$A(I + P)\bar{\mathbf{x}} = (I + D)\mathbf{b} + \mathbf{r}$

The original problem is the "real world" problem, the one we actually want to solve in exact arithmetic. The *machine problem* is the linear system that actually exists inside the computer; there are perturbations P and D (a diagonal matrix) from the original problem. These perturbations might come from reading the numbers a_{ij} and b_i into the computer or they might come from inherent or experimental uncertainty in these numbers. These latter uncertainties are very large compared to machine round-off errors for many real problems. The *solved problem* is a further perturbation due to the inadequacies in the machine arithmetic or algorithm for solving the machine problem. The residual vector **r** represents the total effect of these inadequacies.

We wish to estimate $\bar{\mathbf{x}} - \mathbf{x}$ and we have

$$\mathbf{x} = A^{-1}\mathbf{b}$$

$$\mathbf{x}' = (I + P)^{-1}A^{-1}(I + D)\mathbf{b}$$

$$\bar{\mathbf{x}} = (I + P)^{-1}A^{-1}(I + D)\mathbf{b} + (I + P)^{-1}A^{-1}\mathbf{r}$$

As usual, we assume that P, D, and **r** are relatively small. We can thus use the estimate

$$(I + P)^{-1} \sim I - P$$

and obtain

$$\begin{aligned}\bar{x} &= A^{-1}\mathbf{b} - PA^{-1}\mathbf{b} + A^{-1}D\mathbf{b} + A^{-1}\mathbf{r} - PA^{-1}D\mathbf{b} - PA^{-1}\mathbf{r}\\ &\sim A^{-1}\mathbf{b} - PA^{-1}\mathbf{b} + A^{-1}D\mathbf{b} + A^{-1}\mathbf{r}\end{aligned}$$

Subtracting $\mathbf{x} = A^{-1}\mathbf{b}$ from both sides gives

$$\begin{aligned}\bar{\mathbf{x}} - \mathbf{x} &\sim -PA^{-1}\mathbf{b} + A^{-1}D\mathbf{b} + A^{-1}\mathbf{r}\\ &= -P\mathbf{x} + A^{-1}D\mathbf{b} + A^{-1}\mathbf{r}\end{aligned}$$

and

$$\begin{aligned}\frac{\|\bar{\mathbf{x}} - \mathbf{x}\|}{\|\mathbf{x}\|} &\le \frac{\|P\mathbf{x}\|}{\|\mathbf{x}\|} + \frac{\|A^{-1}D\mathbf{b}\|}{\|\mathbf{x}\|} + \frac{\|A^{-1}\mathbf{r}\|}{\|\mathbf{x}\|}\\ &\le \|P\| + \frac{\|A^{-1}D\mathbf{b}\|}{\|\mathbf{x}\|} + \frac{\|A^{-1}\mathbf{r}\|}{\|\mathbf{x}\|}\end{aligned}$$

This *composite error estimator* is an extension of the Aird-Lynch condition estimate $\|C\mathbf{r}\|/\|\mathbf{x}\|$; two terms have been added to include the effect $\|P\|$ of perturbing the matrix and $\|A^{-1}D\mathbf{b}\|/\|\mathbf{x}\|$ of perturbing the right-hand side. Recall from Chap. 8 that the Aird-Lynch estimate underestimated the actual error in all the examples considered. If one examines these and similar examples in more detail, one sees that the source of the underestimate is that the perturbation errors just due to changing to 48-bit binary numbers were ignored and contributed to the error actually measured. The natural and standard condition numbers also ignore these perturbations, but they so grossly overestimate the error that this did not show up in the examples. One can construct instances where they too underestimate the actual error.

It is feasible to compute the composite error estimator. The norm of P is a data item; one either knows the uncertainty in A or assumes P_{ij} is about machine round-off error. One can estimate $\|A^{-1}Db\|$ and $\|A^{-1}r\|$ rather efficiently, as discussed in Chap. 8, without computing A^{-1}. The next example shows the performance of the composite error estimator for the four examples given in Chap. 8.

Example 9.3: The composite error estimator applied to Examples 8.2 through 8.5 The calculations were made with a CDC 6500 which uses 14+ decimal digit arithmetic. Thus we take EPSA = EPSB = 10^{-14} in the estimate

$$\frac{\|x - \bar{x}\|}{\|x\|} \sim \frac{2\|Cr\|}{\|x\|} + N * \text{EPSA} + \frac{\|A^{-1}d\|\text{EPSB}}{\|x\|}$$

with d a vector $d_i = v * b_i$ where v is a random variable uniformly distributed between 1 and -1. Two cases for d were generated and the largest value of $\|A^{-1}d\|$ used. For ease of comparison we reproduce the data for the natural, standard, and Aird-Lynch condition numbers:

Error estimator	Error estimate	Digits off	Relative cost
Example 8.2: Actual error = 2.770E − 4, solution time = 0.024 second			
Natural	6.434E − 3	1.366	17.5
Standard	1.812E + 5	8.816	17.5
Aird-Lynch	2.693E − 4	−0.012	1.83
Composite	5.383E − 4	0.289	1.08
Example 8.3: Actual error = 1.774E − 3, solution time = 0.005 second			
Natural	1.681E + 2	4.977	3.9
Standard	1.681E + 2	4.977	4.0
Aird-Lynch	1.781E − 7	−3.998	1.4
Composite	8.721E − 3	0.692	1.6
Example 8.4: Actual error = 1.450E − 12, solution time = 0.048 second			
Natural	3.179E − 11	1.34	12.1
Standard	3.179E − 11	1.34	12.2
Aird-Lynch	1.261E − 12	−0.06	1.9
Composite	5.258E − 12	0.56	0.88
Example 8.5: Actual error = 1.529E − 8, solution time = 0.549 second			
Natural	4.009E − 6	2.42	24.0
Standard	1.034E + 3	10.83	24.1
Aird-Lynch	9.147E − 9	−0.22	1.8
Composite	1.830E − 8	0.078	0.43

Table 9.1 Summary performance of error estimators for 52 linear systems with moderately to extremely poor conditioning

Error estimator	Digits off: Maximum	Minimum	Average
Natural	16.3	0.82	7.2
Standard	28.5	3.1	14.6
Aird-Lynch	0.0	−4.0	−0.31
BOUNDS	12.8	0.26	5.3
Composite	12.7	−0.20	1.2

Table 9.2 Summary performance of error estimators for 20 random systems (well conditioned) of order 10 and 25

Error estimator	Digits off: Maximum		Minimum		Average	
	Order = 10	Order = 25	Order = 10	Order = 25	Order = 10	Order = 25
Natural	1.66	2.03	0.47	1.11	1.05	1.47
Standard	3.45	4.38	1.59	2.62	2.57	3.43
Aird-Lynch	0.13	0.02	−0.49	−0.29	−0.06	−0.04
BOUNDS	1.70	1.88	0.68	0.89	1.15	1.33
Composite	1.09	0.96	0.25	0.49	0.67	0.68

These comparisons make the composite error estimator appear attractive; it is always an upper bound and it is the cheapest of the four to compute. Of course, the faster ways of estimating the other condition numbers are faster yet, but not by much. Summaries of two experiments involving a larger number of matrices are given in Tables 9.1 and 9.2.

Algorithm 9.1 given below is one way that the composite error estimator can be incorporated into the solution of $\mathrm{A}\mathbf{x} = \mathbf{b}$ by Gauss elimination. The input to Algorithm 9.1 is A,**b**, EPSA, and EPSB; the output is X, ERROR.

Algorithm 9.1: Gauss elimination with composite error estimator

1. Factor A by Gauss elimination with partial pivoting so that MA = U
2. Compute **x** from $\mathbf{v} = \mathrm{M}\mathbf{b}$, $\mathrm{U}\mathbf{x} = \mathbf{v}$
3. *a.* Compute residual **r** in double precision, truncate to single precision
   b. Compute **y** from $\mathbf{v} = \mathrm{M}\mathbf{r}$, $\mathrm{U}\mathbf{y} = \mathbf{v}$
   c. $\mathbf{x} = \mathbf{x} + \mathbf{y}$

4. *a.* For two times do the following:
   Generate random number α, set $c_i = \alpha b_i$ for $i = 1, 2, \ldots, N$
   Compute $\mathbf{z}$ from $\mathbf{v} = \mathbf{M}\mathbf{c}$, $\mathbf{U}\mathbf{z} = \mathbf{v}$
   b. $\text{ERR1} = 2\|\mathbf{y}\|/\|\mathbf{x}\|$
   $\text{ERR2} = N * \text{EPSA}$
   $\text{ERR3} = 1.3 * \max\,[\|\mathbf{z}\|]/\|\mathbf{x}\| * \text{EPSB}$
5. ERROR = ERR1 + ERR2 + ERR3

Note that this algorithm carries out the first iteration of iterative improvement. Since $\|\mathbf{y}\|$ is needed for the error estimator, it seems plausible to add it to $\mathbf{x}$ at step 3*c*. This will make the error estimator considerably more conservative since ERROR actually estimates the error of the solution obtained at step 2, not the more accurate one actually returned.

It is important to note that the composite error estimator is based on the assumption that A is perturbed to $A(I + P)$ with $|p_{ij}| \leq \text{EPSA}$. This is not the same as a perturbation of A to $A + E$ where $e_{ij} = \alpha a_{ij}$ and α is a random number with $|\alpha| \leq \text{EPSA}$. We see that $P = A^{-1}E$, and thus $\|P\|$ can be much larger than $\|E\|$ if A is ill conditioned. This effect can be observed in practice, and the composite error estimator is *not* a reliable error estimator for EPSA perturbations in individual elements of A. If such perturbations are present, one should use a modified composite estimator:

$$\frac{\|\mathbf{x} - \bar{\mathbf{x}}\|}{\|\mathbf{x}\|} \leq \frac{\|A^{-1}E\mathbf{x}\|}{\|\mathbf{x}\|} + \frac{\|A^{-1}D\mathbf{b}\|}{\|\mathbf{x}\|} + \frac{\|A^{-1}\mathbf{r}\|}{\|\mathbf{x}\|}$$

This estimator is more expensive to compute since $\|A^{-1}E\mathbf{x}\|$ must now be estimated. However, since E is a random matrix, one may estimate $\|A^{-1}E\mathbf{x}\|$ by solving $A\mathbf{z} = \mathbf{e}$ for several random vectors. This is not completely reliable, but it has a high probability of giving an upper bound on the error. This approach is implemented in Algorithm 9.2.

Algorithm 9.2: Gauss elimination with modified composite error estimator

1. Factor A by Gauss elimination with partial pivoting so that MA = U
2. Compute $\mathbf{x}$ from $\mathbf{v} = \mathbf{M}\mathbf{b}$, $\mathbf{U}\mathbf{x} = \mathbf{v}$
3. *a.* Compute residual $\mathbf{r}$ in double precision, truncate to single precision
   b. Compute $\mathbf{y}$ from $\mathbf{v} = \mathbf{M}\mathbf{r}$, $\mathbf{U}\mathbf{y} = \mathbf{v}$
   c. $\mathbf{x} = \mathbf{x} + \mathbf{y}$
4. *a.* For two times do the following:
   Generate random numbers α, β, set $c_i = \alpha b_i$, $d_i = \beta x_i$ for $i = 1, 2, \ldots, N$
   Compute $\mathbf{z}$, $\mathbf{w}$ from $\mathbf{v} = \mathbf{M}\mathbf{c}$, $\mathbf{U}\mathbf{z} = \mathbf{v}$, $\mathbf{u} = \mathbf{M}\mathbf{d}$, $\mathbf{U}\mathbf{w} = \mathbf{u}$
   b. $\text{ERR1} = 2\|\mathbf{y}\|/\|\mathbf{x}\|$
   $\text{ERR2} = 1.3 * \max\,[\|\mathbf{w}\|]/\|\mathbf{x}\| * \text{EPSA}$
   $\text{ERR3} = 1.3 * \max\,[\|\mathbf{z}\|]/\|\mathbf{x}\| * \text{EPSB}$
5. ERROR = ERR1 + ERR2 + ERR3

It is important to note that the error estimates given in this section have the following intuitive interpretation:

Solution uncertainty ~ model uncertainty + data uncertainty + calculation errors

$$\frac{\|\mathbf{x}-\bar{\mathbf{x}}\|}{\|\mathbf{x}\|} \sim \frac{\|A^{-1}E\mathbf{x}\|}{\|\mathbf{x}\|} + \frac{\|A^{-1}D\mathbf{b}\|}{\|\mathbf{x}\|} + \frac{\|A^{-1}\mathbf{r}\|}{\|\mathbf{x}\|}$$

This interprets the matrix as the model of a situation and the right-hand side as the data or forcing function of the model. The intelligent use of these estimates requires one to make judgments about the relative sizes of these uncertainties. Numerical analysis has concentrated on the calculation errors because they can be controlled in the computation. In many real situations, the calculation errors are completely negligible compared to the uncertainties in the model or in the data. Wild answers from calculations normally are only reflecting the high sensitivity of the model (ill conditioning) and do not indicate that the calculation has been done poorly.

There is a common belief that the standard condition number provides a good estimate of the uncertainty in the situation where both A and **b** are perturbed. The validity of this belief depends crucially on the assumptions about the relative sizes of the uncertainties and the nature of the perturbations. Suppose that one assumes that E is "proportional" to A in the sense that $|e_{ij}| \sim |a_{ij}| * \text{EPSA}$. Then one is tempted to estimate

$$\frac{\|A^{-1}E\mathbf{x}\|}{\|\mathbf{x}\|} \text{ by } \|A^{-1}\|\,\|A\|\text{EPSA}$$

which gives the bound

$$\frac{\|\mathbf{x}-\bar{\mathbf{x}}\|}{\|\mathbf{x}\|} \le \|A^{-1}\|\,\|A\|\text{EPSA} + \|A^{-1}\|\text{EPSB} + \frac{\|A^{-1}\mathbf{r}\|}{\|\mathbf{x}\|}$$

The first term often dominates and, in these cases, one might conclude that $\|A^{-1}\|\,\|A\|\text{EPSA}$ is a reliable estimate of the uncertainty in solving $A\mathbf{x} = \mathbf{b}$. However, experiments show that $\|A^{-1}\|\,\|A\|\text{EPSA}$ is *not* a completely reliable estimate of the effect of such perturbations in A. The reason is as follows: The estimate

$$\|A^{-1}E\mathbf{x}\| \le \|A^{-1}\|\,\|E\mathbf{x}\|$$

is, in general, not sharp. Note that the solution **x** is fixed for a particular problem $A\mathbf{x} = \mathbf{b}$, and equality in

$$\|A^{-1}E\mathbf{x}\| = \|A^{-1}\|\,\|E\mathbf{x}\|$$

requires that Ex be a particular vector (the eigenvector of A^{-1} with maximum eigenvalue). That, of course, can be achieved for some matrix E, but it cannot, in general, be achieved with $\|Ex\| = \|x\|EPSA$. Equivalently if Ex is the required vector, then $\|Ex\| = \|x\|EPSA$ is not a sharp estimate.

The last problems at the end of this chapter illustrate the effect that various assumptions on the nature of E have on the sharpness of this estimate. A simple 3 × 3, upper triangular matrix is considered along with the assumptions

$$|e_{ij}| \le |a_{ij}| * EPSA \tag{9.1}$$

$$|e_{ij}| \le \max_{i,j} |a_{ij}| * EPSA \quad \text{if } |a_{ij}| > 0 \tag{9.2}$$

$$= 0 \quad \text{if } |a_{ij}| = 0$$

$$|e_{ij}| \le \|A\| * EPSA \quad \text{if } |a_{ij}| > 0 \tag{9.3}$$

$$= 0 \quad \text{if } |a_{ij}| = 0$$

$$\|E\| \le \|A\| * EPSA \tag{9.4}$$

The lack of sharpness in the estimate discussed above is by a factor of 18.87, 2.75, 1.83, and 1, respectively, for the four different assumptions.

9.D BACKWARD ERROR ANALYSIS

The first and most natural attempt to study the effects of errors on the accuracy of numerical computation is *forward error analysis.* Here one starts with the original problem and follows, step by step, the effect of the computational errors (round-off) and original data uncertainty. If one is skillful enough, one will obtain an estimate of the error in the final result. This is illustrated by Example 9.4.

Example 9.4: Forward error analysis in $ab^2 + \sin(3.1a - b)$ Consider the computation

```
      READ 10, A, B
10    FORMAT (2F8.6)
      ANS = A * B ** 2 + SIN(3.1 * A - B)
      PRINT 20, ANS
20    FORMAT (F15.9)
```

We *assume* a computer with seven decimal digits in its numbers, so the round-off ε is 10^{-7}. We also *assume* that A and B are about 1 in value. The original data error is *assumed* to be as specified by FORMAT 10, so we let $\delta = 10^{-6}$ be the uncertainty in A and B. The Fortran I/O computations also introduce round-off, but we ignore that here.

The actual calculation goes as follows: Compute

$$\text{B**2} = \text{B}^2 + 2\delta\text{B} + \delta^2 + \varepsilon \tag{9.5}$$

$$\begin{aligned}\text{A} * \text{B**2} = {} & \text{AB}^2 + 2\delta\text{AB} + \delta^2\text{A} + \varepsilon\text{A} \\ & + \delta\text{B}^2 + 2\delta^2\text{B} + \delta^2 + \delta\varepsilon + \varepsilon\end{aligned} \tag{9.6}$$

$$3.1 * \text{A} = 3.1\text{A} + 3.1\delta + \varepsilon \tag{9.7}$$

$$3.1 * \text{A} - \text{B} = 3.1\text{A} + 3.1\delta + \varepsilon - \text{B} - \delta + \varepsilon \tag{9.8}$$

$$\text{SIN}\,(3.1 * \text{A} - \text{B}) = \text{SIN}\,(3.1\text{A} + 3.1\delta + \varepsilon - \text{B} - \delta + \varepsilon) + \varepsilon \tag{9.9}$$

$$\begin{aligned}\text{ANS} = {} & \text{AB}^2 + 2\delta\text{AB} + \delta^2\text{A} + \varepsilon\text{A} + \delta\text{B}^2 + 2\delta^2\text{B} \\ & + \delta^2 + \delta\varepsilon + \varepsilon + \text{SIN}\,(3.1\text{A} + 3.1\delta + \varepsilon - \text{B} - \delta + \varepsilon) \\ & + \varepsilon + \varepsilon\end{aligned} \tag{9.10}$$

We now have a big mess, and clearly this detailed approach cannot be carried through for any large computation. So we must make approximations and simplifications as we go. These are primarily (1) to neglect any terms involving the product of two errors, (2) to approximate functions by their tangent line (one term in a Taylor's series), and (3) to combine the ε's and δ's by assuming they are the same number. Redoing the calculation we now get:

$$\text{B} ** 2 = \text{B}^2 + 2\delta\text{B} + \varepsilon \tag{9.5a}$$

$$\text{A} * \text{B} ** 2 = \text{AB}^2 + 2\delta\text{AB} + \varepsilon\text{A} + \delta\text{B}^2 + \varepsilon \tag{9.6a}$$

$$3.1 * \text{A} = 3.1\text{A} + 3.1\delta + \varepsilon \tag{9.7a}$$

$$3.1 * \text{A} - \text{B} = 3.1\text{A} + 3.1\delta + \varepsilon - \text{B} - \delta + \varepsilon \tag{9.8a}$$

$$\begin{aligned}\text{SIN}\,(3.1 * \text{A} - \text{B}) = {} & \text{SIN}\,(3.1\,\text{A} - \text{B}) + \varepsilon \\ & + \text{COS}(3.1\text{A} - \text{B}) * (3.1\delta + \varepsilon - \text{B} - \delta + \varepsilon)\end{aligned} \tag{9.9a}$$

$$\begin{aligned}\text{ANS} = {} & \text{AB}^2 + \text{SIN}\,(3.1\text{A} - \text{B}) \\ & + \varepsilon(\text{A} + 3 + 2\,\text{COS}\,(3.1\text{A} - \text{B})) \\ & + \delta(2\text{AB} + \text{B}^2 + 4.1)\end{aligned} \tag{9.10a}$$

This is a little, but not much, simpler. And now the effect of the errors is substantially exaggerated because we assumed that they all combine to give the worst possible result. That is, $\varepsilon + \varepsilon + \varepsilon$ (the sum of three round-off errors) is very unlikely to be $3 * 10^{-7}$ because (1) actual errors are less than 10^{-7} and (2) some errors are positive and some negative so that cancellation is to be expected.

One of the most famous papers in numerical computation deals with forward error analysis for Gauss elimination (Von Neumann and Goldstein,

1947; see References at end of book). This paper led people to conclude that the accumulated effect of round-off errors made it impossible to solve large (say 100×100) systems of equations. Computers at that time used 10 to 12 decimal digits. In retrospect, we see that this paper also proves that forward error analysis is unlikely to produce much useful information.

Much of the theory of condition and condition numbers is of the spirit of forward error analysis and, while less tedious to carry out, we have seen that these numbers frequently grossly overestimate the effect of computational errors and data uncertainty.

The basic goal of error analysis is to provide an estimate of $\|\bar{\mathbf{x}} - \mathbf{x}^*\|$, where $\mathbf{x}^*$ is the true solution and $\bar{\mathbf{x}}$ is the computed solution. Unfortunately, *realistic estimates of* $\|\bar{\mathbf{x}} - \mathbf{x}^*\|$ *are difficult or impossible to obtain.* We list some questions that one can ask about the effect of errors and data uncertainty on the answers:

1. What is the worst error that can occur?
2. What error actually occurred?
3. What error is expected to occur?
4. How sensitive is the problem to errors?
5. How close is the problem actually solved to the one we wanted to solve?

Forward error analysis and *a priori* error bounds attempts to answer the first question. By and large these answers are hopelessly pessimistic and useful only to show that a problem is very well behaved. Much of the effort in Chap. 8 seems directed toward question 2, but in fact is actually an effort to answer question 4. The true solution $\mathbf{x}^*$ is almost never actually known, so question 2 is almost never answerable. The problem solver must use estimates of the level of data uncertainty and problem sensitivity so as to make a judgment about the validity of the answer; that is, one answers question 3 as best one can. Recall that a good program may well be able to compute the "right" answer to the wrong problem and thus report back that the computation went well. Little is known about what errors to expect beyond the fact that they are often *much* smaller than error estimation procedures suggest. We conclude that the first four of these questions are either unanswerable or provide little information about the actual size of the error $\|\bar{\mathbf{x}} - \mathbf{x}^*\|$.

Question 5 can be answered satisfactorily, and leads to real insight into the validity of many numerical computations. *Backward error analysis* answers this question and can be carried out for linear systems (and many other problems) with relative ease (Wilkinson, 1963; see References at end of book). However, *this analysis does not provide any information about the error* $\|\bar{\mathbf{x}} - \mathbf{x}^*\|$ *and it takes some time to adjust to this viewpoint.* The idea is presented graphically in Fig. 9.5. There may be many data sets whose true solution is $\bar{\mathbf{x}}$; one wants to find data $\mathbf{d}_b$ which make the backward error small.

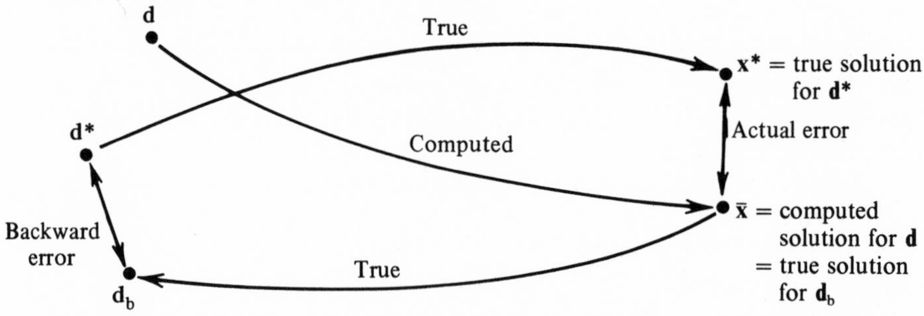

Figure 9.5 Graphical illustration of the backward error estimate. The true data and solution are **d*** and **x***. The data actually used is **d**, and $\bar{x}$ is computed from it. The data $\mathbf{d}_b$ is another set with true solution $\bar{x}$.

Example 9.5: Solving

$$f(x) = 2.23x^2 \cos(x/4) + 2.41x^4 - 5.06e^{-6.4x} + 0.832 = 0$$

Suppose one has attempted to solve this equation and come up with x = 0.256 as a tentative answer. If we substitute 0.256 into f(x) = 0, we find that the residual is

$$f(0.256) = 0.005086$$

This means that 0.256 is the exact solution of

$$2.23x^2 \cos(x/4) + 2.41x^4 - 5.06e^{-6.4x} + 0.82691 = 0$$

$$2.23x^2 \cos(x/4) + 1.22582x^4 - 5.06e^{-6.4x} + 0.832 = 0$$

$$2.23x^2 \cos(x/4) + 2.41x^4 - 5.0338e^{-6.4x} + 0.832 = 0$$

All of these problems have changed the data more than the implied accuracy of three digits in the original problem's coefficients. Thus we are unlikely to accept 0.256 as a solution unless we believe the uncertainty in the original problem is more than indicated by the significance of the given coefficients.

Suppose now that one obtains $\bar{x} = 0.2553$ as a tentative answer. The residual then is

$$f(0.2553) = -0.0002356$$

and thus 0.2553 is the exact solution of

$$2.23x^2 \cos(x/4) + 2.41x^4 - 5.06e^{-6.4x} + 0.8322356 = 0$$

Since it is plausible that the fourth digit of the term 0.832 is unknown, we may as well assume it to be a 2 and then we have the exact answer to a problem which is indistinguishable from the original problem.

If we continue the search to find $\bar{x} = 0.2553295$ with a residual of -0.0000106, then we certainly must accept it as an accurate solution. Here, as the reader probably suspects, everything is going well and all these answers are reasonably close to the "true" answer 0.2553309476. Such is not always the case, as seen from Example 9.6.

Example 9.6: Solving

$$f(x) = x^5 - 7.5x^4 + 22.5x^3 - 33.75x^2 + 25.3125x - 7.59375 = 0$$

Suppose one has obtained 1.33 as a tentative answer. The residual is

$$f(1.33) = -0.000142$$

All the calculations in this example are done with seven-digit decimal arithmetic. This means that 1.33 is the exact solution of

$$x^5 - 7.4995557x^4 + 22.5x^3 - 33.75x^2 + 25.3125x - 7.59375 = 0$$

$$x^5 - 7.5x^4 + 22.500334x^3 - 33.75x^2 + 25.3125x - 7.59375 = 0$$

$$x^5 - 7.5x^4 + 22.5x^3 - 33.75x^2 + 25.3125x - 7.593608 = 0$$

The first two equations seem to be negligible changes from the original problem, and thus we might accept 1.33 as the answer. The third equation has a significant change in the constant term.

An improved solution estimate is 1.4026, which gives a residual of

$$f(1.4026) = -0.000032$$

Thus, 1.4026 is the exact solution of

$$x^5 - 7.5x^4 + 22.500088x^3 - 33.75x^2 + 25.3125x - 7.59375 = 0$$

which is a very small perturbation of the original problem and must be accepted as correct.

However, we might think that the "exact" answer would have an even smaller residual. So we discover that 1.582 has a smaller residual:

$$f(1.582) = -0.000008$$

This residual is zero in the eighth place relative to 33.75, etc., and thus as small as we could hope for using seven-digit arithmetic. So 1.582 must be "the" solution.

However, we should be suspicious because the three tentative solutions have changed quite a bit and each has a small residual. Further calculations show

$$f(1.4) = -0.00001$$

$$f(1.462) = -0.00001$$

$$f(1.5002) = 0.000007$$

$$f(1.55) = -0.000006$$

$$f(1.6) = 0.00001$$

and, in fact, any value for the solution between 1.4 and 1.6 gives a small residual, including dozens of values where the residual is *exactly zero* (using seven-digit arithmetic).

Further examination shows that f(x) is exactly $(x - 1.5)^5$, so the true solution must be 1.5. But what about the other values of x that also make f(x) exactly zero? They surely must be true solutions of this equation. This example is typical of ill-conditioned problems; there are many widely varying "answers" which give small residuals, and each of these are the exact solution of a problem *very* close to the original problem. All these problems are well within the uncertainty of the original problem, and it is meaningless to consider any result as the exact answer.

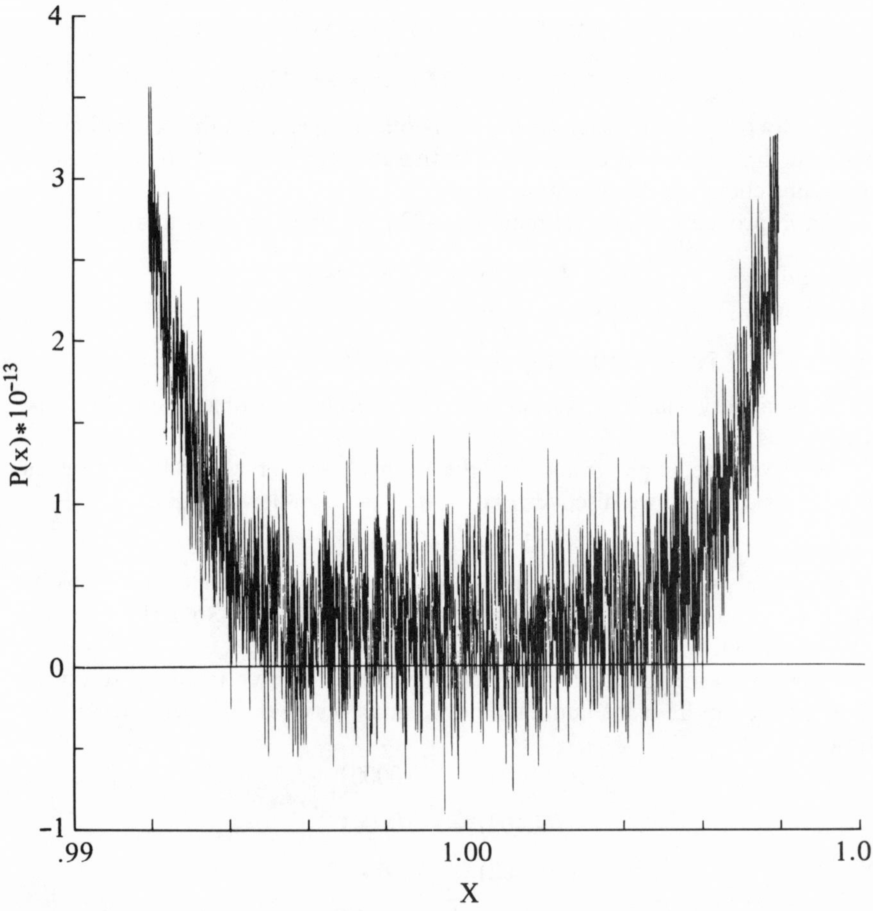

Figure 9.6 Graph of the values of a sixth-degree polynomial evaluated with 14 decimal digit arithmetic.

A similar situation is shown in Fig. 9.6, where the computed values of the sixth degree polynomial

$$P(x) = x^6 - 6x^5 + 15x^4 - 20x^3 + 15x^2 - 6x + 1$$

are plotted. The computation was made with 14-decimal digit arithmetic. We see that there is an *interval of solutions* for the zero of this polynomial, and the uncertainty in any one solution is about 0.01.

The objective of backward error analysis is to stop worrying about whether one has the "exact" answer, because this is not a well-defined thing in most real-world situations. What one wants is to find an answer which is the true mathematical solution to a problem which is within the domain of uncertainty of the original problem. Any result that does this must be acceptable as an answer to the problem, at least with the philosophy of backward error analysis.

To apply backward error analysis to Gauss elimination is not terribly difficult, at least in common cases.

Example 9.7: Backward error analysis for a 3 × 3 linear system We consider Gauss elimination for the system

$$a_{11}x_1 + a_{22}x_2 + a_{13}x_3 = b_1$$

$$a_{21}x_1 + a_{22}x_2 + a_{23}x_3 = b_2$$

$$a_{31}x_1 + a_{32}x_2 + a_{33}x_3 = b_3$$

where all the a_{ij} are approximately 1 in size and no pivoting is required. Let ε denote the size of a typical round-off error. The first two multipliers are computed as

$$m_{21} = a_{21}/a_{11} + \varepsilon \qquad m_{31} = a_{31}/a_{11} + \varepsilon$$

$$= (a_{21} + \varepsilon_1)/a_{11} \qquad = (a_{31} + \varepsilon_2)/a_{11}$$

Since $a_{11} \sim 1$, we see that ε_1 and ε_2 are about ε in size and thus m_{21} and m_{31} are *the exact multipliers* for the problem with a_{21} and a_{31} perturbed by order ε.

Next consider the calculation on the 2 × 2 submatrix to finish the elimination step:

$$a_{22} = a_{22} - m_{21}a_{12} + \varepsilon_3 = (a_{22} + \varepsilon_3) - m_{21}a_{12}$$

$$a_{23} = (a_{23} + \varepsilon_4) - m_{21}a_{13}$$

$$a_{32} = (a_{32} + \varepsilon_5) - m_{31}a_{12}$$

$$a_{33} = (a_{33} + \varepsilon_6) - m_{31}a_{13}$$

Each of the round-off errors ε_3, ε_4, ε_5, and ε_6 are the size of ε since all the numbers are of order 1, and thus the new values form *the exact* 2 × 2 *submatrix* for the problem with a_{ij}, $i = 2, 3$ and $j = 1, 2, 3$, perturbed by order ε.

Put in matrix terms, this says that the result of the first step of Gauss elimination produces the exact result for the matrix $A + E_1$ where E_1 is of the size

$$\begin{pmatrix} 0 & 0 & 0 \\ 1 & 1 & 1 \\ 1 & 1 & 1 \end{pmatrix} \varepsilon$$

The argument is now repeated for the second step of Gauss elimination on the 2×2 submatrix. The result is the exact result for the matrix $(A + E_1) + E_2$ where E_2 is of the size

$$\begin{pmatrix} 0 & 0 & 0 \\ 0 & 0 & 0 \\ 0 & 1 & 1 \end{pmatrix} \varepsilon$$

The first column and row of E_2 are zero because these terms do not enter the calculation. The rest of E_2 is just E_1 shifted down and to the right. We conclude that the total perturbation matrix $E = E_1 + E_2$ is of the size

$$\begin{pmatrix} 0 & 0 & 0 \\ 1 & 1 & 1 \\ 1 & 2 & 2 \end{pmatrix} \varepsilon$$

The application of the multipliers to the right-hand side gives a result just like that of the last column of the matrix. That is, the result is the exact result for a vector $\mathbf{b} + \mathbf{e}_1$, where $\mathbf{e}_1$ is of size $(0, 1, 2)^T\varepsilon$. The back-substitution computations are

$$\begin{aligned} x_3 &= b_3/a_{33} + \varepsilon = (b_3 + \varepsilon)/a_{33} \\ x_2 &= (b_2 - a_{23}x_3 + \varepsilon)/a_{22} + \varepsilon = ((b_2 + 2\varepsilon) - a_{23}x_3)/a_{22} \\ x_1 &= (b_2 - a_{13}x_3 - a_{12}x_2 + 2\varepsilon)/a_{22} + \varepsilon \\ &= ((b_1 + 3\varepsilon) - a_{13}x_3 - a_{12}x_2)/a_{11} \end{aligned}$$

Thus the values for the x_i are the exact values for a right-hand side $\mathbf{b} + \mathbf{e}_1$ perturbed by $\mathbf{e}_2 = (3, 2, 1)^T\varepsilon$.

We conclude then that, with these assumptions, the result $\bar{\mathbf{x}}$ computed by Gauss elimination is the exact solution to the system

$$(A + E)\bar{\mathbf{x}} = \mathbf{b} + \mathbf{e}$$

where the size of E is given above and $\mathbf{e}$ is of the size $(3, 3, 3)^T\varepsilon$.

The common situation is where the elements of A are all about 1 in size and *all* the intermediate elements generated are no larger than this. If Gauss elimination with pivoting is applied to $A\mathbf{x} = \mathbf{b}$, then the result $\bar{\mathbf{x}}$ computed is the true solution of

$$(A + E)\bar{\mathbf{x}} = \mathbf{b} + \mathbf{e}$$

Let ε be the amount of round-off made in one arithmetic operation (an addition, subtraction, or multiplication). Then, *with these assumptions*, E and **e** are no larger (in absolute value) than

$$\begin{pmatrix} 0 & 0 & 0 & 0 & 0 & \dots & 0 \\ 1 & 1 & 1 & 1 & 1 & \dots & 1 \\ 1 & 2 & 2 & 2 & 2 & \dots & 2 \\ 1 & 2 & 3 & 3 & 3 & & 3 \\ 1 & 2 & 3 & 4 & 4 & & 4 \\ 1 & 2 & 3 & 4 & 5 & & 5 \\ \vdots & & & & & & \vdots \\ 1 & 2 & 3 & 4 & 5 & \dots & N-1 \end{pmatrix} \varepsilon \quad \text{and} \quad \begin{pmatrix} N \\ N \\ \vdots \\ \vdots \\ N \\ N \end{pmatrix} \varepsilon$$

In most instances, the matrix A + E is well within the uncertainty of the original problem and the computed answer must be accepted as correct.

Note that this analysis does not apply to all problems because of the assumptions made. Recall from Sec. 5.C.1 the difficulty in scaling a matrix, which shows that one cannot always satisfy the assumption about the size of the elements of A. Furthermore, one cannot guarantee that the size of the elements of A do not grow somewhat during Gauss elimination even though this is very rare (see the discussion at the end of Sec. 5.B).

The philosophy of backward error analysis can be expressed in terms of *fuzzy linear systems*. We define the absolute value of a matrix or vector as the matrix or vector of absolute values; that is,

$$|A| = \begin{pmatrix} |a_{11}| & |a_{12}| & \dots & |a_{1n}| \\ |a_{21}| & & & \vdots \\ \vdots & & & \vdots \\ |a_{m1}| & \dots & \dots & |a_{mn}| \end{pmatrix}$$

$$|\mathbf{x}| = (|x_1|, |x_2|, \dots, |x_n|)^T$$

We say $|\mathbf{x}| \le |\mathbf{y}|$ if $|x_i| \le |y_i|$ for all i; $|A| \le |B|$ if $|a_{ij}| \le |b_{ij}|$ for all i and j. Suppose we are given a matrix vector pair A^* and $\mathbf{b}^*$ along with a perturbation matrix δA and vector $\delta\mathbf{b}$. A *fuzzy system* is then the set of linear equations $A\mathbf{x} = \mathbf{b}$ where

$$|A^* - A| \le \delta A$$

$$|\mathbf{b}^* - \mathbf{b}| \le \delta\mathbf{b}$$

A vector $\bar{\mathbf{x}}$ is called an *acceptable solution of the fuzzy system* if it is a solution of one of the set of linear equations in the fuzzy system. The following result about fuzzy systems was established by Oettle and Prager (1964) (see References at end of book).

Theorem 9.1: *The vector $\bar{x}$ is acceptable if and only if*

$$|\mathbf{b}^* - A^*\bar{\mathbf{x}}| \le \delta\mathbf{b} + \delta A|\bar{\mathbf{x}}|$$

PROOF Suppose $\bar{\mathbf{x}}$ is acceptable, that is, $A\bar{\mathbf{x}} = \mathbf{b}$ with $|A - A^*| \le \delta A$ and $|\mathbf{b} - \mathbf{b}^*| \le \delta\mathbf{b}$. Then we have

$$\begin{aligned} |\mathbf{b}^* - A^*\bar{\mathbf{x}}| &= |\mathbf{b} + (\mathbf{b}^* - \mathbf{b}) - A\bar{\mathbf{x}} - (A^* - A)\bar{\mathbf{x}}| \\ &\le |\mathbf{b} - A\bar{\mathbf{x}}| + |\mathbf{b}^* - \mathbf{b}| + |(A^* - A)\bar{\mathbf{x}}| \\ &\le \delta\mathbf{b} + \delta A|\bar{\mathbf{x}}| \end{aligned}$$

which establishes the first part of the theorem.

Suppose now that $\bar{\mathbf{x}}$ satisfies the inequality of the theorem. Set $\mathbf{r} = \mathbf{b}^* - A^*\bar{\mathbf{x}}$, $\mathbf{s} = \delta\mathbf{b} + \delta A|\bar{\mathbf{x}}|$, and

$$\begin{aligned} t_i &= \frac{r_i}{s_i} \qquad \text{if } s_i \neq 0 \\ &= 0 \qquad \text{if } s_i = 0 \end{aligned}$$

The vector $\mathbf{t}$ clearly satisfies $|\mathbf{t}| \le 1$, and note that if $s_i = 0$ then the inequality $|\mathbf{r}| \le |\mathbf{s}|$ implies $r_i = 0$. Thus we have

$$\begin{aligned} r_i = s_i t_i &= (\delta b_i + \sum_{j=1}^{n} \delta a_{ij} |\bar{x}_j|)t_i \\ &= \delta b_i t_i + \sum_{j=1}^{n} \delta a_{ij} \operatorname{sign}(\bar{x}_j) t_i \bar{x}_j \end{aligned}$$

Define

$$\begin{aligned} \varepsilon_i &= -\delta b_i t_i \\ e_{ij} &= \delta a_{ij} \operatorname{sign}(\bar{x}_j) t_i \end{aligned}$$

and then, from the definition of $\mathbf{r}$, the previous relation becomes

$$r_i = b_i^* - \sum_{j=1}^{n} a_{ij}^* \bar{x}_j = -\varepsilon_i + \sum_{j=1}^{n} e_{ij} \bar{x}_j$$

or, equivalently,

$$\sum_{j=1}^{n} (a_{ij}^* + e_{ij})\bar{x}_j = b_i^* + \varepsilon_i$$

Thus we have $A\bar{\mathbf{x}} = \mathbf{b}$ where $|A^* - A| = |E| \le \delta A$ and $|\mathbf{b} - \mathbf{b}^*| = |\boldsymbol{\varepsilon}| \le \delta\mathbf{b}$. This is the condition for $\bar{\mathbf{x}}$ to be acceptable and concludes the proof.

Example 9.8: Fuzzy system analysis of Wilkinson's triangular (Example 8.3) Let $A^*\mathbf{x} = \mathbf{b}^*$ be the machine problem; that is, the numbers a_{ij} and b_i are converted to 48-bit binary numbers. Let ε be the machine round-off which, in this calculation, is $0.5 * 10^{-14}$. Then we expect the perturbations between the original problem and the machine problem to be

$$\delta A = \begin{pmatrix} \varepsilon & 0 & 0 & 0 \\ \varepsilon & \varepsilon & 0 & 0 \\ \varepsilon & \varepsilon & \varepsilon & 0 \\ \varepsilon & \varepsilon & \varepsilon & \varepsilon \end{pmatrix} \qquad \delta\mathbf{b} = (\varepsilon, \varepsilon, \varepsilon, \varepsilon)^T$$

We now ask: Is $\bar{\mathbf{x}} = (1, 1, 1, 1)^T$ an acceptable solution to the machine problem? The norm of the residual is $1.5 * 10^{-14}$, so we have

$$|\mathbf{b}^* - A^*\bar{\mathbf{x}}| \le (1.5 * 10^{-14}, 1.5 * 10^{-14}, 1.5 * 10^{-14}, 1.5 * 10^{-14})^T = \bar{\mathbf{r}}$$

According to Theorem 9.1, we then ask if the following inequality holds:

$$\bar{\mathbf{r}} \le \delta\mathbf{b} + \delta A\,|\bar{\mathbf{x}}|$$

or

$$\bar{\mathbf{r}} \le (\varepsilon, \varepsilon, \varepsilon, \varepsilon)^T + \begin{pmatrix} \varepsilon & 0 & 0 & 0 \\ \varepsilon & \varepsilon & 0 & 0 \\ \varepsilon & \varepsilon & \varepsilon & 0 \\ \varepsilon & \varepsilon & \varepsilon & \varepsilon \end{pmatrix}\begin{pmatrix} 1 \\ 1 \\ 1 \\ 1 \end{pmatrix} = (\varepsilon, \varepsilon, \varepsilon, \varepsilon)^T + (\varepsilon, 2\varepsilon, 3\varepsilon, 4\varepsilon)^T$$

$$= (2\varepsilon, 3\varepsilon, 4\varepsilon, 5\varepsilon)^T = (1 * 10^{-14}, 1.5 * 10^{-14}, 2 * 10^{-14}, 2.5 * 10^{-14})^T$$

This inequality is *not* satisfied because

$$\bar{r}_1 = 1.5 * 10^{-14} > 2\varepsilon = 1 * 10^{-14}$$

Of course, we should have applied the theorem to the actual value of $\mathbf{r}$ rather than $\bar{\mathbf{r}}$ and, in fact, a further calculation shows that $r_1 = 0$ exactly. Thus $\bar{\mathbf{x}}$ is acceptable because

$$(0, 1.5 * 10^{-14}, 1.5 * 10^{-14}, 1.5 * 10^{-14})^T$$
$$\le (1 * 10^{-14}, 1.5 * 10^{-14}, 2 * 10^{-14}, 2.5 * 10^{-14})^T$$

Example 9.9: Fuzzy system analysis of the LINPACK solution of the Hilbert 10 x 10 (Example 8-2) We now use Theorem 9.1 to approximately answer the question: What are the smallest perturbations δA and $\delta\mathbf{b}$ for which the LINPACK solution is acceptable? Thus we assume that

$$\delta A = \varepsilon_A(a_{ij})$$
$$\delta\mathbf{b} = \varepsilon_b(b_i)^T$$

and we wish to estimate values of ε_A and ε_b so that

$$|\mathbf{b}^* - A^*\bar{\mathbf{x}}| \le \delta\mathbf{b} + \delta A\,|\bar{\mathbf{x}}|$$

Note the backward error analysis says that $(A + E)\bar{\mathbf{x}} = \mathbf{b}$ with $|e_{ij}| \le 9\varepsilon$. With $\varepsilon = 0.5 * 10^{-14}$ and $|a_{ij}| = \frac{1}{19}$, this suggests that $\varepsilon_b = 0$ and $\varepsilon_A = 9.5 * 10^{-14}$ are suitable choices.

Let us bound the residual $\mathbf{r}$ by the constant vector

$$\bar{\mathbf{r}} = (\|\mathbf{r}\|, \|\mathbf{r}\|, \ldots, \|\mathbf{r}\|)^T$$
$$= (2.2 * 10^{-12}, 2.2 * 10^{-12}, \ldots, 2.2 * 10^{-12})^T$$

We need to find values of ε_A and ε_b so that

$$|\bar{\mathbf{r}}| \le (\varepsilon_b, 0, 0, \ldots, 0)^T + \begin{pmatrix} \varepsilon_A & \varepsilon_A/2 & \cdots & \\ \varepsilon_A/2 & & & \vdots \\ \vdots & & \cdots & \varepsilon_A/19 \end{pmatrix} \begin{pmatrix} 100.005711648351 \\ \vdots \\ 924185.572651327 \end{pmatrix}$$

This relationship is a set of 10 ordinary inequalities:

$$2.2 * 10^{-12} \le \varepsilon_b + \varepsilon_A(1, \tfrac{1}{2}, \ldots, \tfrac{1}{9})^T |\bar{\mathbf{x}}|$$
$$2.2 * 10^{-12} \le \qquad \varepsilon_A(\text{row j of A})^T |\bar{\mathbf{x}}| \qquad j = 2, 3, \ldots, 10$$

The dot products (row j of A)^T $|\bar{\mathbf{x}}|$, $j = 2, 3, \ldots, 10$ are

$4.8 * 10^6$, $4.2 * 10^6$, $3.7 * 10^6$, $3.3 * 10^6$, $3.0 * 10^6$,

$2.8 * 10^6$, $2.5 * 10^6$, $2.4 * 10^6$, $2.2 * 10^6$, $2.1 * 10^6$

These values are large because the absolute values have eliminated any cancellation in the dot products. Just $a_{i10}\bar{x}_{10}$ is always at least 48,600, which implies that ε_A need only be greater than $2.2 * 10^{-12}/48{,}600 = 4.5 * 10^{-17}$ in order to have

$$2.2 * 10^{-12} \le \varepsilon_A\, |a_{i10}|\, |\bar{x}_{10}| \le \varepsilon_A(\text{row j of A})^T |\bar{\mathbf{x}}|$$

The last component determines ε_A and ε_b to be

$$\varepsilon_A = \frac{2.2 * 10^{-12}}{2.1 * 10^6} = 10^{-18}$$

and $$\varepsilon_b = 0$$

Thus a 10^{-18} perturbation of A is sufficiently large to satisfy the conditions of Theorem 9.1.

Thus we conclude that the LINPACK solution is acceptable for perturbations *much smaller* than suggested by the ordinary backward error analysis. The conclusion from this example may be rephrased to say that there is perturbation of this problem of order 10^{-18} so that the LINPACK solution is the exact solution of the perturbed problem.

PROBLEMS FOR CHAP. 9

1 Describe the difference between an ill-conditioned problem and an ill-conditioned computation.

2 Suppose you have a tentative solution to

$$x + 2y = 3$$
$$2x + y = 3$$

with a residual of $(0.01, 0.023)^T$. Carry out a backward error analysis for this problem and the tentative solution $(1.012, 0.999)^T$. Do not modify the right-hand side or use the general formula of Example 9.7; apply the backward error analysis idea directly.

3 For each of the linear systems

(*i*) $3x + 7y = 1$, $0.04x + 8y = 24$ (*ii*) $x + y = 401$, $0.01x - 2y = 2$ (*iii*) $7.5x + 10.5y = 18$, $7x + 10y = 17$

do the following:

(*a*) Compute the standard and natural condition numbers.

(*b*) Solve the systems using three-decimal-digit arithmetic and estimate the accuracy of the computed solution using the natural and standard condition numbers.

(*c*) Compute the Aird-Lynch error estimate for the solution obtained in (*b*).

(*d*) Interchange the two equations and repeat part (*b*) without using pivoting.

(*e*) Compare the error estimates with the actual error.

4 Consider the linear system with a parameter θ:

$$x \cot \theta + y \csc \theta = b_1$$
$$-x \csc \theta - y \cot \theta = b_2$$

(*a*) Compute the standard condition number of this matrix.

(*b*) Show that the eigenvalues of the matrix are of size 1.

(*c*) What values of the parameter θ should cause difficulty for this system? What corresponding values of b_1 and b_2 should make the calculation particularly ill conditioned? Give a set of specific values for θ, b_1, and b_2.

5 Consider a function $f(x)$ for $0 \leq x \leq 1$. One way to measure the "size" of $f(x)$ is by

$$\max_{0 \leq x \leq 1} |f(x)|$$

(*a*) What does it mean to say that "$g(x)$ is in a sphere of radius 10^{-3} and with center $f(x)$"?

(*b*) What does it mean to say that "$g(x)$ is in a relative sphere of radius 10^{-3} and with center $f(x)$"?

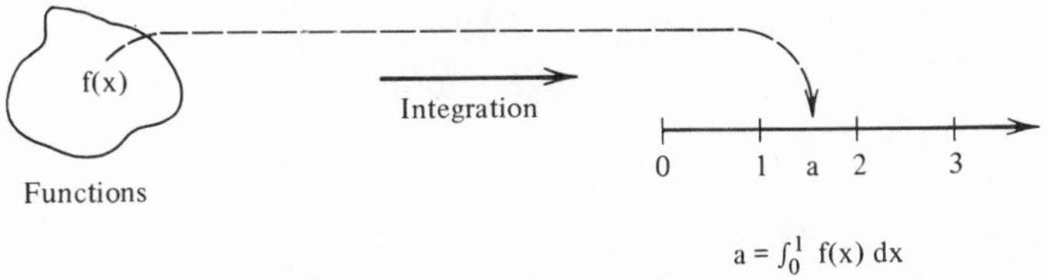

The process of integration, i.e., $a = \int_0^1 f(x)\,dx$, carries us from a space of functions to the space of real numbers

(*c*) What is the absolute condition of this process?

(*d*) What is the relative condition of this process?

(*e*) Replace "integration" by "differentiation" and answer (*c*) and (*d*)—i.e.,

$$a(x) = \frac{df(x)}{dx}$$

Note that the process now carries functions into functions and we must measure sizes as noted at the beginning of the problem.

6 Various kinds of errors or uncertainty can arise in solving $\mathbf{Ax} = \mathbf{b}$, and we have developed a variety of schemes (both backward and forward) to estimate the effect of these uncertainties.

(*a*) List three such schemes or error estimates developed in this book.
(*b*) Describe, in two or three sentences, their objectives or use.
(*c*) Describe, in two or three sentences, their strong and weak points.
(*d*) What do these estimates say, if anything, about the specific problem

$$\mathbf{Ax} = \begin{pmatrix} 0.932 & 0.443 \\ 1.237 & 0.587 \end{pmatrix} \mathbf{x} = \begin{pmatrix} 0.699 \\ 3.242 \end{pmatrix}$$

using six-digit computations?

Note: In some cases, one or more of the following numbers may be useful to express your results:

$$\|A\| \sim 2 \qquad \|A^{-1}\| \sim 2400$$

$$\mathbf{x}_{\text{True}} = (1131.083869, \ -2378.038749)^{\text{T}}$$

$$\mathbf{x}_{\text{Computed}} = (1148.01, \ -2413.66)^{\text{T}}$$

$$\text{Residual} = (0.006, \ -0.028)^{\text{T}}$$

7 Consider the following problem for $\mathbf{Ax} = \mathbf{b}$ using six-decimal digit arithmetic:

$$\begin{pmatrix} 0.932165 & 0.443126 & 0.417632 \\ 0.712345 & 0.915312 & 0.887652 \\ 0.632165 & 0.514217 & 0.493909 \end{pmatrix} \mathbf{x} = \begin{pmatrix} 0.876132 \\ 0.815327 \\ 0.012345 \end{pmatrix} \qquad \|A^{-1}\|_\infty \sim 1.4\text{E} + 5$$

The computed solution

$$\bar{\mathbf{x}} = (0.495702\text{E} + 3, \ -0.236728\text{E} + 5, \ 0.240135\text{E} + 5)^{\text{T}}$$

has residual

$$\mathbf{r} = (0.02721797, 0.07109741, 0.01931627)^{\text{T}}$$

Carry out the following error analysis of this problem:

(*a*) Estimate $\dfrac{\|\mathbf{x} - \bar{\mathbf{x}}\|}{\|\mathbf{x}\|}$ by the standard condition number.

(*b*) Estimate $\dfrac{\|\mathbf{x} - \bar{\mathbf{x}}\|}{\|\mathbf{x}\|}$ by the natural condition number.

(*c*) Make a backward error estimate using the general bounds obtained in Example 9.7.

8 Consider a computation made with four-decimal digit arithmetic (all numbers are $0.xxxx\ 10^{-P}$). Assume the arithmetic unit makes at most $\frac{1}{2}$ unit error in the fourth significant digit in any arithmetic operation. For example, $\zeta_{\text{comp}} = x + y$ differs from ζ_{true} by $\frac{1}{2}$ unit at most in the fourth significant digit. You are to solve $\mathbf{Ax} = \mathbf{b}$ by Gauss elimination for

$$A = \begin{pmatrix} 2.xxx & 1.xxx & 0 \\ 1.xxx & 2.xxx & -1.xxx \\ 0 & 1.xxx & 2.xxx \end{pmatrix}$$

The x's are digits that are known, but not to be used in this problem.

(*a*) Perform a backward error analysis (*for this specific matrix*) for the triangularization of A; do not apply the general formula of Example 9.7.

(*b*) What do you have at this point in the way of error information?

9 Design and carry out a small computational experiment to test the suggestion that the condition of a relative perturbation in the matrix is 1. Specifically, take two matrices (one ill conditioned and one well conditioned) of order 6 and apply perturbations $I + P$ to these where $\|P\|$ is small compared to 1 but large compared to the round-off of the computer you use. Compute

$$\frac{\|\mathbf{x}^* - \bar{\mathbf{x}}\|}{\|\mathbf{x}^*\|}$$

and compare it with $\|P\|$. Repeat for several choices of P.

10 Do a forward error analysis for the Gauss elimination solution of the 3×3 matrix in Example 9.7; use the same assumptions about the calculation.

11 Take A to be the $N \times N$ Hilbert matrix where N is chosen so that you obtain about 1 digit of accuracy in solving $A\mathbf{x} = \mathbf{b}$ on your computer. Take EPSA equal to 10 times the round-off on your machine and perturb A by both $A(I + P)$ with $|p_{ij}| \leq \text{ESPA}$ and $A + E$ with $|e_{ij}| \leq \text{ESPA}$. Take $\mathbf{b} = (1, 1, \ldots, 1)^T$ and solve $A\mathbf{x} = \mathbf{b}$ with and without these perturbations.

(*a*) Compare the changes in the computed solutions produced by the two different perturbations.

(*b*) Compare the changes in the computed solution with the error estimates obtained from the corresponding composite estimators.

12 Apply Theorem 9.1 to the solution obtained in Prob. 3, part (*b*), to obtain a minimal perturbation in the problem so the computed solution becomes the exact solution. Compare this with the result of applying backward error analysis (Example 9.7) to the problem.

13 Suppose that $|e_{ij}| \leq |a_{ij}|$ for all i, j and that $\|\mathbf{x}\|_\infty \leq 1$. Show that

$$\max_E \|E\mathbf{x}\|$$

occurs for $|e_{ij}| = |a_{ij}|$. *Hint:* Note that the components of $E\mathbf{x}$ are linear functions of each of the variables e_{ij}.

14 Consider the vector $\mathbf{b} = (2.5, 1.5, 0.05)^T$ and the matrix

$$A = \begin{pmatrix} 2 & 0 & 1 \\ 0 & 1 & 1 \\ 0 & 0 & 0.1 \end{pmatrix}$$

Let $\mathbf{x}$ be the solution of $A\mathbf{x} = \mathbf{b}$ and E a matrix with $|e_{ij}| \leq |a_{ij}|\text{EPSA}$. Show that $\|E\mathbf{x}\| \leq 2.5$.

(*Hint:* Use Prob. 13.) Compute both sides of the inequality

$$\|A^{-1}E\mathbf{x}\| \leq \|A^{-1}\| \, \|A\| \, \|\mathbf{x}\|\text{EPSA}$$

and show that it fails to be sharp by a factor of over 18. That is, no matter how E might be chosen, the right-hand side is at least 18 times larger than the left-hand side.

15 Consider the A, $\mathbf{x}$, and $\mathbf{b}$ of Prob. 14 and change the assumption on E to be $\|E\| \leq \|A\|\text{EPSA}$. Show that then there is always a matrix E so that

$$\|A^{-1}E\mathbf{x}\| = \|A^{-1}\| \, \|A\| \, \|\mathbf{x}\|\text{EPSA}$$

Hint: The result is true for any A and $\mathbf{x}$. Find a vector $\mathbf{y}$ with $\|\mathbf{y}\| = 1$ so that $\|A^{-1}\mathbf{y}\| = \|A^{-1}\|$ and then a rotation matrix R with $\|R\| = 1$ so that $R\mathbf{x} = \|\mathbf{x}\|\mathbf{y}$. Construct E from R.

16 Do Prob. 14 with the assumption on E changed to

$$|e_{ij}| \le \max_{i,j} |a_{ij}| * \text{EPSA} \qquad \text{if } |a_{ij}| > 0$$
$$= 0 \qquad \text{if } |a_{ij}| = 0$$

Show that the factor is 2.75.

17 Do Prob. 14 with the assumption on E changed to

$$|e_{ij}| \le \|A\| * \text{EPSA} \qquad \text{if } |a_{ij}| > 0$$
$$= 0 \qquad \text{if } |a_{ij}| = 0$$

Show that the factor is 1.8333.

CHAPTER

TEN

ITERATIVE METHODS

The Gauss elimination algorithms for solving $Ax = \mathbf{b}$ is a finite or *direct method*. One has, ignoring round-off errors, the exact answer at the end of the computation. Iterative methods for $Ax = \mathbf{b}$ are infinite methods and produce only approximate answers. They are easy to define and widely used. However, they should be used only in special circumstances and therefore here we just outline the basic ideas and provide a guide as to when they might be appropriate. If one thinks iterative methods should be used, then a more thorough study of the problem and particular methods is advised. Iterative methods are attractive for sparse matrices because they use much less memory than direct methods, so they might be used even though they require more execution time. Partial differential equations often lead to large sparse linear systems where iterative methods are attractive.

10.A INTRODUCTION TO ITERATIVE METHODS

We start with two old and simple methods; the first is the *Jacobi method*, illustrated with the following linear system:

$$\begin{aligned} 3x_1 + 4x_2 - x_3 &= 7 \\ 2x_1 + 6x_2 + 3x_3 &= -2 \\ -x_1 + x_2 + 4x_3 &= 4 \end{aligned}$$

We can rewrite this system $\mathbf{Ax} = \mathbf{b}$ in the form

$$x_1 = \tfrac{1}{3}[\ 7 - 4x_2 + \ x_3]$$
$$x_2 = \tfrac{1}{6}[-2 - 2x_1 - 3x_2]$$
$$x_3 = \tfrac{1}{4}[\ 4 + \ x_1 - \ x_2]$$

which is of the form $\mathbf{x} = \mathbf{Bx} + \mathbf{g}$ where

$$B = \begin{pmatrix} 0 & -\frac{4}{3} & \frac{1}{3} \\ -\frac{2}{6} & 0 & -\frac{3}{6} \\ \frac{1}{4} & -\frac{1}{4} & 0 \end{pmatrix}$$

and $\mathbf{g} = (\frac{7}{3}, -\frac{2}{6}, \frac{4}{4})^T$. We see that we have solved the jth equation explicitly for the jth unknown and put everything else on the right-hand side. The Jacobi method is now to guess at $\mathbf{x}$, say $\mathbf{x}^{(0)}$, and apply the iteration

$$\mathbf{x}^{(K+1)} = \mathbf{Bx}^{(K)} + \mathbf{g} \qquad K = 0, 1, 2, \ldots$$

This method depends on having the right numbering of the equations and unknowns.

The second old method is the *Gauss-Seidel method.* (We observe as an aside that the method was unknown to Seidel and scorned by Gauss as worthless; such are the vagaries of historical accuracy in science.) We rewrite the same system used above as

$$\begin{aligned} 3x_1 \qquad\qquad &= \ \ 7 - 4x_2 + x_3 \\ 2x_1 + 6x_2 \qquad &= -2 - 3x_3 \\ -x_1 + \ x_2 + 4x_3 &= \ \ 4 \end{aligned}$$

In the jth equation we have moved to the right-hand side all terms involving x_k with $k > j$. This is of the form $(\mathbf{L} + \mathbf{D})\mathbf{x} = \mathbf{Ux} + \mathbf{g}$ where

$$L + D = \begin{pmatrix} 3 & 0 & 0 \\ 2 & 6 & 0 \\ -1 & 1 & 4 \end{pmatrix} \qquad U = \begin{pmatrix} 0 & 4 & -1 \\ 0 & 0 & 3 \\ 0 & 0 & 0 \end{pmatrix} \qquad \mathbf{g} = \mathbf{b}$$

D denotes the diagonal of A, U the upper triangular part, and L the lower triangular part. We then apply the iteration

$$(\mathbf{L} + \mathbf{D})\mathbf{x}^{(K+1)} = -\mathbf{Ux}^{(K)} + \mathbf{g} \qquad K = 0, 1, 2, \ldots$$

after making an initial guess $\mathbf{x}^{(0)}$. Note that the calculation here is almost exactly the same as the Jacobi method. The difference is that new values for the x_i are used here as soon as generated, while in the Jacobi method they are not used until the next iteration.

10.A.1 Basic Convergence Analysis

Iterative methods are usually studied in one of two standard forms

$$\mathbf{x}^{(K+1)} = \mathbf{x}^{(K)} + H^{(K)}[\mathbf{b} - A\mathbf{x}^{(K)}] \qquad \text{(uses residual)}$$

or

$$\mathbf{x}^{(K+1)} = B^{(K)}\mathbf{x}^{(K)} + \mathbf{g}^{(K)}$$

where $H^{(K)}$, $B^{(K)}$, and $\mathbf{g}^{(K)}$ might vary with K. An iteration is called *stationary* if $H^{(K)}$, $B^{(K)}$, and $g^{(K)}$ are constant, i.e., do not depend on K. Both the Jacobi and Gauss-Seidel methods are stationary. A method that is any good must have

$$\mathbf{x}^* = \mathbf{x}^* + H^{(K)}[\mathbf{b} - A\mathbf{x}^*] \qquad \text{as } K \to \infty$$

$$\mathbf{x}^* = B^{(K)}\mathbf{x}^* + g^{(K)} \qquad \text{as } K \to \infty$$

where $\mathbf{x}^*$ is the true solution of $A\mathbf{x} = \mathbf{b}$. If we set the error $\varepsilon_K = \mathbf{x}^* - \mathbf{x}^{(K)}$, we have, after a short calculation,

$$\varepsilon_{K+1} = [I - H^{(K)}A]\varepsilon_K$$

or

$$\varepsilon_{K+1} = B^{(K)}\varepsilon_K$$

Recall that $\rho(A)$ denotes the spectral radius of A, which is the absolute value of the largest (in absolute value) eigenvalue of the matrix A. We state without proof the basic theorem which shows that the matrices $I - HA$ and B govern the convergence of an iterative method.

Theorem 10.1: *A necessary and sufficient condition for a stationary iteration to converge is*

$$\rho(I - HA) < 1$$

or

$$\rho(B) < 1$$

A similar result holds for a nonstationary iteration where these conditions must hold for all sufficiently large values of K. Note that these iterative methods are a form of fixed point iteration $\mathbf{x}_{m+1} = f(\mathbf{x}_m)$, and Theorem 10.1 is just a generalization of the fact that $|f'(x)| < 1$ is required for convergence.

One can use any means available to estimate $\rho(B)$ and attempt to determine if a particular method is convergent. Recall that $\rho(B) \le \|B\|$ for any norm, and the simplest norms to try are the row-sum or column-sum norms. For the *Jacobi process* we have

$$\mathbf{x}^{(K+1)} = -D^{-1}(A - D)\mathbf{x}^{(K)} + D^{-1}\mathbf{b}$$

that is, $B = -D^{-1}(A - D) = I - D^{-1}A$. The row-sum and column-sum norms lead to the convergence criteria of *diagonal dominance:*

$$|a_{ii}| > \sum_{\substack{j=1 \\ j \ne i}}^{N} |a_{ij}| \qquad \text{or} \qquad |a_{jj}| > \sum_{\substack{i=1 \\ i \ne j}}^{N} |a_{ij}|$$

If A is diagonally dominant, then $\|B\| < 1$, and the Jacobi iteration converges. For the *Gauss-Seidel process* we have

$$\begin{aligned}\mathbf{x}^{(K+1)} &= -(D+L)^{-1}U\mathbf{x}^{(K)} + (D+L)^{-1}\mathbf{b} \\ &= [I-(D+L)^{-1}A]\mathbf{x}^{(K)} + (D+L)^{-1}\mathbf{b}\end{aligned}$$

that is, $B = I - (D+L)^{-1}A$. In terms of the residual $\mathbf{r} = \mathbf{b} - A\mathbf{x}$ we have

$$\mathbf{x}^{(K+1)} = \mathbf{x}^{(K)} - (D+L)^{-1}[\mathbf{b} - A\mathbf{x}^{(K)}]$$

so $H = (D+L)^{-1}$.

Convergence occurs when the matrices B or I − HA are "small." For the Jacobi method this means $D^{-1}A - I$ is small or that D^{-1} is a fair approximation to A^{-1}. For Gauss-Seidel, $(D+L)^{-1}A - I$ is to be small or $(D+L)^{-1}$ is a fair approximation to A^{-1}. This may be restated as saying: The Jacobi iteration assumes that A is "nearly diagonal" and the Gauss-Seidel iteration assumes that A is "nearly lower triangular."

10.A.2 Three Common Errors in Belief

There are three widely held beliefs that are completely wrong. The first two are not particularly serious, but the third is. The three statements below correct these errors.

1. *Diagonal dominance is not required for either the Jacobi or Gauss-Seidel methods to converge.* One merely needs to try the matrix

$$A = \begin{pmatrix} 8 & 2 & 1 \\ 10 & 4 & 1 \\ 50 & 25 & 2 \end{pmatrix}$$

to see that Gauss-Seidel can converge very rapidly without diagonal dominance. A must be "nearly diagonal" for the Jacobi method to converge, but this is not quite the same as diagonal dominance. Note that *column diagonal dominance*

$$|a_{ii}| > \sum_{j \neq i} |a_{ji}|$$

is also sufficient for convergence, and it is easy to construct matrices which have one but not the other of these properties. With a little more effort, one can find examples without either kind of diagonal dominance where the Jacobi method converges.

2. *It is not true that if the Jacobi method works, then Gauss-Seidel works even better.* There are examples where Jacobi converges and Gauss-Seidel diverges. The source of this error in belief is the fact that *if A is symmetric and positive definite* then Gauss-Seidel converges twice as fast as Jacobi.

3. *Iterative methods are no better for ill-conditioned problems than Gauss elimination.* It is often believed that the source of trouble in Gauss elimination for ill-conditioned problems is the steady accumulation of thousands or millions of errors during the computation. This is not so—the inaccuracy often arises almost entirely in one single arithmetic step of elimination. In any case, iterative methods applied to ill-conditioned problems produce the same amount of garbage as direct methods do.

10.B WHEN ITERATIVE METHODS SHOULD BE CONSIDERED

Iterative methods are used primarily when A (and hence B and H) are large and sparse. If B or H is sparse, say it has p nonzero elements per row, then one iteration requires about pn operations for a matrix of order n. Thus K iterations require about pKn operations and, for comparison with Gauss elimination for full matrices, we have K iterations cheaper if

$$K < \frac{n^2}{3p}$$

If A is a band matrix of width d (small compared to n), then the work for Gauss elimination is about d^2n while K iterations require work of about 2dnK. Thus for iteration to pay off by reducing arithmetic, the number K of iterations for a band matrix must satisfy

$$K < \frac{d}{2}$$

For matrices derived from partial differential equations, the bandwidth is usually about $\sqrt{n}$, but the band is itself sparse so that p is 4 or 6 or so. In this situation, the work for Gauss elimination is n^2 while the work for K iterations is perhaps 6Kn. Thus iterative methods should require less than n/6 iterations to be considered. However, the overriding consideration might be the memory required, which is about n^2 for Gauss elimination and pn for an iterative method. For these problems one may have n in the range of 100 to 1,000,000 with 100,000 a not unusual case.

10.B.1 SOR and Component Suppression Methods

If one thinks an iterative method might be useful, then one should study two additional methods. The first is *systematic overrelaxation*, or SOR for short.

The idea is to take the change produced in a Gauss-Seidel step and extrapolate it by an amount q. One might think of this symbolically as

$$\mathbf{x}^{(K+1)} = \mathbf{x}^{(K)} + Q[\mathbf{x}_{GS}^{(K+1)} - \mathbf{x}^{(K)}]$$

where Q is a diagonal extrapolation matrix and $\mathbf{x}_{GS}^{(K+1)}$ indicates the Gauss-Seidel result. SOR is slightly different in that new values of **x** are used as soon as they are computed; the iteration is

$$\mathbf{x}^{(K+1)} = \mathbf{x}^{(K)} + QD^{-1}[\mathbf{b} - (D + U)\mathbf{x}^{(K)} - L\mathbf{x}^{(K+1)}]$$

The matrix governing convergence is

$$(I + QD^{-1}L)^{-1}[I - QD^{-1}(D + U)]$$

or

$$(D + QL)^{-1}(D - DQ - QU)$$

The famous result by David Young relates the rate of convergence of SOR to that of the Jacobi process for a certain class of "block tridiagonal matrices." The delicate point—both in theory and practice—is to be able to correctly choose the extrapolation (overrelaxation) coefficients in the matrix Q.

For the case of the standard finite difference approximation for Laplace's equation $U_{xx} + U_{yy} = 0$ on a rectangle, one obtains a block tridiagonal matrix of the right kind which has bandwidth $\sqrt{n}$ and five nonzero coefficients per row. One can show that about $\sqrt{n}$ iterations are required to reduce the error in the linear equations to the same size as the truncation error in approximating Laplace's equation. Thus we get that the SOR work is order $n^{3/2}$ while the Gauss-elimination work is order n^2—*provided we know the optimum overrelaxation factors* (in the Q matrix). These are known in this particular case, but other cases may have a much different optimum relaxation factor. Not only does one save in work, but one also saves on memory used. For a complete discussion of such methods see Young (1971); more elementary discussions are presented in works by Forsythe and Wasow (1960), Fox (1965, chap. 8), and Varga (1962, chap. 4) (see References at end of book).

The second method, or class of methods, is *component suppression* (the name is not standardized). These methods are technically complicated but also quite powerful at times. The idea is to have an iteration

$$\mathbf{x}^{(K+1)} = \mathbf{x}^{(K)} + f(A)[\mathbf{b} - A\mathbf{x}^{(K)}]$$

where f(A) is a function (usually polynomial) of the matrix A. Again let $\varepsilon_K = \mathbf{x}^* - \mathbf{x}^{(K)}$ and we have

$$\varepsilon_{K+1} = -[I - Af(A)]\varepsilon_K = g(A)\varepsilon_K$$

If g(A) is a nice function (e.g., polynomial or analytic), then $g(A) * \text{eigenvector} = g(\text{eigenvalue})$. Now suppose we happen to know something about the eigenvalues of A, say that they are all contained in a region Z. We can choose g(A) so that it is small on Z and then we do not care what it is anywhere else—except for one point: *We must have* $g(0) = 1$; *otherwise the function* $f(A)$ *involves* A^{-1} and the iteration is not practical.

The most widely known special case of this method is the *Tchebycheff semi-iterative method* for positive-definite matrices. In this case the set Z is the interval [a, T] on the real line and the "best" function g is the Tchebycheff polynomial associated with [a, T]. It is possible to arrange the computation so that this polynomial in A is never explicitly formed and the amount of work is reasonable.

This approach includes many other specialized methods and a good exposition of it is in chap. 9 of the old work by Faddeev and Faddeeva (1963) (see References at end of book), where they are called *universal methods.*

PROBLEMS FOR CHAP. 10

1 Write a program to use the Gauss-Seidel iteration to solve the system

$$\begin{aligned} 2x_1 - x_2 \qquad\qquad &= 1 \\ -x_{i-1} + 2x_i - x_{i+1} &= 0 \qquad i = 2, 3, \ldots, n-1 \\ -x_{n-1} + 2x_n &= 1 \end{aligned}$$

for n = 20. Start with $\mathbf{x}^{(0)} = 0$ and terminate the iteration when

$$\frac{\|\mathbf{x}^{(k)} - \mathbf{x}^{(k-1)}\|_\infty}{\|\mathbf{x}^{(k)}\|_\infty} < 10^{-6}$$

The exact solution is $x_i = 1$ for all i. What is the accuracy achieved?

2 Compare the computer time required to solve the system in Prob. 1 by Gauss-Seidel with that required by Gauss elimination. Gauss-Seidel for Prob. 1 converges in about 466 iterations.

3 Apply the Jacobi method to Prob. 1 for 100 iterations and find the number of Gauss-Seidel iterations that gives the same accuracy.

4 Let A be $N \times N$ and upper triangular with $a_{ii} = 0$ for all i. Show that $A^N = 0$. Use this to show that both Jacobi and Gauss-Seidel converge in a finite number of iterations whenever A is upper triangular (and nonsingular). How many iterations does it take for Gauss-Seidel to converge if A is lower triangular?

5 Consider a system of linear equations whose coefficient matrix is partitioned into four matrices and the solution and right-hand side vectors are partitioned into two vectors each, that is,

$$\begin{pmatrix} A & B \\ C & D \end{pmatrix} \begin{pmatrix} \mathbf{x} \\ \mathbf{y} \end{pmatrix} = \begin{pmatrix} \mathbf{c}_1 \\ \mathbf{c}_2 \end{pmatrix}$$

We define a *block-Jacobi* iteration as follows:

Iterate: Step 1. Guess at **y** and solve for **x** from the system $A\mathbf{x} = \mathbf{c}_1 - B\mathbf{y}$.
Step 2. Use the resulting **x** and solve for **y** from the system $D\mathbf{y} = \mathbf{c}_2 - C\mathbf{x}$. Use this as the next guess at **y**.

(*a*) Formulate this iteration in matrix terms.

(*b*) Give an example of a 5×5 system (A is 3×3 and D is 2×2) where one would expect this method to converge rapidly.

(*c*) Give the matrix that governs the convergence of this method.

6 Suppose you have run Gauss-Seidel iteration to solve $A\mathbf{x} = \mathbf{b}$ and on the last iteration the difference $\mathbf{x}^{198} - \mathbf{x}^{197}$ is less than 10^{-10} in each component. The matrix A is 500×500 with at most 50 nonzero elements per equation and the a_{ij} and b_i are all of the size 1. Carry out a backward error analysis for this situation.

7 To solve $A\mathbf{x} = \mathbf{b}$ by iteration, you partition A into three parts: T is the tridiagonal part, U is the part above T, and L is the part below T. Your iteration scheme is to guess at $\mathbf{x}$, put this into the L and U parts of A, move these to the right-hand side, solve the resulting tridiagonal system for a better estimate of $\mathbf{x}$, and then overrelax this iteration (or extrapolate the change in the estimates) by a factor w. The final result is the next estimate of $\mathbf{x}$.

(*a*) Formulate this iterative method in matrix terms.
(*b*) Find the matrix which governs the convergence of the iteration.
(*c*) Give the operation count for one iteration of this method.

8 Suppose that you are required to try to solve the following system by Gauss-Seidel iteration:

$$2x + y - \tfrac{1}{2}z + 8w = 4$$

$$6x + 2y + 8z + 14w = 12$$

$$x - 6y + 10z + 9w = -1$$

$$2x + 11y + 3z - 4w = 4$$

(*a*) Describe what you would do first.
(*b*) Carry out several iterations (with initial guess = 0) and estimate approximately how many iterations it would take to get six digits correct in the solution.

9 Apply Jacobi and Gauss-Seidel iteration to the problem $A\mathbf{x} = (8, 8, 29)^T$ with initial guess $= (-1, 1, 0)^T$ and A the matrix from Sec. 10.A.2. How many iterations does it take for these to converge to 10^{-4} accuracy?

10 Consider a system of equations that "almost" breaks up into two parts:

$$\sum_{j=1}^{n} a_{ij}x_j + \sum_{j=1}^{m} e_{ij}y_j = c_i \qquad i = 1, 2, \ldots, n$$

$$\sum_{j=1}^{n} h_{ij}x_j + \sum_{j=1}^{m} b_{ij}y_j = c_{i+n} \qquad i = 1, 2, \ldots, m$$

The matrices $E = (e_{ij})$ and $H = (h_{ij})$ are "small" compared to A and B. One notes that A is much smaller than B and that B is heavily diagonally dominant. So one proceeds to apply the following scheme:

Step 1. Guess at $\mathbf{y}$ and solve for $\mathbf{x}$ exactly from the first set of equations.
Step 2. Given this $\mathbf{x}$, solve for an improved estimate of $\mathbf{y}$ by one iteration of Gauss-Seidel on the second set of equations.

Then iterate steps 1 and 2 to take a vector pair $(\mathbf{x}^{(k)}, \mathbf{y}^{(k)})$ into $(\mathbf{x}^{(k+1)}, \mathbf{y}^{(k+1)})$.

(*a*) Express the original linear system in matrix form.
(*b*) Express each of steps 1 and 2 in matrix form.
(*c*) Express the iteration scheme in matrix form as a stationary iteration.
(*d*) Exhibit the matrix which governs the convergence of this scheme.

CHAPTER

ELEVEN

LINEAR LEAST SQUARES AND REGRESSION

The linear least-squares or statistical regression problem is a problem of optimization. One has some parameters or coefficients to choose and one wants to find the "best" ones in some sense, namely the least-squares sense. The choice of the least-squares criterion is not, as many people believe, especially natural nor is it justifiable in practice just because of the elaborate theoretical machinery that exists for it. Arguments for the "principle of least squares" based on "normally distributed random errors" are suspect because one very rarely knows much, if anything, about the distribution of errors in a real problem. However, the fact remains that the least-squares criterion for "best" is perfectly adequate in a wide variety of situations—just as long as one realizes that it is inadequate in a certain proportion of the applications that arise. The great and enduring strength of the least-squares criterion is that one can solve the resulting optimization problems by the direct application of matrix computation methods and software. We outline how this is done in this chapter.

The mathematical machinery for least squares heavily involves orthogonality, and the reader may want to review the relevant background concepts from Chap. 2.

11.A THE LEAST-SQUARES PROBLEM

We describe three somewhat different contexts which lead to the same mathematical problem.

11.A.1 Overdetermined Systems of Equations

Suppose one has N linear equations but only M < N variables. There are more conditions (equations) to be satisfied than degrees of freedom (variables), and it is unlikely that they can all be satisfied. Pictorially, the linear system appears as follows:

$$
\begin{bmatrix} \text{Matrix} \\ \text{A} \end{bmatrix} \begin{bmatrix} \mathbf{x} \end{bmatrix} = \begin{bmatrix} \mathbf{b} \end{bmatrix} \Big\} \, N
$$

$$
\longleftrightarrow \\ M
$$

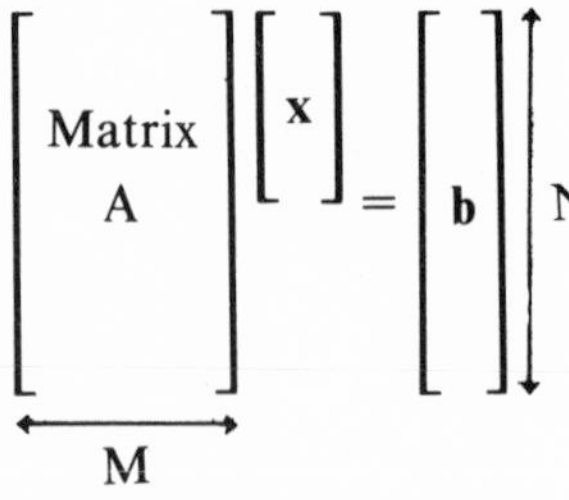

Since the equations cannot be satisfied exactly, we may attempt to satisfy them as best we can—that is, make the size of the residual vector **r** with components

$$
r_j = b_j - \sum_{i=1}^{M} a_{ij} x_i \qquad j = 1, 2, \ldots, N
$$

as small as possible. The least-squares criterion is the use of the Euclidean (or least-squares) norm for the size of **r**; that is, minimize

$$
\sqrt{\sum_{j=1}^{N} r_j^2} = \|\mathbf{r}\|_2
$$

11.A.2 Least-Squares Functional Approximation

Consider writing a Fortran compiler and the implementation of the standard functions, SIN (T), TAN (T), etc. Obviously, the implementation must use ordinary arithmetic operations, which means, for example, that we may want to have

$$
\sin(t) \sim \text{polynomial of degree } M - 1 \text{ in } t
$$

We can introduce the residual function r(t) as

$$
r(t) = \sin(t) - \sum_{i=1}^{M} x_i t^{i-1} \qquad \text{for } t\varepsilon[0, \pi/2]
$$

We clearly cannot make r(t) zero everywhere, so we attempt to make it as small as possible in the sense that

$$
\sqrt{\int_0^{\pi/2} r(t)^2 \, dt} = \text{minimum}
$$

The least-squares problem is then to choose the polynomial coefficients x_i to accomplish this. It may be awkward (or impossible) to evaluate the integrals when sin (t) is replaced by arctan (t) or a Bessel function, so one might choose the x_i instead to have

$$\sqrt{\sum_{j=1}^{101} r(t_j)^2} = \text{minimum}$$

where the t_j are equally spaced in the interval $[0, \pi/2]$.

For actual Fortran standard functions, a different, more natural, and more difficult criterion is used; namely, one chooses the x_i so that

$$\max |r(t)| = \text{minimum}$$

11.A.3 Regression and Mathematical Modeling

Consider the study of a phenomenon which involves one independent variable and one dependent variable. Examples of this are weight of cows as a function of age, repair costs of cars as a function of mileage, lifetime income as a function of education obtained. In each case we know or believe or hope there are several different factors that influence this relationship. Let t be the independent variable and let $f_i(t)$ express how these factors may vary (i.e., the amount of corn or hay fed the cows as a function of time; the amount of maintenance or farm use of cars as a function of mileage; the type of training or geographical location as a function of years of education). Finally, let d(t) be the dependent variable and set up the linear mathematical model

$$d(t) = \sum_{i=1}^{M} x_i f_i(t)$$

Theoretically, there should be values of the coefficients x_i which make this model exact.

Suppose now that we go out and make a large number of measurements (take observations) and obtain values d_j for t values t_j, $j = 1, 2, \ldots, N$. If $N = M$, we just solve the linear system

$$d_j = d_j(t_j) = \sum_{i=1}^{M} x_i f_i(t_j) \qquad j = 1, 2, .., N = M$$

for the unknown coefficients x_i. However, life is usually not so simple and if we take N larger than M we find that the coefficients x_i cannot be chosen to make the model exact for all observations. The discrepancy may be due to errors in the observations, incompleteness of the model, or inherent randomness in the phenomenon (or a combination of all three factors).

In order to get the "best" model possible, we decide to make the residual

$$r_j = d_j - \sum_{i=1}^{M} x_i f_i(t_j) \qquad j = 1, 2, \ldots, N$$

as small as possible. If we choose the least-squares criterion, then we want

$$\sqrt{\sum_{j=1}^{N} r_j^2} = \text{minimum}$$

In summary, we have three problems that lead to minimizing the square root of the sum of the squares of the residuals. Now it is easy to see that one can minimize the square root of something by simply minimizing the thing itself, so we attempt to do that.

11.B THE NORMAL EQUATIONS APPROACH

We used different notations for each of these examples, but we see that the second two can be put into the notation of the first example. Just set $a_{ij} = t_j^{i-1}$ for the polynomial approximation problem and $a_{ij} = f_i(t_j)$ for the regression problem. Thus we wish to have

$$E = E(x_1, x_2, \ldots, x_M) = \sum_{j=1}^{N} \left[b_j - \sum_{i=1}^{M} x_i a_{ij} \right]^2 = \text{minimum}$$

and we apply calculus to this minimization problem. That is, set the derivatives of E with respect to the x_i equal to zero. We have, for $k = 1, 2, \ldots, M$,

$$0 = \frac{\partial E}{\partial x_k} = \frac{\partial \sum \left[b_j - \sum x_i a_{ij} \right]^2}{\partial x_k} = 2 \sum \left[b_j - \sum x_i a_{ij} \right] a_{kj}$$

This may be rewritten, for $k = 1, 2, \ldots, M$, as

$$\sum_{j=1}^{N} b_j a_{kj} = \sum_{j=1}^{N} \sum_{i=1}^{M} x_i a_{ij} a_{kj} = \sum_{i=1}^{M} x_i \sum_{j=1}^{N} a_{ij} a_{kj}$$

This is now M linear equations in the M unknowns x_i and may be expressed in matrix terms as

$$A^T A \mathbf{x} = A^T \mathbf{b}$$

These are the *normal equations.*

We can roughly estimate the work to form and solve the normal equations as follows. To compute one entry of A^TA requires N operations (one operation = one add + one multiply), and $M^2/2$ of them must be found (A^TA is symmetric, so only half of the elements need be computed). Since the normal equations are symmetric, one can apply the Cholesky method to solve them, which requires the order of $M^3/6$ operations. Thus the total work, for M and N large, is $M^2N/2 + M^3/6$.

We are about to discuss two other ways to do the least-squares problem. The normal equations approach is so simple that, unless there was something wrong with it, we would not consider another approach. The basic problem is that common modeling choices lead to ill-conditioned matrices A^TA, so bad that the solutions are random numbers unrelated to the original problem. Recall the discussion involving the Hilbert matrix in Example 8.1. Of course, this does not always happen; it just happens often enough to make the approach unreliable. Note that the condition number of A^TA is the condition number of A *squared.*

A secondary, but still important, weakness of this approach is that it is so simple that many users never see the real source of trouble: nearly linearly dependent basis vectors (columns of A). Thus a model for school children's athletic or physical characteristics might contain as variables:

> age, weight, height, and strength

These are obviously highly correlated and thus nearly linearly dependent. A model for a car's fuel economy might contain as variables:

> weight, speed, engine horsepower, engine displacement, wind resistance, rolling friction, and tire inflation

Again, there are high correlations between some of these factors (e.g., speed, wind resistance, rolling friction).

Finally, there is the not uncommon and potentially disastrous approach exemplified by the attitude:

> "I really don't know which variables affect the thing I'm interested in; so I'll throw in everything I can imagine and let the computer sort them out."

It does not always work out as hoped; one may get garbage or find that small random variations in the data in fact determine which variables are selected as important.

11.C THE GRAM-SCHMIDT ORTHOGONALIZATION APPROACH

If we have vectors $\mathbf{a}_i$, $i = 1, 2, \ldots, M$, which are orthogonal (these are the columns of A), then the least-squares problem is trivial to solve. To see this, A^TA would be diagonal since the rows of A^T are just the columns of A and the only nonzero dot products are the $\mathbf{a}_i^T\mathbf{a}_i$ on the diagonal of A^TA. Thus we can give an explicit solution for the best coefficients in this case as

$$x_i = \frac{\mathbf{b}^T\mathbf{a}_i}{\mathbf{a}_i^T\mathbf{a}_i}$$

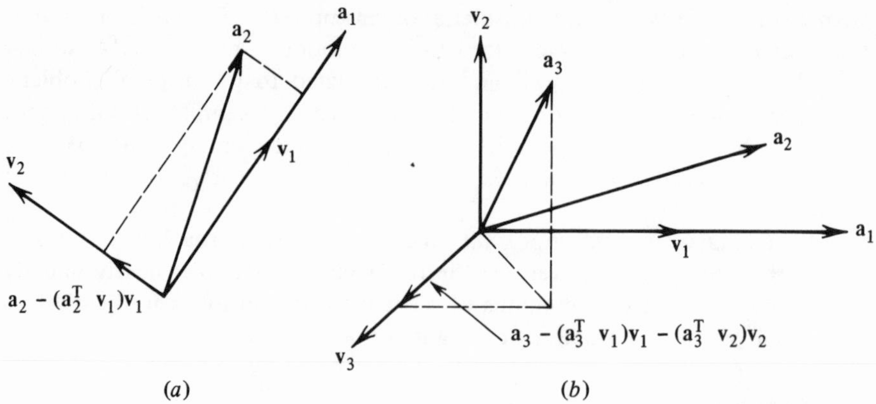

Figure 11.1 The geometric visualization of the Gram-Schmidt process for (*a*) two and (*b*) three vectors.

So we can attempt to make the columns of A orthogonal instead of forming and solving the normal equations. The classical method to do this is *Gram-Schmidt orthogonalization.* Explicitly the problem is: Given vectors $\mathbf{a}_1$, $\mathbf{a}_2, \ldots, \mathbf{a}_M$ find an equivalent set $\mathbf{v}_1, \mathbf{v}_2, \ldots, \mathbf{v}_M$ which are orthonormal. Making the $\mathbf{v}_i$ have length 1 simplifies the computation and later use of the vectors. The idea is quite simple. We take $\mathbf{a}_1$ and divide by its Euclidean length $\|\mathbf{a}_1\| = (\mathbf{a}_1^T\mathbf{a}_1)^{1/2}$ to get $\mathbf{v}_1$. We now subtract off the component of $\mathbf{a}_2$ in the direction of $\mathbf{v}_1$ and the remainder is orthogonal to $\mathbf{v}_1$. See the diagram in Fig. 11.1. This remainder vector is now normalized by dividing by its length, which gives us $\mathbf{v}_2$. In algebraic terms we have

$$\mathbf{v}_1 = \frac{\mathbf{a}_1}{\|\mathbf{a}_1\|}$$

$$\mathbf{v}_2 = \frac{\mathbf{a}_2 - (\mathbf{a}_2^T\mathbf{v}_1)\mathbf{v}_1}{\|\mathbf{a}_2 - (\mathbf{a}_2^T\mathbf{v}_1)\mathbf{v}_1\|}$$

The process is continued by subtracting off the components of $\mathbf{a}_3$ in the directions $\mathbf{v}_1$ and $\mathbf{v}_2$ and obtaining the remainder. This is normalized to obtain $\mathbf{v}_3$ (see Fig. 11.1). In algebraic terms we have

$$\mathbf{v}_3' = \mathbf{a}_3 - (\mathbf{a}_3^T\mathbf{v}_1)\mathbf{v}_1 - (\mathbf{a}_3^T\mathbf{v}_2)\mathbf{v}_2$$

$$\mathbf{v}_3 = \mathbf{v}_3'/\|\mathbf{v}_3'\|$$

It is evident now that the general step is

$$\mathbf{v}_k' = \mathbf{a}_k - \sum_{j=1}^{k-1} (\mathbf{a}_k^T\mathbf{v}_j)\mathbf{v}_j$$

$$\mathbf{v}_k = \mathbf{v}_k'/\|\mathbf{v}_k'\|$$

Algorithm 11.1: Gram-Schmidt orthogonalization

For k = 1 to M do

$$\mathbf{v}'_k = \mathbf{a}_k - \sum_{j=1}^{k-1} (\mathbf{a}_k^T \mathbf{v}_j)\mathbf{v}_j$$

$$\mathbf{v}_k = \mathbf{v}'_k / \|\mathbf{v}_k\|$$

end of k-loop

The coefficients y_i of the orthogonal vectors $\mathbf{v}_k$ are simply $\mathbf{v}_i^T\mathbf{b}$. To calculate the x_i (if desired), one uses back substitution on the triangular system relating the $\mathbf{a}_k$ and $\mathbf{v}_k$ (see Prob. 18 at end of this chapter).

We can estimate the amount of work for Gram-Schmidt as follows: There are $M^2/2$ terms of the form $(\mathbf{a}_k^T\mathbf{v}_j)\mathbf{v}_j$ to process. Each one requires N operations (add + multiply) for the dot product and N operations (add + multiply) for the vector subtraction. The work to actually compute the x_i is M dot products of N-vectors or MN operations, which is small compared to the orthogonalization work. The total is thus M^2N. If N is about the same size as M, then this is about 50 percent more work than using the normal equations. If N is very large compared to M, a not unusual case, then Gram-Schmidt is about twice as much work as using the normal equations.

There are three advantages to using this method over the normal equations approach:

1. The condition number of the problem is not squared in the process. This helps for a certain number (relatively small) of cases.
2. When you are going to get garbage instead of the solution, you know where and why it arises. Let us assume that the $\mathbf{a}_i$ are all about 1 in size (if they are not, it is a good practice to make them so). Then if one of the $\mathbf{v}'_k$ is of the order of round-off error in size, you have lost all information about it. You can test for this happening and report back to the user that the first k vectors are linearly dependent to within round-off error.
3. You can introduce another tolerance (an estimate of observational error or model uncertainty) and simply skip vectors $\mathbf{v}'_k$ whose length is less than this tolerance. You can report to the user that these vectors (columns of A) have been dropped from the model (matrix A) because they are linearly dependent on the previously processed vectors.

There is a modern version of Gram-Schmidt called *modified Gram-Schmidt orthogonalization* (Rice, 1966, see References at end of the book), which is simply a rearrangement of the order of doing the calculation. It is analogous to the Crout variant of Gauss elimination in this sense. The algorithm for it is:

Algorithm 11.2: Modified Gram-Schmidt orthogonalization

For k = 1 to M do

$$\mathbf{a}_k = \mathbf{a}_k / \|\mathbf{a}_k\|$$

$$\mathbf{a}_j = \mathbf{a}_j - (\mathbf{a}_j^T \mathbf{a}_k)\mathbf{a}_k \qquad \text{for } j = k + 1, k + 2, \ldots, M$$

end of k-loop

This method's advantages over the classical Gram-Schmidt are

1. It requires less storage. Note that the formulas do not use a different name for the new vectors $\mathbf{v}_i$—they are computed and placed in the same storage as the original vectors.
2. It is easier to program.
3. It is a numerically stable method; that is, the answers are as accurate as one can reasonably expect from any computational method [see Bjorck (1967) in References at end of book].
4. One can use a "pivoting" strategy—namely, choose the largest remaining vector as the one to be processed next. This is useful in a small number of cases and examples can be constructed where this pivoting is as valuable as pivoting is in Gauss elimination.

11.D THE ORTHOGONAL MATRIX FACTORIZATION APPROACH

We have seen that, if we can find M and U (lower and upper triangular) so that MA = U, then we can easily solve the problem $A\mathbf{x} = \mathbf{b}$. There is another factorization that is attractive—namely, find an orthogonal matrix Q and an upper triangular matrix R so that

$$QA = R$$

Then to solve $A\mathbf{x} = \mathbf{b}$ we multiply by Q on both sides to obtain

$$QA\mathbf{x} = Q\mathbf{b} = R\mathbf{x}$$

and thus $\mathbf{x}$ may be obtained by back substitution on the vector $Q\mathbf{b}$. Note that $Q^T = Q^{-1}$ does not play an essential role in this even though we do have $A = Q^T R$ as a factorization of A.

The attraction of orthogonal factorization lies with the fact that multiplying A or $\mathbf{b}$ by Q does not change the size of anything, i.e., does not magnify any round-off errors or uncertainties associated with the matrix A or vector $\mathbf{b}$. It is a process with condition number 1, the best we could hope for. To see this, note that $\|Q\mathbf{x}\| = \|\mathbf{x}\|$ for any vector $\mathbf{x}$ from the analysis

$$\|Q\mathbf{x}\|^2 = (Q\mathbf{x})^T Q\mathbf{x} = \mathbf{x}^T Q^T Q\mathbf{x} = \mathbf{x}^T\mathbf{x} = \|\mathbf{x}\|^2$$

since $Q^T Q = I$. Recall the discussion of pivoting in Gauss elimination as a means to control error magnification; such a process is not needed here.

There are two different orthogonal factorization schemes, plane rotations and elementary reflections (Householder transformations), and we briefly outline each of them.

11.D.1 Orthogonal Factorization with Plane Rotations

One may rotate the coordinate system in any plane, just as ordinary three-dimensional Euclidean space may be rotated. As in ordinary three-dimensional space, things stay the same in the axis of rotation. It is geometrically clear that such a transformation does not change the size of vectors. What we want to do is find rotations that zero out certain entries in A so we can obtain the upper triangular matrix R.

An *elementary plane rotation* (Givens transformation) is represented by the matrix

$$R_{ij} = \begin{bmatrix} 1 & & & & & & & & & & & & & \\ & 1 & & & & & & & & & & & & \\ & & 1 & & & & & & & & & & & \\ & & & 1 & & & & & & & & & & \\ & & & & 1 & & & & & & & & & \\ & & & & & c & \cdots & & & s & & & & \\ & & & & & \vdots & 1 & & & \vdots & & & & \\ & & & & & \vdots & & 1 & & \vdots & & & & \\ & & & & & \vdots & & & 1 & \vdots & & & & \\ & & & & & -s & \cdots & & & c & & & & \\ & & & & & & & & & & 1 & & & \\ & & & & & & & & & & & 1 & & \\ & & & & & & & & & & & & 1 & \\ & & & & & & & & & & & & & 1 \end{bmatrix} \begin{matrix} \\ \\ \\ \\ \\ \leftarrow \text{i row} \\ \\ \\ \\ \leftarrow \text{j row} \\ \\ \\ \\ \\ \end{matrix}$$

where $c^2 + s^2 = 1$ and $c = \cos(\theta)$, $s = \sin(\theta)$ with θ the angle of rotation in the i, j coordinate plane. By direct verification we can see that $R_{ij}A$ only has four elements different from A, namely, the (i, i), (i, j), (j, i), and (j, j) elements.

We consider in detail $R_{1j}A$ and see how to choose the values of c and s so that the resulting (j, 1) elements are zero. We have

$$(R_{ij}A)\ \text{j,1 component} = -sa_{11} + ca_{j1}$$

and we can choose θ so that this component is zero, i.e.,

$$\frac{s}{c} = \tan\theta = \frac{a_{j1}}{a_{11}}$$

Thus we can apply R_{1j} to A for j = 2, 3, ..., N with θ chosen each time to zero out a_{j1}, and then we have the same form of the matrix as after Gauss elimination on the first column of A.

There are various ways to explicitly solve for c and s (we really do not need to know θ itself). The most obvious is

$$r = \pm\sqrt{a_{11}^2 + a_{j1}^2}$$

$$c = a_{11}/r \qquad s = a_{j1}/r$$

which requires four multiplications/divisions, two additions, and one square root. This is substantially more than the work of one step of Gauss elimination. A clever, but complicated to describe, scheme has been found by Gentleman (1973) (see References at end of book) which only requires two multiplications/divisions, two additions, and no square roots. This scheme then only requires twice the work of Gauss elimination and is implemented in the BLAS (see Appendix).

11.D.2 Orthogonal Factorization with Elementary Reflections

Consider reflecting the space with respect to some plane, as in Fig. 11.2. The idea here is to choose the plane so that $\mathbf{a} = (a_1, a_2, \ldots, a_N)^T$ is reflected onto the first coordinate axis, that is, $\mathbf{Ha} = (-\sigma, 0, 0, \ldots, 0)^T$ where H represents the reflection. This linear transformation is then applied to $\mathbf{a}_1$, the first column of the matrix A.

The matrix H, which represents this elementary reflection (*Householder transformation*), is easily found as follows. Let $\mathbf{e}_1 = (1, 0, 0, \ldots, 0)^T$ = first coordinate vector, $\sigma = \pm 1$ and then set

$$\mathbf{u} = \mathbf{a}_1 + \sigma\mathbf{e}_1$$

$$c = \tfrac{1}{2}\|\mathbf{u}\|^2$$

$$H = I - \frac{\mathbf{u}\mathbf{u}^T}{c}$$

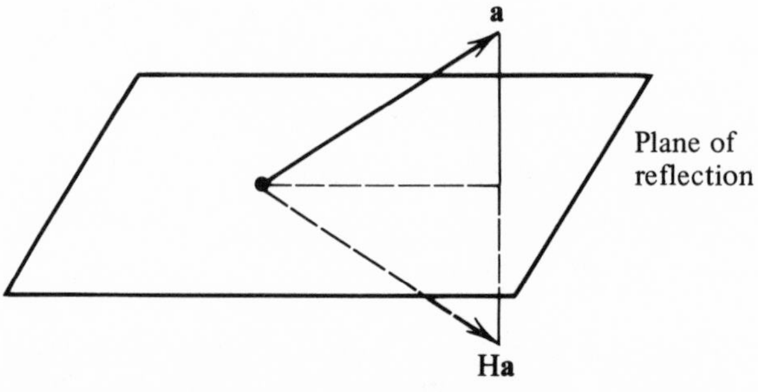

Figure 11.2 The reflection of a vector with respect to a plane.

Note that $\mathbf{u}\mathbf{u}^T$ is a full matrix, whereas $\mathbf{u}^T\mathbf{u}$ is just one number. We leave it to the reader to verify that H is an orthogonal matrix ($H^TH = I$) and $H\mathbf{a}_1 = -\sigma\mathbf{e}_1$.

Thus HA has its first column of the same form as the first column of A by Gauss elimination. One must apply H to the other columns of A also and then, as in Gauss elimination, one applies the same scheme to the $(N - 1) \times (N - 1)$ matrix left. Note that one never explicitly forms the matrix H; one computes the result HA as follows:

$$\mathbf{u} = \mathbf{a}_1 + \sigma\mathbf{e}_1$$

$$c = \tfrac{1}{2}\|\mathbf{u}\|^2$$

$$\mathbf{a}_1 = -\sigma\mathbf{e}_1$$

For $j = 2, 3, \ldots, N$ do

$$d_j = \mathbf{u}^T\mathbf{a}_j/c$$

$$\mathbf{a}_j = \mathbf{a}_j - d_j\mathbf{u}$$

end of j-loop

A careful operations count shows that this computation also takes twice as much arithmetic as the corresponding phase of Gauss elimination. A careful implementation of these Householder transformations is included in the BLAS and the least-squares software of Lawson-Hanson (see Appendix).

An estimate of the work for each of these methods yields about $M^2N - M^3/3$ operations (one add + one multiply). If N is about the same size as M, then this is about the same work as using the normal equations. If N is large compared to M, then the orthogonal factorization involves about the same work as Gram-Schmidt and twice the work of using the normal equations.

This method's advantages are:

1. It is a numerically stable method; that is, the answers are as accurate as one can reasonably expect from any computational method.
2. One may apply the *singular value analysis* (a topic not discussed here) to the matrix R to obtain detailed insight into the linear dependencies that may exist in the original problem.

11.E THE LAWSON-HANSON BOOK: SOLVING LEAST-SQUARES PROBLEMS

So far we have just introduced the basic ideas of least squares. There are many books which present the theory of least squares in great detail, but there is one which is entirely devoted to the theory and practice of solving least-squares problems: Lawson and Hanson (1974) (see References at end of book). This is a treatise which thoroughly covers all the questions that arise in the practical solution of least-squares problems. They discuss mundane items such as the different terminology used in numerical computation, statistics, and electrical engineering for the same theory; hard practical problems such as how to handle very large data sets (say N = 10,000,000, M = 20) in a real computer system; and complicated theoretical questions like error analysis for factorization methods. They show that, whatever "tricks" exist to handle a problem (such as multiple data sets for the same model) with one of the above approaches, there is an equivalent trick for the other two. These authors believe that, on balance, the orthogonal factorization approach (using elementary reflections) is the best and they analyze its use in a wide variety of contexts, including nonlinear least squares. Anyone doing serious least-squares computations should have access to this book. The software presented at the end of the Lawson and Hanson book is discussed in the Appendix.

PROBLEMS FOR CHAP. 11

1 Give a definition of the *residual* of a least-squares solution of $A\mathbf{x} = \mathbf{b}$. Show that the residual is orthogonal to the columns of A.

2 Let $\mathbf{b} = (0.01, 0, 1)^T$, $\bar{\mathbf{b}} = (0.0101, 0, 1)^T$ and

$$A = \begin{pmatrix} 1 & 0 \\ 0 & 1 \\ 0 & 0 \end{pmatrix}$$

(*a*) Compute the least-squares solutions $\mathbf{x}$ and $\bar{\mathbf{x}}$ to $A\mathbf{x} = \mathbf{b}$, $A\bar{\mathbf{x}} = \bar{\mathbf{b}}$.

(*b*) What is the relative difference in size between $\mathbf{b}$ and $\bar{\mathbf{b}}$? between $\mathbf{x}$ and $\bar{\mathbf{x}}$? Explain how these differences can be so far apart.

(*c*) Give an example of $\mathbf{b}$ and $\bar{\mathbf{b}}$ where the relative difference in $\mathbf{x}$ and $\bar{\mathbf{x}}$ is 10^5 times that of $\mathbf{b}$ and $\bar{\mathbf{b}}$.

3 Consider

$$A = \begin{pmatrix} 1.000 & 1.050 \\ 1.000 & 1.000 \\ 1.000 & 1.000 \end{pmatrix} \qquad A + E = \begin{pmatrix} 1.000 & 1.051 \\ 1.000 & 1.001 \\ 1.000 & 1.000 \end{pmatrix}$$

$$\mathbf{b} = (2.050, 2.000, 2.000)^T \qquad \bar{\mathbf{b}} = (2.050, 1.500, 2.500)^T$$

(*a*) Show that $(1.000, 1.000)^T$ is the least-squares solution to both $A\mathbf{x} = \mathbf{b}$ and $A\mathbf{x} = \bar{\mathbf{b}}$.

(*b*) Show that the least-squares solutions $\mathbf{x}_E$ and $\bar{\mathbf{x}}_E$ to $(A + E)\mathbf{x} = \mathbf{b}$ and $(A + E)\mathbf{x} = \bar{\mathbf{b}}$ are $\mathbf{x}_E = (1.0097, 0.9898)^T$ and $\bar{\mathbf{x}}_E = (1.3088, 0.6958)^T$.

(*c*) Compute relative differences in size between A and A + E, between $\mathbf{x}$ and $\mathbf{x}_E$, and between $\bar{\mathbf{x}}$ and $\bar{\mathbf{x}}_E$.

(*d*) It is technically complicated to explain "why" such large variations in these differences can occur. However, what lesson should you draw from this example?

4 Consider

$$A = \begin{pmatrix} 1.000 & 1.000 \\ 1.000 & 1.040 \\ 1.000 & 1.000 \end{pmatrix} \qquad A + E = \begin{pmatrix} 1.000 & 1.001 \\ 1.000 & 1.041 \\ 1.000 & 1.000 \end{pmatrix}$$

$$\mathbf{b} = (2.000, 2.040, 2.000)^T \qquad \bar{\mathbf{b}} = (1.500, 2.040, 2.500)^T$$

(*a*) Show that $(1.000, 1.000)^T$ is the least-squares solution to both $A\mathbf{x} = \mathbf{b}$ and $A\mathbf{x} = \bar{\mathbf{b}}$.

(*b*) Compute the least-squares solutions $\mathbf{x}_E$ and $\bar{\mathbf{x}}_E$ to $(A + E)\mathbf{x}_E = \mathbf{b}$ and $(A + E)\bar{\mathbf{x}}_E = \bar{\mathbf{b}}$.

(*c*) Compute the relative differences in size between A and A + E, between $\mathbf{x}$ and $\mathbf{x}_E$, and between $\bar{\mathbf{x}}$ and $\bar{\mathbf{x}}_E$. Compare the size of these differences and give a discussion about the sensitivity of the least-squares solution to perturbations in the matrix A.

5 In the Gram-Schmidt orthogonalization, the vectors are normalized at each step. Describe the variant of Gram-Schmidt where the vectors are not normalized until the end of the algorithm. Explain why this variant is less efficient.

6 Give the calling sequence for a good design of a Fortran library routine for the linear least-squares problem $A\mathbf{x} = \mathbf{b}$. Explicitly state the algorithmic and software objectives of the design and which ones were weighted most heavily. Define all the variables that appear in the calling sequence. Describe an example application where this design is weak compared to some reasonable alternative (briefly describe the alternative).

7 Perform a detailed operation count for Gram-Schmidt orthogonalization of m vectors of length n. What steps correspond to back substitution in Gauss elimination?

8 Show how Gram-Schmidt orthogonalization can be used to solve $A\mathbf{x} = \mathbf{b}$ by orthogonalizing the columns of A and then using the method for orthogonal matrices.

9 In this book we have studied the following four linear algebra problems: (1) Solve $A\mathbf{x} = \mathbf{b}$; (2) compute A^{-1}; (3) find the least-squares solution to $A\mathbf{x} = \mathbf{b}$; and (4) compute det (A). Discuss in a comparative manner the following points for these problems:

(*a*) The difficulty of the matrix theory underlying the computation

(*b*) The actual amount of computation required to solve the problems (i.e., the amount of execution time for comparable sized matrices)

(*c*) The amount of preliminary analysis that one would expect to make in order to write a library subroutine to solve each of these problems for a large class of matrices A.

10 Write a Fortran subroutine to carry out Gram-Schmidt orthogonalization and apply it to solve least-squares problems. There specific examples to be used are

(*a*) $\mathbf{a}_i = \left(\frac{1}{i+1}, \frac{1}{i+2}, \ldots, \frac{1}{i+n}\right)^T$ for $i = 1, 2, \ldots, 10$ and $n = 20$

$b_j = 1$ for all j

(*b*) $\mathbf{a}_i = (\sin(i/n), \sin(2i/n), \sin(3i/n), \ldots, \sin(i))^T$ for $i = 1, 2, \ldots, 10$ and $n = 10$

$b_1 = 1$ and $b_j = 0$ for $j > 1$

(*c*) $\mathbf{a}_i$ = random vector of length n for $i = 1, 2, \ldots, N$

b_j = random number

11 Repeat Prob. 9 for modified Gram-Schmidt orthogonalization.

12 Compare the lengths and difficulty of writing the Fortran subroutines of Probs. 10 and 11. Compare the computed values for each of the three least-squares problems.

13 Modify the subroutine of Prob. 10 (or 11) to include a test for linear dependency of the vectors. Make the tolerance (estimate of model uncertainty) an input variable. If the tolerance is zero, then the subroutine should reset it to the round-off level of the computer used (times a small constant). What effect does this tolerance have on least-squares problem (*a*) of Prob. 10? Make some runs with varying tolerances and report on the effects.

14 Describe an algorithm for solving the least-squares problem using elementary rotations. The level of detail should be the same as Algorithm 5.1.

15 Implement the algorithm of Prob. 14 as a Fortran subroutine and apply it to the least-squares problems of Prob. 10.

16 Repeat Prob. 14 for elementary reflections.

17 Implement the algorithm of Prob. 16 as a Fortran subroutine and apply it to the least-squares problems of Prob. 10.

18 Suppose the vectors $\mathbf{a}_k$ have been orthogonalized by Algorithm 11.1. Give an algorithm to compute the coefficients x_i from the quantities $\mathbf{b}^T\mathbf{v}_k$. *Hint:* Save information generated in Algorithm 11.1 and use it.

CHAPTER

TWELVE

PROJECTS

This chapter contains a number of computational projects with the following features:

1. They include some analysis and/or algorithm development.
2. They require considerable programming and computer use.
3. They require the collection and analysis of experimental data from computations.

The projects are appropriate for a group of three or four students to do over a period of 4 to 6 weeks. Some of the projects are somewhat "open-ended" and students could spend large amounts of effort digging deeper into the phenomena under study. Assignments of such projects should warn the students of this situation and state that they are expected to obtain results commensurate with the period allowed for the assignment. Of course, the projects can be done by one or two students over proportionally longer times.

The projects are useful not only for learning about matrix computations and mathematical software, but also as an introduction to cooperative programming efforts and for practice in scientific analysis. For the latter use, the assignment should include a final report that is evaluated as a scientific document. Typical points to consider in its evaluation are:

Analysis: correctness of mathematical analysis; correctness of algorithms developed

Software: correctness; style and documentation; efficiency

Computations: appropriateness of experiments; proper collection of data, accurate measurements, and proper summary and analysis of data

Report: style of English and scientific presentation; soundness of, and reasoning for, conclusions reached

PROJECT 1: STUDY OF GAUSS ELIMINATION

Write and debug a subprogram which uses Gauss elimination with partial pivoting to solve $\mathbf{Ax} = \mathbf{b}$ and to compute A^{-1}. Design the subprogram so that the choice of what to do is governed by a simple switch. For this subprogram, carry out the following tasks:

A. Make an operations count for the program.
B. Give the storage requirements for the program variables in terms of the size parameters of the problem. Do not include the code for the algorithm itself.
C. Give the storage requirements for the algorithm code.
D. Compare the program's speed performance with two other similar programs. Choose the programs from the local library, the IMSL library (LEQT1F and LINV1F, for example), or from LINPACK (SGECO, SGESL, and SGEDI, for example). Design and carry out an experiment that covers the range of matrix sizes from 2 to 30. Present the results with composite performance profiles.
E. Evaluate the program's accuracy performance for well-conditioned matrices with orders between 2 and 30. Use random matrices, pick the true solutions $\mathbf{x}^*$, and generate the right-hand side from $\mathbf{x}^*$. Discuss the accuracy of the computed solutions $\bar{\mathbf{x}}$ as a function of the matrix size.
F. Repeat task E for ill-conditioned matrices (see Chap. 8 for examples) of order 4 to 12 or 15. Examine the elimination pivots used for any particular trends. Compare them with pivots for well-conditioned problems. Examine the quantities in the back-substitution calculation

$$x_j = \frac{b_j - A_j^T \mathbf{s}}{a_{jj}}$$

where $\mathbf{s}$ is the partial solution vector $(0, \ldots, 0, x_{j+1}, \ldots, x_n)^T$ and A_j is the jth row of A. Display some of the results by performance profiles involving condition numbers.
G. Repeat task E for a comparable library program and then compare the performance of the programs.
H. Repeat task F for a comparable library program and then compare the performance of the programs.

PROJECT 2: PROGRAMMING LANGUAGE EFFECTS ON LINEAR EQUATIONS SOFTWARE

This project involves seven programs; the first four are to be written:

1. Fortran subprogram to
   a. Solve **Ax** = **b** by Gauss elimination with partial pivoting and allowing for multiple right-hand sides
   b. Compute A^{-1}
2. Pascal program for the same tasks
3. Basic or Algol or PL/1 (your choice) program for the same tasks
4. Double-precision Fortran program for the same tasks
5. A comparable program from the local computing center library
6. A comparable commercial library program (e.g., LEQT1F from IMSL)
7. A comparable LINPACK program (SGEFA plus SGESL, for example)

In order to make the first four programs as identical as possible, the algorithm should be expressed in some programming-language-independent form (e.g., flowcharted) and then each program written from this specification. These four programs should be well-structured, high-quality programs with good documentation.

Carry out the following tasks with the programs:

A. Estimate the time to specify the algorithm and to code and debug each program. Give the length of each program in terms of statements (both with and without comments).
B. Justify the design of the user interface chosen.
C. Measure the compile time (if applicable) of each program.
D. Design and carry out an experiment to evaluate the speed and memory performance of all seven programs. Use full matrices of orders between 3 and 40. Present your results as performance profiles. Explain the observed differences.

PROJECT 3: STUDY OF BAND MATRIX SOLVERS

This project involves four programs, two to be written:

1. A sub-program to solve **Ax** = **b** where A is an n × n matrix of bandwidth k. Use Gauss elimination without pivoting and an economical storage scheme for the band matrix.
2. A similar program that uses partial pivoting.

3. Two comparable library programs—for example, SGBCO and SGBSL from LINPACK or LEQT1B from IMSL or something else from the local computing center library.

Carry out the following tasks:

A. Show that program 2 with partial pivoting requires twice the storage of program 1.
B. Justify the design of the user interface of programs 1 and 2. This includes the band matrix storage scheme chosen.
C. Compare qualitatively the difficulty of programming Gauss elimination for full matrices with that of program 1 and compare these in turn with writing program 2.
D. Compare the speed of these four programs over a range of problems with up to 8000 elements in the band of the matrices. Display the performance in terms of the size parameters n and k. Do the observed results agree with the behavior one expects from an operations count?
E. Repeat task D for memory requirements instead of speed.
F. Locate some ill-conditioned band systems and carry out an experiment of your design to show the value of pivoting in the solution of these systems. Also, exhibit a nonsingular band matrix for which program 1 fails.

PROJECT 4: PROGRAMMING LANGUAGES AND STYLE EFFECTS ON MATHEMATICAL SOFTWARE

The objective is to study mathematical software accuracy, efficiency, and implementation effects as a function of the following variables: compiler, language, precision, and modularization level. Three mathematical software computations are defined to be implemented in the following ways:

1. Fortran in single precision. Three different compilers are to be used.
2. Fortran in double precision with one compiler.
3. Algol.
4. Pascal.
5. Basic.
6. Little modularization (your choice of one language) with a maximum of one level of subprogram (except for functions).
7. Extreme modularization in Fortran and one of Pascal or Algol. Some hints about the modularization are given with each computation.

At least one of the implementations should have good style and documentation.

You are to design an experiment to assess the effects of the four variables on the three software qualities using these six implementations. Care is to be taken that the programs carry out the same computations within the constraints imposed on the implementations. The experiment is to include the following tasks:

A. Rate the ease of programming and debugging of each implementation on a scale of 0 to 10, with 0 comparable to assembly language programming and 10 being extremely quick and simple.
B. Measure the programming and debugging time, the lengths of the programs, their compilation times (if applicable), and their times to execute the computations. Analyze these as a function of the four variables.
C. Compare the precisions of the computed results.
D. Consider two different machines, one where double precision is 10 per cent slower than single precision and the other where double precision is 300 per cent slower than single precision. Estimate the effects that the use of these two machines would have on the measurements made and the balance in the choice between accuracy and speed.
E. Discuss how the execution time measurements are made and how confident you are of their validity.
F. Discuss the effect of interpretive execution (Basic) versus compile and execute implementations.
G. Choose one program and insert a large amount of intermediate output. Compare the execution time with a run with no output and discuss the relative costs of I/O and arithmetic.
H. Present an overall assessment of the strengths and weaknesses of these languages for mathematical software.

The three computations specified below are typical of numerical computations even though they are somewhat artificial because a lot of computation and potential modularity is desired in a short program. The computations involve four functions:

$$f_1(x) = \sin \frac{x}{2}$$

$$f_2(x) = \frac{1}{1 + 66x^4}$$

$$f_3(x) = \min [\sin (5x), 0.75]$$

$$f_4(x) = \sin \frac{x}{2} + 10^{-6} * (\text{RANF}(0) - \tfrac{1}{2})$$

where RANF(0) is a uniformly distributed random variable on (0, 1).

Computation 1: Gram-Schmidt Orthogonalization

```
For f1(x), f2(x), and f4(x) do
  For N = 2 to 12 with step 3 do
    For M = N + 1 to N =26 with step 5 do
          1) Create vectors xj = f(j • x) for x = i/M, i = 0, 1, ..., M and for j = 1, 2, ..., N.
          2) Orthogonalize these vectors by Gram-Schmidt to obtain vectors vj.
          3) Find the maximum value of vj^T vk for j ≠ k.
  end of M- and N-loops
  Print a table of the maximum dot products found as a function of N and M. Format the
  table nicely with a heading.
end of f(x)-loop
```

For the extreme modularization case use at least one module (subprogram) for each of

Multiplying a vector by a constant
Printing a vector (row of a table)
Finding the maximum of a vector
The inner loop calculations for an N, M pair
The outer loop calculations for a value of N
The entire calculation for one f(x)
Normalizing a vector
Vector subtraction
Forming a vector
A dot product
The sum in Gram-Schmidt

Computation 2: Gauss Elimination

```
For f1(x), f2(x), and f4(x) do
  For n = 2 to 15 with step 3 do
        1) Create a matrix of order N with aij = f(i • j/N).
        2) Create a true solution vector and corresponding right-hand side vector b.
        3) Solve the system Ax = b by Gauss elimination to find x̄.
        4) Compute ||x - x̄||/||x|| and ||r|| where r is the residual for x̄.
  end of N-loop
Print a table of ||x - x̄||/||x|| and ||r|| for each f(x) and N. Format the table nicely with a
heading.
end of f(x)-loop
```

For the extreme modularization case use at least one module (subprogram) for each of

The entire calculation for one f(x)
The inner loop for one value of N
Creating the true solution vector
Computing one component of **b**
Computing a vector norm
Processing one column in Gauss elimination
Computing the multipliers
Processing one row in Gauss elimination
Processing the right-hand side
Computing a_{ij}
Computing **b**
Creating a row of A
Creating A
Computing **r**
Gauss elimination
Testing to pivot
Doing the pivoting
Back substitution

Computation 3: Romberg Integration on $(-2, 2)$

```
For f1(x), f2(x), f3(x), and f4(x) do
  For H = 1.0, .5, 0.25, ..., 0.015625 do
     1) Form the array F(N, M) = f(-2 + (N - 1)2^(1-M)) for M = 1 to 7 and for N = 1 to 2^(M+1)
     2) For NEXTRAP = 1 to 7 do
          Form the array TRAP(M, NEXTRAP) for M = 1, ..., 7 where TRAP(M, 1) is the
          trapezoidal rule estimate of ∫_{-2}^{2} f(x) dx based on 2^(M+1) intervals. TRAP(M, K) is
          then the Romberg extrapolation of the K - 1 column.
        end of NEXTRAP-loop
  end of H-loop
  Print a table of the integral estimates and their errors. For f4(x) assume that
  ∫_{-2}^{2} (RANFL(0) - 1/2)dx = 0.
end of f(x)-loop
```

For the extreme modularization case use at least one module (subprogram) for each of

A single extrapolation	One column of F with H fixed
A column of the TRAP table	Forming the F array
A trapezoidal rule estimate	Forming the TRAP array
Computing one error	Printing the table for one f(x)
The whole computation for one f(x)	Printing one row of the table
The computation for one H value	Computing one entry in the F table

PROJECT 5: ROBUSTNESS OF LINEAR EQUATION SOLVERS

Select as many linear equation solvers as practical (at least three) from the library and misuse them in various ways. Then give your evaluation of how robust each program is and how much additional effort would be required to make the program highly robust. Typical of the misuses to attempt are

1. Arguments of wrong type, e.g., integers that are real or complex or logical or function names, arrays that are not arrays, integer arrays
2. Illegal arguments, e.g., matrix orders of 0 or -1, negative number of right-hand sides, invalid switches for programs with choices
3. Incompatible dimensions, e.g., 20 equations with a 10×10 matrix, actual and specified dimensions are different
4. Extreme cases of arguments, e.g., matrix order 1, matrix order 1,000,000, 1,000,000 right-hand sides, matrix entries near underflow or overflow
5. Unsolvable problems, e.g., matrix identically zero or less obvious singularities, the system

$$x - y = \sigma$$

$$x - 1.0001y = \sigma + 1$$

where σ is nearly the largest representable number in the machine

PROJECT 6: EVALUATION OF LIBRARY LINEAR EQUATION SOLVERS

Select for evaluation a reasonable number (at least three) library programs for solving $\mathbf{Ax} = \mathbf{b}$. The programs should represent a variety of sources. These programs are to be evaluated on the following qualities:

1. Documentation for users. It should be clearly written, with no ambiguities and with well-defined variables. Do the instructions contain an example, do the choice of words and names suggest the right things?
2. Documentation for maintenance. If something should need to be changed, do the internal comments provide a good basis for understanding the algorithm?
3. Design of the user interface. Are the variables and their names well chosen? Are there any variables whose values are difficult to know?
4. Execution speed. Prepare a performance profile for each program of execution time versus matrix size.
5. Memory usage. Prepare a performance profile for each program of total memory used versus matrix size.
6. Accuracy for ill-conditioned problems. Choose two families of ill-conditioned matrices (such as the Hilbert matrices) and prepare a performance profile for each program and each family of accuracy versus matrix size.

Once these evaluations have been made, make an overall assessment of each program and rank them according to suitability as library programs. Explain the criteria, weighting, and procedure used to make the ranking. Discuss the shortcomings of this evaluation from two points of view: weaknesses in the evaluation of the six qualities above and other considerations not included in the assessment.

PROJECT 7: DIRECT AND ITERATIVE METHODS FOR LINEAR SYSTEMS FROM DIFFERENTIAL EQUATIONS BOUNDARY VALUE PROBLEMS

The discretization of ordinary differential equations by finite differences leads to linear equations; if it is a boundary value problem, the equations form a simultaneous linear system. Three examples of such systems are

$$y'' = 1 \qquad y(0) = 1 \qquad y(2) = 2$$

with solution $y(x) = x^2/2$

$$y'' + \frac{\pi^2}{4} y = 0 \qquad y(0) = 0 \qquad y(0.5) = \sqrt{2}/2$$

with solution $y(x) = \sin(\pi x/2)$

$$y'' + \frac{1}{x} y' \left(1 - \frac{1}{x^2}\right) y = 0 \qquad y(1) = J_1(1) \qquad y(2) = J_1(2)$$

with solution $y(x) = J_1(x)$

where $J_1(x)$ is the Bessel function of order 1.

For one or all of these equations carry out the following tasks:

A. Display the system of finite difference equations.
B. Estimate the computational work required to evaluate the analytic solutions to six decimal digits at 100 and at 1000 points in the interval. Locate and use Taylor's series expansions for this evaluation.
C. Estimate, before doing any computation, the computational effort to solve the finite difference equations at 100 and at 1000 points by
   1. Gauss elimination
   2. Jordan iteration
   3. Gauss-Seidel iteration
D. Compute the solutions of the finite difference equations by each of the three methods in task C. Compare the actual effort with the estimate in task C.
E. Make an evaluation of the suitability of various methods for approximately solving differential equation boundary value problems.

PROJECT 8: SOLUTION OF LINEAR EQUATIONS FROM PARTIAL DIFFERENTIAL EQUATION BOUNDARY VALUE PROBLEMS

The technique of finite differences can be applied to the partial differential equation

$$u_{xx} + u_{yy} = 6xye^x e^y(xy + x + y - 3)$$

in much the same way as for ordinary differential equations. Carry out the following tasks for this approach:

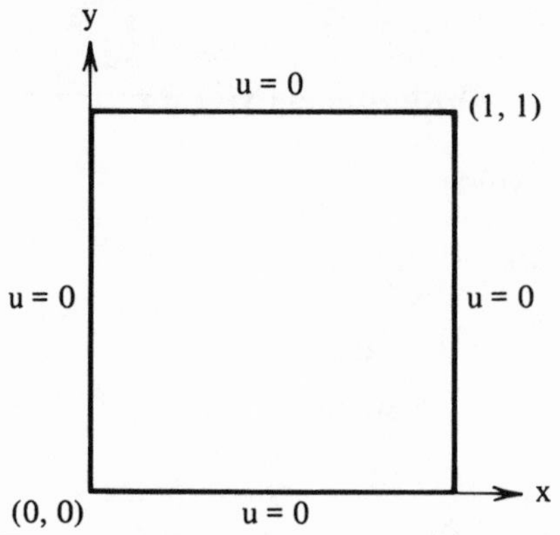

SOLUTION
$u = 3e^x e^y (x - x^2)(y - y^2)$

A. Derive the system of linear equations obtained when this partial differential equation is discretized. Explain how the boundary values are entered into the system. Use the same sized step h for each variable x and y.
B. Show how to apply a library program for band matrices to the linear system obtained. Note that pivoting is not required.
C. Use the library program to plot a small performance profile of error versus the finite difference step h. Find a formula which approximates this profile. Also plot a performance profile of execution time versus h. Use values of h between 0.25 and 0.05.
D. Write a program to apply Gauss-Seidel iteration to the linear system of task A. Determine a satisfactory method to terminate the iteration when the accuracy in solving the linear system is only slightly higher than the error in approximate solution to the partial differential equation.
E. Compare the performance of the two methods in Tasks C and D with respect to execution time and memory used.

PROJECT 9: DIRECT AND ITERATIVE METHODS FOR ILL-CONDITIONED LINEAR SYSTEMS

The object of this project is to compare the accuracy achieved by direct and iterative methods on ill-conditioned problems. Locate several (at least four) matrices of order 6 to 12 where Gauss-Seidel converges and which are poorly conditioned. Select true solution vectors and generate corresponding right-hand sides for the equation $\mathbf{Ax} = \mathbf{b}$. Then carry out the following tasks:

A. Solve the system by Gauss elimination.
B. Apply Gauss-Seidel iteration to the systems, continuing the iteration until no further improvement in accuracy occurs.
C. Examine and discuss the behavior of the iteration after improvement in accuracy stops.

D. Take the true solution as initial guess for Gauss-Seidel and discuss the resulting iterations.
E. Compare the accuracy obtained by Gauss elimination and Gauss-Seidel iteration.

PROJECT 10: ELEMENTARY REFLECTIONS FOR $\mathbf{Ax} = \mathbf{b}$

It was remarked in Chap. 11 that elementary reflections can be used to solve a linear system $\mathbf{Ax} = \mathbf{b}$. This project is to develop and evaluate that method. The tasks to do are

A. Give a detailed description of the algorithm for solving $\mathbf{Ax} = \mathbf{b}$.
B. Make a detailed operations count for the algorithm.
C. Write a program to solve $\mathbf{Ax} = \mathbf{b}$ using this algorithm. Discuss the design of the user interface and prepare a set of instructions for the program's use.
D. Compare the speed of this program with a library program that uses Gauss elimination with partial pivoting. Prepare performance profiles for execution time versus matrix order for up to 25×25 matrices.
E. Continue the comparison of task D with accuracy for well-conditioned problems. Use random matrices for the comparison.
F. Continue the comparison for ill-conditioned problems. Prepare performance profiles of accuracy versus condition number for each program.
G. Make an overall comparison of the two programs and justify your choice of one of them for a program library.

PROJECT 11: ELEMENTARY ROTATIONS FOR $\mathbf{Ax} = \mathbf{b}$

Repeat Project 10 for the use of elementary rotations to solve $\mathbf{Ax} = \mathbf{b}$.

PROJECT 12: JORDAN ELIMINATION FOR $\mathbf{Ax} = \mathbf{b}$

Once Gauss elimination has been used to reduce A to triangular form U, the elimination can continue to reduce U to diagonal form. For example, appropriate multiples of the last row can be subtracted from the preceding rows to put zeros in the last column of U. Then the next-to-last row of U can be used to put zeros in the next-to-last column, and so forth. The object of this project is to develop and evaluate this method. The tasks are

A. Give a detailed description of the algorithm. Show how to save all the multipliers for later use in processing the right-hand side.
B. Finish the project with tasks B through G of Project 10.

PROJECT 13: EXPERIMENTAL DETERMINATION OF OPTIMUM SOR OVERRELAXATION FACTOR

There is a theory of SOR iteration that allows one to analytically determine the optimum overrelaxation factor (the matrix Q in Chap. 10 has constants q on the diagonal). In many applications, the factor q must be determined experimentally. An unsophisticated way to do that is to systematically evaluate the rate of convergence for various values and then pick the best. That is the aim of this project. The tasks are

A. Consider two matrices: A_1 is tridiagonal with 2 on the diagonal and -1 above and below the diagonal, A_2 is five-diagonal with 2 on the diagonal, -1 above and below the diagonal, and $\frac{1}{2}$ on the next upper and lower diagonals. Construct right-hand side vectors so that $\mathbf{x} = (1, 1, \ldots, 1)^T$ is the true solution for each system $A_1\mathbf{x} = \mathbf{b}_1$, $A_2\mathbf{x} = \mathbf{b}_2$.
B. For each value of $q = 1, 1.1, 1.2, \ldots, 1.9, 2.0$, apply 100 iterations of SOR starting with $\mathbf{x}^{(0)} = 0$. Do this for A_1 and A_2 of order 10, 20, and 50. Measure the error at the end of 100 iterations, call it e, and set $p = \sqrt[100]{e}$. The value of p is the "average" rate of convergence of the iteration; the error was reduced by this much on each iteration. Note that the error of $\mathbf{x}^{(0)}$ is 1.
C. For each of the six cases make a performance plot of p versus q and estimate the optimum value for q. If the plot is too coarse, make additional runs to fill in the gaps.
D. Discuss the behavior of the performance profiles and their implications for the difficulty of finding optimum SOR factors.

PROJECT: 14: EXPERIMENTS WITH GAUSS-SEIDEL AND JACOBI ITERATION

This project is to explore various ways that one part of a matrix dominates another and how this affects iterative methods. The tasks are

A. Write two programs, one to implement Jacobi iteration and one for Gauss-Seidel.
B. Write a program to generate random matrices A of order N of the form L + U where L is lower triangular and U is upper triangular. This program has two other parameters MODE and SIGMA. The following relationships are to be satisfied:

$$\text{MODE} = 1 \qquad \sum_{ij} |l_{ij}| = \text{SIGMA} * \sum_{ij} |u_{ij}|$$

$$\text{MODE} = 2 \qquad \sum_{j=1}^{i} |l_{ij}| = \text{SIGMA} * \sum_{j=i+1}^{N} |u_{ij}| \qquad \text{for } i = 1, 2, \ldots, N$$

$$\text{MODE} = 3 \qquad |l_{ij}| = \text{SIGMA} * |u_{ji}| \qquad \text{for } i \neq j$$

Thus L can "dominate" U in three different ways.

C. Design an experiment to explore the effect of SIGMA and MODE on the convergence of the two methods. Select a couple of moderate values of N and a range of values of SIGMA for each value of MODE.
D. Carry out the experiment and report the percentage of convergence of the two methods as a function of SIGMA and MODE. Discuss the relationships that you observe.

PROJECT 15: DIRECTED GAUSS-SEIDEL VERSUS GAUSS-SEIDEL

Directed Gauss-Seidel means that the next iteration is made on the equation where the residual is largest. Under normal circumstances it is prohibitively expensive to evaluate *all* the residuals at each iteration. However, for very sparse matrices with a regular structure, this may be quite practical. Carry out the following tasks:

A. Describe situations where the work of reevaluating residuals is practical. Give specific procedures for the systems that arise from Projects 7 and 8.
B. Describe how to use a heap to keep track efficiently of which equation has the largest residual.
C. Write a program to implement directed Gauss-Seidel. Use the procedure developed in task B to direct the iteration. Update the residuals after each iteration by a straightforward scheme; it is not necessary to attempt efficiency on this point for this project.
D. Design and carry out an experiment to compare directed Gauss-Seidel with the regular Gauss-Seidel. Use matrices of order between 5 and 20 and measure "rate of convergence" as indicated in task B of Project 13.
E. Discuss the gain in rate of convergence that directed Gauss-Seidel achieves and how much "expense" one can afford in the "directing" and still be more efficient than regular Gauss-Seidel.

PROJECT 16: STUDY OF GRAM-SCHMIDT AND MODIFIED GRAM-SCHMIDT

A. Give detailed algorithms for Gram-Schmidt and modified Gram-Schmidt.
B. Give an arithmetic operations count for each algorithm in terms of the number N of vectors of length M.
C. Design and write a subprogram to implement each algorithm. Justify your design and prepare a set of user's instructions for each of them (they could be nearly the same).
D. Give the total storage requirements for each program as a function of N and M.
E. Design and carry out an experiment to evaluate the speed of each program. Prepare performance profiles that show the behavior of each program.
F. Generate vectors of lengths N = 20 and 40 by the formula

$$\mathbf{x}_k = \left(\left(\frac{1}{N}\right)^k, \left(\frac{2}{N}\right)^k, \ldots, \left(\frac{N}{N}\right)^k\right)^T$$

Use them to test the accuracy of the programs by checking the dot products of the resulting vectors.
G. Outline how to use one of these programs to solve $\mathbf{Ax} = \mathbf{b}$.

PROJECT 17: EVALUATION OF LINEAR LEAST-SQUARES METHODS

The object of this project is to compare the three essentially different methods for solving the linear least-squares problem. The tasks to be carried out are

A. Design and write a subprogram for solving $\mathbf{Ax} = \mathbf{b}$ in the least-squares sense by modified Gram-Schmidt. Justify your design and prepare a set of user's instructions for the program.
B. Repeat task A using the normal equations approach; use a library Gauss elimination program to actually solve the normal equations.
C. Get the appropriate Lawson-Hanson program for the same problem.
D. Design and carry out an experiment to compare the speed of the three programs. Use N vectors of length M with $5 \leq N \leq 20$ and $10 \leq M \leq 50$. Prepare performance profiles that illustrate the behavior of each method; discuss the relationship between the actual computation times and the operations counts mentioned in Chap. 11?
E. Similarly compare the accuracy of the three programs. Use the vectors of task F of Project 16 as columns of A and measure the accuracy of the computed results.
F. Give an overall assessment of the three programs based on these observations. Discuss any shortcomings the evaluation might have and propose (but do not carry out) further experiments that would help differentiate between the programs.

PROJECT 18: MODIFIED GRAM-SCHMIDT WITH PIVOTING

Consider the modified Gram-Schmidt algorithm (MGS) changed so that each stage the next vector brought into the orthogonal set is the remaining vector of largest size. To evaluate this variant carry out the following tasks:

A. Give a detailed description of this algorithm. Estimate the additional work of this algorithm compared to MGS.
B. Construct an example of three vectors of length 5 where MGS produces on one "correct" orthogonalized vector and this variant produces two "correct" orthogonalized vectors. The example will contain two nearly linearly dependent vectors.
C. Design and write a program that uses this variant to orthogonalize vectors. Justify the design and prepare a set of user's instructions for it. Insert a switch in the program to enable or disable the pivoting.
D. Design and carry out an experiment to test the effectiveness of the pivoting. Include ill-conditioned set of vectors of the following types:
   1. The columns of the Hilbert matrix
   2. The vectors of task F of Project 16
   3. The vectors of Computation 1 of Project 4 for $f_2(x)$
   4. A random mixture of the vectors of Computation 1 of Project 4 for $f_1(x)$ and $f_2(x)$
E. Make an evaluation of the value of pivoting in MGS.

APPENDIX

STANDARD LINEAR ALGEBRA SOFTWARE

A. The BLAS: Basic Linear Algebra Subroutines
B. The LINPACK Programs
C. The IMSL Library Programs for Linear Algebraic Equations
D. The NAG Library Programs for Simultaneous Linear Equations
E. The Lawson-Hanson Least Squares Programs
F. EISPACK—Matrix Eigensystem Routines
G. The Local Computing Center Library—Purdue Example

APPENDIX

STANDARD LINEAR ALGEBRA SOFTWARE

We discuss seven groups of matrix computation programs in this Appendix and all but one are standard software available to the entire computing community. The exception is the Purdue University Computing Center library which is presented as an example of what one will find in a well-supported computing center library.

The presentations are very abbreviated and not intended to serve as a user's guide or a reference. Just enough detail is given to show the flavor, scope, organization, and use of these software sets. References are given for those who wish to obtain more information or to use the software; much of the material here is directly reproduced from these sources in order to show their nature.

Each of the standard matrix software items is available from the source listed. It is not required that students have access to all, or even any, of these programs. Any small library of matrix computation software is sufficient to do most of the problems and projects in this book. If some of this software is available locally, then this presentation will serve as a first introduction. These examples illustrate the various ways that matrix computation software can be organized; the local computing center probably uses yet another organization.

APPENDIX

A

THE BLAS: BASIC LINEAR ALGEBRA SUBROUTINES

This package contains thirty-eight Fortran-callable subprograms for basic, low-level operations of numerical linear algebra. They were developed by C. L. Lawson, R. J. Hanson, D. R. Kincaid, and F. T. Krogh as a SIGNUM-sponsored (ACM Special Interest Group for Numerical Mathematics) project during 1973–1977 and the basic reference on them is their paper [Lawson et al. 1979]. The programs are available as Algorithm 539 from the ACM Algorithms Distribution Service, Sixth Floor, GNB Building, 7500 Bellaire Blvd., Houston, Texas 77036. The cost is nominal. The programs in this package are available in portable Fortran or assembly language for the IBM 360/67, CDC 6600–7600 and Univac 1108.

The reasons for developing this package are:

1. It serves as a conceptual aid in the design and coding of large programs and provides modularization.
2. It improves the self-documentation of code to have standard names.
3. A significant portion of the execution time of many large programs is spent in these low-level operations and assembly language versions may reduce costs substantially.
4. Some of these operations involve algorithmic and implementation subtleties which are likely to be ignored in typical applications programming environments.

Table A.1 gives a summary of the operations implemented and their naming conventions. Each operation has a root name (e.g., DOT for dot products) and a prefix indicates the operand types (e.g., I for integer). Suffixes on the dot product names indicate variants. *The rest of this section (up to the examples) is directly reproduced from* Lawson et al. (1979).†

† Copyright © 1979 by the Association for Computing Machinery, Inc. Reprinted by permission of The Association for Computing Machinery, Inc., from Lawson et al., Basic linear algebra subprograms for Fortran usage, *ACM Transactions on Mathematical Software*, vol. 5, no. 3, September 1979, pp. 310, 312–317.

Table I. Summary of Functions and Names of the BLAS Subprograms

Function	Prefix and suffix of name								Root of name
Dot product	SDS-	DS-	DQ-I	DQ-A	C-U	C-C	D-	S-	-DOT-
Constant times a vector plus a vector						C-	D-	S-	-AXPY
Set up Givens rotation							D-	S-	-ROTG
Apply rotation							D-	S-	-ROT
Set up modified Givens rotation							D-	S-	-ROTMG
Apply modified rotation							D-	S-	-ROTM
Copy x into y						C-	D-	S-	-COPY
Swap x and y						C-	D-	S-	-SWAP
2-norm (Euclidean length)						SC-	D-	S-	-NRM2
Sum of absolute values[a]						SC-	D-	S-	-ASUM
Constant times a vector					CS-	C-	D-	S-	-SCAL
Index of element having maximum absolute value[a]						IC-	ID-	IS-	-AMAX

[a] For complex components $z_j = x_j + iy_j$ these subprograms compute $|x_j| + |y_j|$ instead of $(x_j^2 + y_j^2)^{1/2}$.

4. PROGRAMMING CONVENTIONS

Vector arguments are permitted to have a storage spacing between elements. This spacing is specified by an increment parameter. For example, suppose a vector x having components x_i, $i = 1, \ldots, N$, is stored in a DOUBLE PRECISION array DX( ) with increment parameter INCX. If INCX ≥ 0 then x_i is stored in DX(1 + $(i - 1) *$ INCX). If INCX < 0 then x_i is stored in DX(1 + (N $-$ $i) * |$INCX$|$). This method of indexing when INCX < 0 avoids negative indices in the array DX( ) and thus permits the subprograms to be written in Fortran. Only positive values of INCX are allowed for operations 26–38 in Section 5 that each have a single vector argument.

It is intended that the loops in all subprograms process the elements of vector arguments in order of increasing vector component indices, i.e. in the order x_i, $i = 1, \ldots, N$. This implies processing in reverse storage order when INCX < 0. If these subprograms are implemented on a computer having parallel processing capability, it is recommended that this order of processing be adhered to as nearly as is reasonable.

5. SPECIFICATION OF THE BLAS SUBPROGRAMS

Type and dimension information for variables occurring in the subprogram specifications are as follows:

$$mx = \max(1, N * |INCX|), \qquad my = \max(1, N * |INCY|).$$

```
INTEGER  N, INCX, INCY, IMAX, QC(10)
REAL  SX(mx), SY(my), SA, SB, SC, SS
REAL  SD1, SD2, SB1, SB2, SPARAM(5), SW
DOUBLE PRECISION  DX(mx), DY(my), DA, DB, DC, DS
DOUBLE PRECISION  DD1, DD2, DB1, DB2, DPARAM(5), DW
COMPLEX  CX(mx), CY(my), CA, CW
```

Type declarations for function names are as follows:

INTEGER ISAMAX, IDAMAX, ICAMAX
REAL SDOT, SDSDOT, SNRM2, SCNRM2, SASUM, SCASUM
DOUBLE PRECISION DSDOT, DDOT, DQDOTI, DQDOTA, DNRM2, DASUM
COMPLEX CDOTC CDOTU

Dot Product Subprograms

1. SW = SDOT(N, SX, INCX, SY, INCY),

$$w := \sum_{i=1}^{N} x_i y_i.$$

2. DW = DSDOT(N, SX, INCX, SY, INCY),

$$w := \sum_{i=1}^{N} x_i y_i.$$

Double precision accumulation is used within the subprogram DSDOT.

3. SW = SDSDOT(N, SB, SX, INCX, SY, INCY),

$$w := b + \sum_{i=1}^{N} x_i y_i.$$

The accumulation of the inner product and the addition of b are in double precision. The conversion of the final result to single precision is done in the same way as the intrinsic function SNGL( ).

4. DW = DDOT(N, DX, INCX, DY, INCY),

$$w := \sum_{i=1}^{N} x_i y_i.$$

5. DW = DQDOTI(N, DB, QC, DX, INCX, DY, INCY),

$$w := b + \sum_{i=1}^{N} x_i y_i.$$

The input data, b, x, and y, are converted internally to extended precision. The result is stored in extended precision form in QC( ) and returned in double precision form as the value of the function DQDOTI.

6. DW = DQDOTA(N, DB, QC, DX, INCX, DY, INCY),

$$w := c := b + c + \sum_{i=1}^{N} x_i y_i.$$

The input value of c in QC( ) is in extended precision. The value c must have resulted from a previous execution of DQDOTI or DQDOTA since no other way is provided for defining an extended precision number. The computation is done in extended precision arithmetic and the result is stored in extended precision form in QC( ) and is returned in double precision form as the function value DQDOTA.

7. CW = CDOTC(N, CX, INCX, CY, INCY),

$$w := \sum_{i=1}^{N} \bar{x}_i y_i.$$

The suffix C on CDOTC indicates that the complex conjugates of the components x_i are used.

8. CW = CDOTU(N, CX, INCX, CY, INCY),

$$w := \sum_{i=1}^{N} x_i y_i.$$

The suffix U on CDOTU indicates that the vector components x_i are used unconjugated.

In the preceding eight subprograms the value of $\sum_{i=1}^{N}$ will be set to zero if $N \le 0$.

Elementary Vector Operation: $y := ax + y$

9. CALL SAXPY(N, SA, SX, INCX, SY, INCY).
10. CALL DAXPY(N, DA, DX, INCX, DY, INCY).
11. CALL CAXPY(N, CA, CX, INCX, CY, INCY).

If $a = 0$ or if $N \le 0$ these subroutines return immediately.

Construct Givens Plane Rotation

12. CALL SROTG(SA, SB, SC, SS).
13. CALL DROTG(DA, DB, DC, DS).

Given a and b, each of these subroutines computes

$$\sigma = \begin{cases} \operatorname{sgn}(a) & \text{if } |a| > |b|, \\ \operatorname{sgn}(b) & \text{if } |b| \ge |a|, \end{cases} \qquad r = \sigma(a^2 + b^2)^{1/2},$$

$$c = \begin{cases} a/r & \text{if } r \ne 0, \\ 1 & \text{if } r = 0, \end{cases} \qquad s = \begin{cases} b/r & \text{if } r \ne 0, \\ 0 & \text{if } r = 0. \end{cases}$$

The numbers c, s, and r then satisfy the matrix equation

$$\begin{bmatrix} c & s \\ -s & c \end{bmatrix} \cdot \begin{bmatrix} a \\ b \end{bmatrix} = \begin{bmatrix} r \\ 0 \end{bmatrix}.$$

The introduction of σ is not essential to the computation of a Givens rotation matrix, but its use permits later stable reconstruction of c and s from just one stored number, an idea due to Stewart [15]. For this purpose the subroutine also computes

$$z = \begin{cases} s & \text{if } |a| > |b|, \\ 1/c & \text{if } |b| \ge |a| \text{ and } c \ne 0, \\ 1 & \text{if } c = 0. \end{cases}$$

The subroutines return r overwriting a, and z overwriting b, as well as returning c and s.

If the user later wishes to reconstruct c and s from z, it can be done as follows:

If $z = 1$ set $c = 0$ and $s = 1$.
If $|z| < 1$ set $c = (1 - z^2)^{1/2}$ and $s = z$.
If $|z| > 1$ set $c = 1/z$ and $s = (1 - c^2)^{1/2}$.

Apply a Plane Rotation

14. CALL SROT(N, SX, INCX, SY, INCY, SC, SS).
15. CALL DROT(N, DX, INCX, DY, INCY, DC, DS).

Each of these subroutines computes

$$\begin{bmatrix} x_i \\ y_i \end{bmatrix} := \begin{bmatrix} c & s \\ -s & c \end{bmatrix} \cdot \begin{bmatrix} x_i \\ y_i \end{bmatrix} \quad \text{for} \quad i = 1, \ldots, \text{N}.$$

If $\text{N} \le 0$ or if $c = 1$ and $s = 0$ the subroutines return immediately.

Construct a Modified Givens Transformation

16. CALL SROTMG(SD1, SD2, SB1, SB2, SPARAM).
17. CALL DROTMG(DD1, DD2, DB1, DB2, DPARAM).

The input quantities d_1, d_2, b_1, and b_2 define a 2-vector $[a_1, a_2]^T$ in partitioned form as

$$\begin{bmatrix} a_1 \\ a_2 \end{bmatrix} = \begin{bmatrix} d_1^{1/2} & 0 \\ 0 & d_2^{1/2} \end{bmatrix} \cdot \begin{bmatrix} b_1 \\ b_2 \end{bmatrix}.$$

The subroutine determines the modified Givens rotation matrix H, as defined in eqs. (A6) and (A7) of the Appendix, that transforms b_2, and thus a_2, to zero. A representation of this matrix is stored in the array SPARAM( ) or DPARAM( ) as follows. Locations in PARAM not listed are left unchanged.

PARAM(1) = 1, case of eq. (A7)	PARAM(1) = 0, case of eq. (A6)	PARAM(1) = −1, case of rescaling
$h_{12} = 1$, $h_{21} = -1$	$h_{11} = h_{22} = 1$	PARAM(2) = h_{11}
PARAM(2) = h_{11}	PARAM(3) = h_{21}	PARAM(3) = h_{21}
PARAM(5) = h_{22}	PARAM(4) = h_{12}	PARAM(4) = h_{12}
		PARAM(5) = h_{22}

In addition PARAM(1) = −2 indicates $H = I$.

The values of d_1, d_2, and b_1 are changed to represent the effect of the transformation. The quantity b_2 which would be zeroed by the transformation is left unchanged in storage.

The input value of d_1 should be nonnegative, but d_2 can be negative for the purpose of removing data from a least squares problem. Further details can be found in the Appendix.

Apply a Modified Givens Transformation

18. CALL SROTM(N, SX, INCX, SY, INCY, SPARAM).
19. CALL DROTM(N, DX, INCX, DY, INCY, DPARAM).

Let H denote the modified Givens transformation defined by the parameter array SPARAM( ) or DPARAM( ). The subroutines compute

$$\begin{bmatrix} x_i \\ y_i \end{bmatrix} := H \begin{bmatrix} x_i \\ y_i \end{bmatrix} \quad \text{for} \quad i = 1, \ldots, \text{N}.$$

If $\text{N} \le 0$ or if H is an identity matrix the subroutines return immediately. See the Appendix for further details.

Copy a Vector x to y: y := x

20. CALL SCOPY(N, SX, INCX, SY, INCY).
21. CALL DCOPY(N, DX, INCX, DY, INCY).
22. CALL CCOPY(N, CX, INCX, CY, INCY).

Return immediately if N ≤ 0.

Interchange Vectors x and y: x :=: y

23. CALL SSWAP(N, SX, INCX, SY, INCY).
24. CALL DSWAP(N, DX, INCX, DY, INCY).
25. CALL CSWAP(N, CX, INCX, CY, INCY).

Return immediately if N ≤ 0.

Euclidean Length or ℓ_2 Norm of a Vector

$$w := \left[\sum_{i=1}^{N} |x_i|^2 \right]^{1/2}$$

26. SW = SNRM2(N, SX, INCX).
27. DW = DNRM2(N, DX, INCX).
28. SW = SCNRM2(N, CX, INCX).

If N ≤ 0 the result is set to zero.

Sum of Magnitudes of Vector Components

29. SW = SASUM(N, SX, INCX).
30. DW = DASUM(N, DX, INCX).
31. SW = SCASUM(N, CX, INCX).

The functions SASUM and DASUM compute $w := \sum_{i=1}^{N} |x_i|$. The function SCASUM computes

$$w := \sum_{i=1}^{N} \{|\mathrm{Re}(x_i)| + |\mathrm{Im}(x_i)|\}.$$

These functions return immediately with the result set to zero if N ≤ 0.

Vector Scaling: x := ax

32. CALL SSCAL(N, SA, SX, INCX).
33. CALL DSCAL(N, DA, DX, INCX).
34. CALL CSCAL(N, CA, CX, INCX).
35. CALL CSSCAL(N, SA, CX, INCX).

Return immediately if N ≤ 0.

Find Largest Component of a Vector

36. IMAX = ISAMAX(N, SX, INCX).
37. IMAX = IDAMAX(N, DX, INCX).
38. IMAX = ICAMAX(N, CX, INCX).

The functions ISAMAX and IDAMAX determine the smallest index i such that $|x_i| = \max\{|x_j| : j = 1, \ldots, N\}$.

The function ICAMAX determines the smallest index i such that $|x_i| = \max\{|\mathrm{Re}(x_j)| + |\mathrm{Im}(x_j)| : j = 1, \ldots, N\}$.

These functions set the result to zero and return immediately if N ≤ 0.

6. IMPLEMENTATION

In addition to the Fortran versions, all of the subprograms except DQDOTI and DQDOTA are also supplied in assembler language for the Univac 1108, the IBM 360/67, and the CDC 6600 and 7600. The Fortran versions of DQDOTI and DQDOTA use part of Brent's multiple precision package [6]. Assembler language modules for these two subprograms are given only for the Univac 1108.

Only four of the assembly routines for the CDC 6600 and 7600 take advantage of the pipeline architecture of these machines. The four routines SDOT( ), SAXPY( ), SROT( ), and SROTM( ) are those typically used in the innermost loop of computations. Some timing results are given in Section 8.

7. RELATION TO THE ANSI FORTRAN STANDARD

American National Standard Fortran, ANSI X3.9-1966 [1, 3, 4], which will be referred to as 1966 FORTRAN, is widely supported by existing Fortran compilers. We will refer to American National Standard Fortran, ANSI X3.9-1977 [2], as FORTRAN 77.

The calling sequences of the BLAS subprograms would require that the subprograms contain declarations of the form

REAL SX(MAX0(1, N*IABS(INCX)))

to precisely specify the array lengths. Neither 1966 FORTRAN nor FORTRAN 77 permits such a statement. A statement of the form REAL SX(1) is permitted by major Fortran compilers to cover cases in which it is inconvenient to specify an exact dimension. This latter form is used in the BLAS subprograms even though it does not conform to 1966 FORTRAN. FORTRAN 77 allows the form REAL SX(*) for this situation. Thus the BLAS package can be made to conform to FORTRAN 77 by changing 1's to *'s in the subprogram array declarations.

EXAMPLE A.1: The matrix product C=AB Given M × K and K × N matrices A and B, compute the M × N product matrix C = AB.

The coding technique for this computation is based on the fact that each element c_{IJ} of C is the dot product of row I of A and column J of B.

```
      DIMENSION A(20,20),B(15,10),C(20,15)
C
      MDA=20
      MDB=15
      MDC=20
C
      M=10
      K=15
      N=10
C
C     FORM THE DOT PRODUCT OF ROW I OF A WITH COLUMN J OF B. EACH OF THESE
C     VECTORS IS OF LENGTH K. THE VALUE OF MDA IS THE STORAGE INCREMENT
C     BETWEEN ELEMENTS OF ROW VECTORS OF A.
C
                         DO 10 I=1,M
                         DO 10 J=1,N
10                       C(I,J)=SDOT(K,A(I,1),MDA,B(1,J),1)
```

EXAMPLE A.2: The solution of Ax = b where A is upper triangular Solve an N × N upper triangular nonsingular system of algebraic equations, **Ax** = **b**. The method used is based on the observation that if we compute the component $x_N = b_N/a_{NN}$, then we have a new problem in N − 1 unknowns, still upper triangular, with the new right-side vector $(b_1 - a_{1N}x_N, \ldots, b_{N-1} - a_{N-1,N}x_N)^T$. In this example the solution vector **x** overwrites the vector **b** in the array B(∗).

```
      DO 20 II=1,N
      I=N+1-II
      B(I)=B(I)/A(I,I)
20    CALL SAXPY (I-1,-B(I),A(1,I),1,B,1)
```

EXAMPLE A.3: Scale the rows of a matrix Row-equilibrate an N × N matrix A. (Divide each nonzero row vector of A by the entry in that row of maximum magnitude.) Here MDA is the first dimensioning parameter of the array A(∗,∗).

```
      DO 40 I=1,N
      JMAX=ISAMAX(N,A(I,1),MDA)
      T=A(I,JMAX)
      IF(T.EQ.0.E0) GO TO 40
      CALL SSCAL(N,1.E0/T,A(I,1),MDA)
40    CONTINUE
```

When using ISAMAX( ) to choose row pivots in Gaussian elimination, for example, the major loop contains a statement of the form

```
      IMAX=ISAMAX(N-J+1,A(J,J),1)+J-1
```

At that point IMAX corresponds to the row that will be interchanged with row J. Thus the offset value J − 1 must be added to the computed value of ISAMAX( ) to get the actual row number to interchange.

EXAMPLE A.4: Set A to the identity, then set B=A Set an N × N matrix A to the N × N identity matrix. Then set B = A. Notice that a storage increment value of 0 for the first vector argument of SCOPY( ) is used. This "broadcasts" the values of 0.E0 and 1.E0 into the second vector argument.

Here MDA is the first dimensioning parameter of the array A(∗,∗).

```
      DO 50 J=1,N
50    CALL SCOPY(N,0.E0,0,A(1,J),1)

      CALL SCOPY(N,1.E0,0,A,MDA+1)

      DO 60 J=1,N
60    CALL SCOPY(N,A(1,J),1,B(1,J),1)
```

EXAMPLE A.5: Interchange the columns of a matrix Interchange or swap the columns of an M × N matrix C. The column to be interchanged with column J is in a type INTEGER array IP(*), and has the value IP(J).

```
      DO 70 J=1,N
      L=IP(J)
      IF(J.NE.L) CALL SSWAP(M,C(1,J),1,C(1,L),1)
70    CONTINUE
```

EXAMPLE A.6: Transpose a matrix in place In this example we want to transpose an N × N matrix A in-place (*in situ*), where N > 1. Here MDA is the first dimensioning parameter of the array A(*,*).

```
      NM1=N-1
      DO 80 J=1,NM1
80    CALL SSWAP(N-J,A(J,J+1),MDA,A(J+1,J),1)
```

APPENDIX

B

THE LINPACK PROGRAMS

LINPACK is a collection of Fortran programs for solving various types of linear systems. The package is concerned with general, banded, symmetric indefinite, symmetric positive definite, triangular, and tridiagonal square matrices, as well as with least squares problems and the QR and singular value decompositions of rectangular matrices. The routines are designed to be completely machine independent, fully portable, and to run with satisfactory efficiency in most operating environments. See Dongarra et al. (1979) for complete details. They are available at a nominal cost from IMSL, Inc., Sixth Floor, GNB Building, 7500 Bellaire Blvd., Houston, TX 77036.

LINPACK is one of several (including EISPACK described later) significant software projects of NATS (National Activity to Test Software) supported by the National Science Foundation and the Department of Energy. The principal contributors to LINPACK are J. J. Dongarra, J. R. Bunch, C. B. Moler, and G. W. Stewart.

The overall design of LINPACK has been strongly influenced by TAMPR and the BLAS. TAMPR is a software development system created by Jim Boyle and Ken Dritz at Argonne National Laboratories. It manipulates and formats structured Fortran programs to clarify the structure, and it can take one basic program and automatically provide several variants targeted for different environments. The "master" LINPACK subroutines use complex arithmetic, and TAMPR produces the versions which use single precision, double precision, and double precision complex arithmetic.

The BLAS (described in the preceding section) contribute to the modularity and clarity of the LINPACK subroutines, as well as to its execution time efficiency. However, using TAMPR it is possible to produce a version of LINPACK which does not use the BLAS, or which uses some other collection of basic vector operations such as a collection for a parallel computer.

An unusual feature of the LINPACK algorithms is that they are strongly column oriented rather than having the usual row orientations. This results in much greater efficiency in virtual memory computers due to the interaction between the column orientation of Fortran and the paging scheme of the computer.

The scope of the LINPACK project is seen from the following description of the program names and table of subroutines to be implemented. *The remainder of this section is directly reproduced from* Dongarra et al.†

A subroutine naming convention is employed in which each subroutine name is a coded specification of the computation done by that subroutine. All names consist of five letters in the form TXXYY . The first letter, T , indicates the matrix data type. Standard Fortran allows the use of three such types:

S	REAL
D	DOUBLE PRECISION
C	COMPLEX

In addition, some Fortran systems allow a double precision complex type:

Z	COMPLEX*16

The next two letters, XX , indicate the form of the matrix or its decomposition:

GE	General
GB	General band
PO	Positive definite
PP	Positive definite packed
PB	Positive definite band
SI	Symmetric indefinite
SP	Symmetric indefinite packed
HI	Hermitian indefinite
HP	Hermitian indefinite packed
TR	Triangular
GT	General tridiagonal
PT	Positive definite tridiagonal
CH	Cholesky decomposition
QR	Orthogonal-triangular decomposition
SV	Singular value decomposition

The final two letters, YY , indicate the computation done by a particular subroutine:

FA	Factor
CO	Factor and estimate condition
SL	Solve
DI	Determinant and/or inverse and/or inertia
DC	Decompose
UD	Update
DD	Downdate
EX	Exchange

† Copyright © 1979 by the Society for Industrial and Applied Mathematics. Reprinted by permission from J. J. Dongarra et al., *LINPACK Users' Guide*, Society of Industrial and Applied Mathematics, Philadelphia, pp. I.2–I.7, 1.2–1.8, C.1, and C.5.

The following chart shows all the LINPACK subroutines. The initial S in the names may be replaced by D , C or Z and the initial C in the complex-only names may be replaced by a Z .

	CO	FA	SL	DI
SGE	✓	✓	✓	✓
SGB	✓	✓	✓	✓
SPO	✓	✓	✓	✓
SPP	✓	✓	✓	✓
SPB	✓	✓	✓	✓
SSI	✓	✓	✓	✓
SSP	✓	✓	✓	✓
CHI	✓	✓	✓	✓
CHP	✓	✓	✓	✓
STR	✓		✓	✓
SGT			✓	
SPT			✓	

	DC	SL	UD	DD	EX
SCH	✓		✓	✓	✓
SQR	✓	✓			
SSV	✓				

The remaining sections of this Introduction cover some software design and numerical analysis topics which apply to the entire package. Each of the chapters 1 through 11 describes a particular group of subroutines, ordered roughly as indicated by the preceding chart. Each chapter includes Overview, Usage and Examples sections which are intended for all users. In addition many chapters include additional sections on Algorithms, Programming Details and Performance which are intended for users requiring more specific information. In order to make each chapter fairly self-contained, some material is repeated in several related chapters.

2. Software Design

The overall design of LINPACK has been strongly influenced by TAMPR and by the BLAS. TAMPR is a software development system created by Boyle and Dritz (1974). It manipulates and formats Fortran programs to clarify their structure. It also generates variants of programs. The "master versions" of all the LINPACK subroutines are those which use complex arithmetic; versions which use single precision, double precision, and double precision complex arithmetic have been produced automatically by TAMPR. A user may thus convert from one type of arithmetic to another by simply changing the declarations in his program and changing the first letter of the LINPACK subroutines being used.

Anyone reading the Fortran source code for LINPACK subroutines should find the loops and logical structures clearly delineated by the indentation generated by TAMPR.

The BLAS are the Basic Linear Algebra Subprograms designed by Lawson, Hanson, Kincaid and Krogh (1978). They contribute to the speed as well as to the modularity and clarity of the LINPACK subroutines. LINPACK is distributed with versions of the BLAS written in standard Fortran which are intended to provide reasonably efficient execution in most operating environments. However, a particular computing installation may substitute machine language versions of the BLAS and thereby perhaps improve efficiency.

LINPACK is designed to be completely machine independent. There are no machine dependent constants, no input/output statements, no character manipulation, no COMMON or EQUIVALENCE statements, and no mixed-mode arithmetic. All the subroutines (except those whose names begin with Z) use the portable subset of Fortran defined by the PFORT verifier of Ryder (1974).

There is no need for machine dependent constants because there is very little need to check for "small" numbers. For example, candidates for pivots in Gaussian elimination are checked against an exact zero rather than against some small quantity. The test for singularity is made instead by estimating the condition of the matrix; this is not only machine independent, but also far more reliable. The convergence of the iteration in the singular value decomposition is tested in a machine independent manner by statements of the form

```
TEST1 = something not small
TEST2 = TEST1 + something possibly small
IF (TEST1 .EQ. TEST2) ...
```

The absence of mixed-mode arithmetic implies that the single precision subroutines do not use any double precision arithmetic and hence that the double precision subroutines do not require any kind of extended precision. It also implies that LINPACK does not include a subroutine for iterative improvement; however, an example in Chapter 1 indicates how such a subroutine could be added by anyone with easy access to mixed-mode arithmetic. (Some of the BLAS involve mixed-mode arithmetic, but they are not used by LINPACK.)

Floating point underflows and overflows may occur in some of the LINPACK subroutines. Any underflows which occur are harmless. We hope that the operating system sets underflowed quantities to zero and continues operation without producing any error messages. With some operating systems, it may be necessary to insert control cards or call special system subroutines to achieve this type of underflow handling.

Overflows, if they occur, are much more serious. They must be regarded as error situations resulting from improper use of the subroutines or from unusual scaling. Many precautions against overflow have been taken in LINPACK, but it is impossible to absolutely prevent overflow without seriously degrading performance on reasonably scaled problems. It is expected that overflows will cause the operating system to terminate the computation and that the user will have to correct the program or rescale the problem before continuing.

Fortran stores matrices by columns and so programs in which the inner loop goes up or down a column, such as

```
      DO 20 J = 1, N
         DO 10 I = 1, N
            A(I,J) = ...
   10    CONTINUE
   20 CONTINUE
```

generate sequential access to memory. Programs in which the inner loop goes across a row cause non-sequential access. Sequential access is preferable on operating systems which employ virtual memory or other forms of paging. LINPACK is consequentially "column oriented". Almost all the inner loops occur within the BLAS and, although the BLAS allow a matrix to be accessed by rows, this provision is never used by LINPACK. The column orientation requires revision of some conventional algorithms, but results in significant improvement in performance on operating systems with paging and cache memory.

All square matrices which are parameters of LINPACK subroutines are specified in the calling sequences by three arguments, for example

```
      CALL SGEFA(A,LDA,N,...)
```

Here A is the name of a two-dimensional Fortran array, LDA is the leading dimension of that array, and N is the order of the matrix stored in the array or in a portion of the array. The two parameters LDA and N have different meanings and need not have the same value. The amount of storage reserved for the array A is determined by a declaration in the user's program and LDA refers to the leading, or first, dimension as specified in this declaration. For example, the declaration

```
      REAL A(50,50)
```

or

```
      DIMENSION A(50,50)
```

should be accompanied by the initialization

```
      DATA LDA/50/
```

or the statement

```
      LDA = 50
```

The value of LDA should not be changed unless the declaration is changed. The order N of a particular coefficient matrix may be any value not exceeding the leading dimension of the array, that is $N \le LDA$. The value of N may be changed by the user's program as systems of different orders are processed.

Rectangular matrices require a fourth argument, for example

```
CALL SQRDC(X,LDX,N,P,...)
```

Here the matrix is called X to adhere to the notation common in statistics, LDX is the leading dimension of the two-dimensional array, N is the number of rows in the matrix, and P is the number of columns. Note that the default Fortran typing conventions must be overridden by declaring P to be an integer. This conforms to usual statistical notation and is the only argument of a LINPACK subroutine which does not have the default type.

Many of the LINPACK subroutines have one or two arguments with the names JOB and INFO . JOB is always an input parameter. It is set by the user, often by simply including an integer constant in the call, to specify which of several possible computations are to be carried out. For example, SGESL solves a system of equations involving either the factored matrix or its transpose, and JOB should be zero or nonzero accordingly.

INFO is always an output parameter. It is used to return various kinds of diagnostic information from LINPACK routines. In some situations, INFO may be regarded as an error parameter. For example, in SPOFA , it is used to indicate that the matrix is not positive definite. In other situations, INFO may be one of the primary output quantities. For example, in SCHDC , it is an indication of the rank of a semi-definite matrix.

A few LINPACK subroutines require more space for storage of intermediate results than is provided by the primary parameters. These subroutines have a parameter WORK which is a one-dimensional array whose length is usually the number of rows or columns of the matrix being processed. The user will rarely be interested in the contents of WORK and so must merely provide the appropriate declaration.

Most of the LINPACK subroutines do not call any other LINPACK subroutine. The only set of exceptions involves the condition estimator subroutines, with names ending in CO , each of which calls the corresponding FA routine to factor the matrix. However, almost all the LINPACK subroutines call one or more of the BLAS. To facilitate construction of libraries, the source code for each LINPACK subroutine includes comments which list all of the BLAS and Fortran-supplied functions required by that subroutine.

2. Usage

Single precision, general matrices. The four subroutines for single precision, general matrices are SGECO, SGEFA, SGESL, and SGEDI. Ordinarily, SGECO or SGEFA will be called once to factor a particular matrix and then SGESL and SGEDI will be called to apply the factorization as many times as needed.

SGECO uses Gaussian elimination with partial pivoting to compute the LU factorization of a matrix and then estimates its condition. The calling sequence is

```
CALL SGECO(A,LDA,N,IPVT,RCOND,Z) .
```

On entry,

- A — is a doubly subscripted array with dimension (LDA,N) which contains the matrix whose factorization is to be computed.
- LDA — is the leading dimension of the array A .
- N — is the order of the matrix A and the number of elements in the vectors IPVT and Z .

On return,

- A — contains in its upper triangle an upper triangular matrix U and in its strict lower triangle the multipliers necessary to construct a matrix L so that A = LU .
- IPVT — is a singly subscripted integer array of dimension N which contains the pivot information necessary to construct the permutations in L . Specifically, IPVT(K) is the index of the K-th pivot row.
- RCOND — is an estimate of the reciprocal condition, $1/\kappa(A)$. If RCOND is so small that the logical expression 1.0 + RCOND .EQ. 1.0 is true, then A can usually be regarded as singular to working precision. If RCOND is exactly zero, then SGESL and SGEDI may divide by zero.
- Z — is a singly subscripted array of dimension N used for work space. If A is close to a singular matrix, then Z will contain an approximate null vector in the sense that $\|Az\| = \text{RCOND}\cdot\|A\|\cdot\|z\|$ (see Section 4).

SGEFA should be used in place of SGECO if the condition estimate is not needed. The calling sequence is

```
CALL SGEFA(A,LDA,N,IPVT,INFO) ,
```

On entry,

A — is a doubly subscripted array with dimension (LDA,N) which contains the matrix whose factorization is to be computed.

LDA — is the leading dimension of the array A .

N — is the order of the matrix A and the number of elements in the vector IPVT .

On return,

A — contains in its upper triangle an upper triangular matrix U and in its strict lower triangle the multipliers necessary to construct a matrix L so that A = LU .

IPVT — is a singly subscripted integer array of dimension N which contains the pivot information necessary to construct the permutations in L . Specifically, IPVT(K) is the index of the K-th pivot row.

INFO — is an integer returned by SGEFA which, if it is 0 , indicates that SGESL and SGEDI can be safely used. If INFO = K ≠ 0 , then SGESL and SGEDI may divide by U(K,K) = 0.0 . If U has several zero diagonal elements, K will be the index of the last one. Although a nonzero INFO technically indicates singularity, RCOND is a more reliable indicator.

SGECO is usually called first to factor the matrix and estimate its condition. The actual factorization is done by SGEFA which can be called in place of SGECO if the condition estimate is not needed. The time required by SGECO is roughly (1 + 9/N) times the time required by SGEFA . Thus when N = 9 , SGECO costs twice as much as SGEFA , but when N = 90 , SGECO costs 10 percent more.

Since any matrix has an LU factorization, there is no error return from SGECO or SGEFA . However, the factors can be singular and consequently unusable by SGESL and SGEDI . Either RCOND or INFO should be tested before calling SGESL .

SGESL uses the LU factorization of a matrix A to solve linear systems of the form

$$Ax = b$$

or

$$A^T x = b$$

where A^T is the transpose of A . The calling sequence is

```
CALL SGESL(A,LDA,N,IPVT,B,JOB) .
```

On entry,

A is a doubly subscripted array with dimension (LDA,N) which contains the factorization computed by SGECO or SGEFA . It is not changed by SGESL .

LDA is the leading dimension of the array A .

N is the order of the matrix A and the number of elements in the vectors B and IPVT .

IPVT is a singly subscripted integer array of dimension N which contains the pivot information from SGECO or SGEFA .

B is a singly subscripted array of dimension N which contains the right hand side b of a system of simultaneous linear equations $Ax = b$ or $A^T x = b$.

JOB indicates what is to be computed. If JOB is 0 , the system $Ax = b$ is solved and if JOB is nonzero, the system $A^T x = b$ is solved.

On return,

B contains the solution, x .

Double precision, general matrices. The calling sequences of the double precision, general subroutines DGECO , DGEFA , DGESL and DGEDI are the same as those of the corresponding single precision "S" subroutines except that A , B , RCOND , DET , Z and WORK are DOUBLE PRECISION variables.

Complex, general matrices. The calling sequences of the complex, general subroutines CGECO , CGEFA , CGESL and CGEDI are the same as those of the corresponding single precision "S" subroutines except that A , B , DET , Z and WORK are COMPLEX variables, RCOND is a REAL variable and the system solved by CGESL when JOB is nonzero involves the complex conjugate transpose of A .

Double precision complex, general matrices. In those computing systems where they are available, the calling sequences of the double precision complex, general subroutines ZGECO , ZGEFA , ZGESL and ZGEDI are the same as those of the corresponding single precision "S" subroutines except that A , B , DET , Z and WORK are COMPLEX*16 variables, RCOND is a DOUBLE PRECISION variable and the system solved by ZGESL when JOB is nonzero involves the complex conjugate transpose of A .

3. Examples

The following program segments illustrate the use of the single precision subroutines for general matrices. Examples showing the use of the "D" , "C" and "Z" subroutines could be obtained by changing the subroutine names and type declarations.

The first program factors a matrix, tests for near singularity and then solves a single system $Ax = b$.

```
      REAL A(50,50),B(50),Z(50),T,RCOND
      INTEGER IPVT(50)
      DATA LDA /50/
      N = ...
      DO 20 J = 1, N
         DO 10 I = 1, N
            A(I,J) = ...
   10    CONTINUE
   20 CONTINUE
      CALL SGECO(A,LDA,N,IPVT,RCOND,Z)
      WRITE(..., ...) RCOND
      T = 1.0 + RCOND
      IF (T .EQ. 1.0) GO TO 90
      DO 30 I = 1, N
         B(I) = ...
   30 CONTINUE
      CALL SGESL(A,LDA,N,IPVT,B,0)
      DO 40 I = 1, N
         WRITE(..., ...) B(I)
   40 CONTINUE
      STOP
   90 WRITE(..., 99)
   99 FORMAT(40H MATRIX IS SINGULAR TO WORKING PRECISION)
      STOP
      END
```

The next program segment replaces C , a matrix with K columns by $A^{-1}C$ without explicitly forming A^{-1} .

```
      CALL SGEFA(A,LDA,N,IPVT,INFO)
      IF (INFO .NE. 0) GO TO ...
      DO 10 J = 1, K
         CALL SGESL(A,LDA,N,IPVT,C(1,J),0)
   10 CONTINUE
```

The next program segment replaces C , a matrix with K rows by CA^{-1} without explicitly forming A^{-1} . Since this involves the rows rather than the columns of C , the device used in the previous example is not applicable.

```
      CALL SGEFA(A,LDA,N,IPVT,INFO)
      IF (INFO .NE. 0) GO TO ...
      DO 30 I = 1, K
         DO 10 J = 1, N
            Z(J) = C(I,J)
   10    CONTINUE
         CALL SGESL(A,LDA,N,IPVT,Z,1)
         DO 20 J = 1, N
            C(I,J) = Z(J)
   20    CONTINUE
   30 CONTINUE
```

The next segment prints out the condition number and the determinant of a matrix. The determinant is printed with a simulated E format that allows a four-digit exponent and avoids underflow/overflow difficulties.

```
      CALL SGECO(A,LDA,N,IPVT,RCOND,Z)
      IF (RCOND .EQ. 0.0) GO TO ...
      COND = 1.0/RCOND
      CALL SGEDI(A,LDA,N,IPVT,DET,Z,10)
      K = INT(DET(2))
      WRITE(..., 10) COND,DET(1),K
   10 FORMAT(13H CONDITION = , E15.5/15H DETERMINANT = , F20.15, 1HE, I5)
```

The next example illustrates how the actual condition number, COND , of a matrix might be computed by forming the matrix inverse. Such a computation would be of interest primarily to numerical analysts who wish to investigate the claim that RCOND returned by SGECO is a good estimate of 1/COND .

```
      ANORM = 0.0
      DO 10 J = 1, N
         ANORM = AMAX1(ANORM, SASUM(N,A(1,J),1) )
   10 CONTINUE
      CALL SGECO(A,LDA,N,IPVT,RCOND,Z)
      IF (RCOND .EQ. 0.0) GO TO ...
      CALL SGEDI(A,LDA,N,IPVT,DUMMY,WORK,1)
      AINORM = 0.0
      DO 20 J = 1, N
         AINORM = AMAX1(AINORM, SASUM(N,A(1,J),1) )
   20 CONTINUE
      COND = ANORM*AINORM
      RATIO = RCOND*COND
```

The Basic Linear Algebra Subprogram expression

```
      SASUM(N,A(1,J),1)
```

computes

$$\sum_{I=1}^{N} |A(I,J)| .$$

Appendix C: Program Listings

```
      SUBROUTINE SGECO(A,LDA,N,IPVT,RCOND,Z)
      INTEGER LDA,N,IPVT(1)
      REAL A(LDA,1),Z(1)
      REAL RCOND
C
C     SGECO FACTORS A REAL MATRIX BY GAUSSIAN ELIMINATION
C     AND ESTIMATES THE CONDITION OF THE MATRIX.
C
C     IF  RCOND  IS NOT NEEDED, SGEFA IS SLIGHTLY FASTER.
C     TO SOLVE  A*X = B , FOLLOW SGECO BY SGESL.
C     TO COMPUTE  INVERSE(A)*C , FOLLOW SGECO BY SGESL.
C     TO COMPUTE  DETERMINANT(A) , FOLLOW SGECO BY SGEDI.
C     TO COMPUTE  INVERSE(A) , FOLLOW SGECO BY SGEDI.
C
C     ON ENTRY
C
C        A       REAL(LDA, N)
C                THE MATRIX TO BE FACTORED.
C
C        LDA     INTEGER
C                THE LEADING DIMENSION OF THE ARRAY  A .
C
C        N       INTEGER
C                THE ORDER OF THE MATRIX  A .
C
C     ON RETURN
C
C        A       AN UPPER TRIANGULAR MATRIX AND THE MULTIPLIERS
C                WHICH WERE USED TO OBTAIN IT.
C                THE FACTORIZATION CAN BE WRITTEN  A = L*U  WHERE
C                L  IS A PRODUCT OF PERMUTATION AND UNIT LOWER
C                TRIANGULAR MATRICES AND  U  IS UPPER TRIANGULAR.
C
C        IPVT    INTEGER(N)
C                AN INTEGER VECTOR OF PIVOT INDICES.
C
C        RCOND   REAL
C                AN ESTIMATE OF THE RECIPROCAL CONDITION OF  A .
C                FOR THE SYSTEM  A*X = B , RELATIVE PERTURBATIONS
C                IN  A  AND  B  OF SIZE  EPSILON  MAY CAUSE
C                RELATIVE PERTURBATIONS IN  X  OF SIZE  EPSILON/RCOND .
C                IF  RCOND  IS SO SMALL THAT THE LOGICAL EXPRESSION
C                           1.0 + RCOND .EQ. 1.0
C                IS TRUE, THEN  A  MAY BE SINGULAR TO WORKING
C                PRECISION.  IN PARTICULAR,  RCOND  IS ZERO  IF
C                EXACT SINGULARITY IS DETECTED OR THE ESTIMATE
C                UNDERFLOWS.
C
C        Z       REAL(N)
C                A WORK VECTOR WHOSE CONTENTS ARE USUALLY UNIMPORTANT.
C                IF  A  IS CLOSE TO A SINGULAR MATRIX, THEN  Z  IS
C                AN APPROXIMATE NULL VECTOR IN THE SENSE THAT
C                NORM(A*Z) = RCOND*NORM(A)*NORM(Z) .
C
C     LINPACK. THIS VERSION DATED 08/14/78 .
C     CLEVE MOLER, UNIVERSITY OF NEW MEXICO, ARGONNE NATIONAL LAB.
C
C     SUBROUTINES AND FUNCTIONS
C
C     LINPACK SGEFA
C     BLAS SAXPY,SDOT,SSCAL,SASUM
```

```
      SUBROUTINE SGEFA(A,LDA,N,IPVT,INFO)
      INTEGER LDA,N,IPVT(1),INFO
      REAL A(LDA,1)
C
C     SGEFA FACTORS A REAL MATRIX BY GAUSSIAN ELIMINATION.
C
C     SGEFA IS USUALLY CALLED BY SGECO, BUT IT CAN BE CALLED
C     DIRECTLY WITH A SAVING IN TIME IF  RCOND  IS NOT NEEDED.
C     (TIME FOR SGECO) = (1 + 9/N)*(TIME FOR SGEFA) .
C
C     ON ENTRY
C
C        A       REAL(LDA, N)
C                THE MATRIX TO BE FACTORED.
C
C        LDA     INTEGER
C                THE LEADING DIMENSION OF THE ARRAY  A .
C
C        N       INTEGER
C                THE ORDER OF THE MATRIX  A .
C
C     ON RETURN
C
C        A       AN UPPER TRIANGULAR MATRIX AND THE MULTIPLIERS
C                WHICH WERE USED TO OBTAIN IT.
C                THE FACTORIZATION CAN BE WRITTEN  A = L*U  WHERE
C                L  IS A PRODUCT OF PERMUTATION AND UNIT LOWER
C                TRIANGULAR MATRICES AND  U  IS UPPER TRIANGULAR.
C
C        IPVT    INTEGER(N)
C                AN INTEGER VECTOR OF PIVOT INDICES.
C
C        INFO    INTEGER
C                = 0  NORMAL VALUE.
C                = K  IF  U(K,K) .EQ. 0.0 .  THIS IS NOT AN ERROR
C                     CONDITION FOR THIS SUBROUTINE, BUT IT DOES
C                     INDICATE THAT SGESL OR SGEDI WILL DIVIDE BY ZERO
C                     IF CALLED.  USE  RCOND  IN SGECO FOR A RELIABLE
C                     INDICATION OF SINGULARITY.
C
C     LINPACK. THIS VERSION DATED 08/14/78 .
C     CLEVE MOLER, UNIVERSITY OF NEW MEXICO, ARGONNE NATIONAL LAB.
C
C     SUBROUTINES AND FUNCTIONS
C
C     BLAS SAXPY,SSCAL,ISAMAX
C
C     INTERNAL VARIABLES
C
      REAL T
      INTEGER ISAMAX,J,K,KP1,L,NM1
C
C
C     GAUSSIAN ELIMINATION WITH PARTIAL PIVOTING
C
      INFO = 0
      NM1 = N - 1
      IF (NM1 .LT. 1) GO TO 70
      DO 60 K = 1, NM1
         KP1 = K + 1
C
C        FIND L = PIVOT INDEX
C
```

APPENDIX

C

THE IMSL LIBRARY PROGRAMS FOR LINEAR ALGEBRAIC EQUATIONS

IMSL stands for International Mathematical and Statistical Libraries, Inc., which markets a large mathematical software library. Their philosophy is that a low cost and a resultant high volume will achieve commercial success. The library has over 400 subroutines and specific versions are available for computers from Burroughs, CDC, Data General, DEC, Hewlett-Packard, Honeywell, IBM, Univac, and Xerox. The library is leased for about $100 per month and updated every 12 to 18 months. For further information about the library and its contents see *IMSL Library General Information*, vol. 1, published by International Mathematical and Statistical Libraries, Inc., Sixth Floor, GNB Building, 7500 Bellaire Blvd., Houston, TX 77036; telephone: (713) 772-1927.

C.1 THE IMSL USER QUICK REFERENCE GUIDE

The reference manual for a library should be a self-contained user's guide. We reproduce the introductory material for Linear Algebraic Equations here to illustrate their approach to providing user documentation.†

† Copyright © 1979 by International Mathematical and Statistical Libraries, Inc. Reprinted by permission of International Mathematical and Statistical Libraries, Inc. from *Linear Algebraic Equations*, pp. L-1 to 6, LETQ1B-1 to 3, LETQ1F-1 to 3.

LINEAR ALGEBRAIC EQUATIONS

This chapter contains subroutines for solving systems of linear algebraic equations. Routines to solve linear least square problems, and to perform a singular value decomposition, are also included. The following discussion summarizes and clarifies the abilities that are included in Chapter L.

<u>Quick Reference Guide to Chapter Abilities</u>

This chapter contains the following subroutines:

Solutions of Linear Equations

Full storage mode, real matrices
LEQT1F - Space economizer solution
LEQT2F - High accuracy solution

Positive definite matrices - symmetric storage mode
LEQT1P - Space economizer solution
LEQT2P - High accuracy solution

Positive definite matrices - band symmetric storage mode
LEQ1PB - Space economizer solution
LEQ2PB - High accuracy solution

Indefinite symmetric matrices
LEQ1S - Space economizer solution
LEQ2S - High accuracy solution

Full storage mode, complex matrices
LEQT1C - Space economizer solution
LEQ2C - High accuracy solution

Band matrices - band storage mode, real matrices
LEQT1B - Space economizer solution
LEQT2B - High accuracy solution

Matrix Inversion

Full storage mode, real matrices
LINV1F - Space economizer solution
LINV2F - High accuracy solution

Positive definite matrices - symmetric storage mode
LINV1P - Space economizer solution
LINV2P - High accuracy solution

Positive definite matrices - band symmetric storage mode
LIN1PB - Space economizer solution
LIN2PB - High accuracy solution

Indefinite symmetric matrices
LEQ1S - Space economizer solution
LEQ2S - High accuracy solution

In place inversion and/or solution
LINV3F - Full storage mode
LINV3P - Symmetric storage mode - positive definite

Full storage mode, complex matrices
LEQT1C - Space economizer solution
LEQ2C - High accuracy solution

Band matrices - band storage mode, real matrices
LEQT1B - Space economizer solution
LEQT2B - High accuracy solution

Decomposition, Substitution, Improvement
Full storage mode
LUDATF - Decomposition
LUELMF - Substitution
LUREFF - Improvement

Positive definite matrices - symmetric storage mode
LUDECP - Decomposition
LUELMP - Substitution
LUREFP - Improvement

Positive definite matrices - band symmetric storage mode
LUDAPB - Decomposition
LUELPB - Substitution
LUREPB - Improvement

Rectangular Matrix Abilities
LLSQF - Solution of a linear least squares problem
LSVDF - Pseudo-inverse
LSVDF - Singular value decomposition

Note: Routines LUDAPB, LUDATF, and LUDECP can be used to compute the determinant of a matrix, and LSVDB can be used to compute a singular value decomposition of a bidiagonal (main diagonal plus one upper diagonal) matrix.

Featured Abilities

IMSL subroutines LEQT1F and LEQT2F contain many features not normally found in linear equation solvers. These features include:

1. Row equilibration.
2. Partial pivoting.
3. Optional a posteriori accuracy testing.
4. The use of iterative improvement - only if required.

Until James Bunch's 1969 Ph.D. thesis (University of California - Berkeley) was published, there was no numerically stable algorithm for symmetric indefinite matrices which retained symmetry throughout the code. IMSL has implemented this algorithm in subroutines LEQ1S and LEQ2S.

Subroutines LLSQF, LSVDF, and LSVDB are based on routines from the book, Lawson, C., and Hanson, R., Solving Least Squares Problems, Prentice-Hall, Inc., Englewood Cliffs, NJ, 1974.

Name Conventions for This Chapter

All names in this chapter start with L. All names end in one of the following:

F = Matrix is in full storage mode

P = Matrix is in symmetric storage mode and is positive definite

PB = Matrix is in band symmetric storage mode and is positive definite

S = Matrix is in symmetric storage mode

C = Matrix is complex in full storage mode

B = Matrix is in band storage mode

Special Instructions on Usage

The various matrix storage modes used by Chapter L routines, e.g., symmetric, band symmetric, band, are discussed in the Introduction under the heading "5.6 Matrix/Vector Storage Modes".

Some of the IMSL linear equation solvers have an input parameter IDGT, the number of decimal places of accuracy in the elements of the matrix A. The treatment of this parameter varies slightly from one routine to another. To understand this parameter, we now look at its use in the individual routines.

LEQT1F: If IDGT is greater than zero, this routine computes an approximate solution $\overline{X}$ to AX=B. Let $\overline{x}$ be a column of matrix $\overline{X}$ and b be the corresponding column of matrix B. The question is asked; "Is $\overline{x}$ the exact solution to some set of linear equations $\overline{A}\overline{x}=\overline{b}$ where A agrees with A, element by element, in the first IDGT digits and $\overline{b}$ agrees with b in the first IDGT digits?". If $\overline{x}$ is such an exact solution, it is accepted as a good answer. Otherwise a warning is produced. In this way, the user is assured of his answer (if indeed, assurance should be given). If IDGT equals 0, this accuracy test is bypassed.

For instance, suppose IDGT=3. Then the user obtains either,

(a) a solution to the perturbed problem where the perturbations do not affect the first three digits of the elements of A and b, or

(b) a warning message.

LEQT2F: This routine proceeds in the same manner as LEQT1F. If the computed solution does not pass the above test, a warning is produced and the routine tries iterative improvement. Iterative improvement is costly in both time and space. Thus, LEQT2F calls on iterative improvement only if needed. Once invoked, iterative improvement will successively refine the answer until it is correct to working precision. If the matrix is so ill-conditioned that improvement does not converge, a terminal error is produced. If IDGT equals 0, LEQT2F will bypass the accuracy test and perform iterative improvement.

LEQT1P, LEQT2P: The input parameter IDGT is also included in the calling sequence of these routines. For the present edition it is unused in LEQT1P. In LEQT2P, IDGT is an output variable giving the number of digits in the largest element in absolute value of the solution vector which were unchanged in the first improvement iteration.

LINV1F, LINV2F, LINV1P, LINV2P: IDGT is included as a parameter to the inversion routines since each one in turn calls a linear equation solver.

For further information on the concept of accuracy testing, the user is referred to B. A. Chartres and J. C. Geuder, "Computable error bounds for direct solution of linear equations", JACM, Volume 14, January, 1967, pp. 63-71.

Subtleties to Note

In many subroutines in this chapter there are error returns which state "the matrix is algorithmically singular" or "the matrix is algorithmically not positive definite". The numerical notions of singularity and definiteness are not the same as the mathematical notions. Numerical singularity (or algorithmic singularity) simply means that the algorithm failed because a small pivot (small or negative for routines for positive definite matrices) was encountered. The data matrix may or may not be mathematically singular. If the data matrix is mathematically singular, it will most likely obtain the error return. Likewise, a matrix that is mathematically positive definite but nearly singular may obtain the error return declaring it algorithmically not positive definite. A matrix that is not positive definite will most likely obtain the error return.

The user may desire an independent check of whether or not a given approximate solution $x \approx A^{-1}b$ can be accepted. The following discussion is intended to provide some basic information about this topic. Further details can be found in the references.

It is assumed that an n by n matrix A and right hand side vector b are given and that an approximate solution $x \approx A^{-1}b$ has been computed. A performance index p can be defined as follows:

$$p = \max_{1 \le i \le n} \left[\frac{\left| b_i - \sum_{j=1}^{n} a_{ij} x_j \right|}{BN + AN \cdot \sum_{j=1}^{n} |x_j|} \right]$$

where $BN = \max_{1 \le i \le n} |b_i|$,

$AN = \max_{1 \le i, j \le n} |a_{ij}|$.

If p is small, relative to working precision, then x is the exact solution of a problem with coefficient matrix A+E and right hand side b+f where

$$E = (e_{ij}), \quad |e_{ij}| \leq p \cdot AN,$$

and $$f = (f_i), \quad |f_i| \leq p \cdot BN.$$

Likewise, if such an E and f exists, p is small. In most cases, the matrix A and vector b are subject to input roundoff error, computational roundoff in the evaluation of their elements, or error in the experimental determination of their elements. In these cases, a small performance index is adequate justification for the approximate solution x to be accepted.

The "space economizer" versions of Chapter L linear equation solvers usually return an approximate solution x that has a small performance index. However, examples exists, for which this is not true. See [3, p. 78] for one such example. When LEQT1F or LEQT2F are called, and the IDGT accuracy test is passed, p is guaranteed to be smaller than 10^{-IDGT}.

The "high accuracy" versions of Chapter L linear equation solvers produce either an accurate (to working precision) approximate solution or a warning message. (There is no proof for this statement, nor have any counter-examples been produced.)

Occasionally, it may be desirable to compute an upper bound on the error of an approximate solution x. If an approximate inverse $C \cong A^{-1}$ is available (this can be computed by one of Chapter L inverters), the following formula produces such a bound:

$$||x-A^{-1}b|| \leq \frac{||C(b-Ax)||}{1 - ||CA-I||}$$

where $||CA-I|| < 1$, $||\cdot||$ is any vector-matrix compatible norm with $||I||=1$. It is advisable to use double working precision for evaluating this formula. See [4] for further details.

See references:

1. Forsythe, G. E., and Moler, C. E., Computer Solution of Linear Algebraic Systems, Prentice-Hall, Englewood Cliffs, New Jersey, 1967.

2. Wilkinson, J. H., Rounding Errors in Algebraic Processes, Prentice-Hall, Englewood Cliffs, New Jersey, 1963.

3. Wilkinson, J. H., "The solution of ill-conditioned linear equations", Mathematical Methods for Digital Computers, Editors, A. Ralston and H. Wilf, John Wiley, New York, 1967, Chapter 3.

4. Aird, T. J. and Lynch, R. E., "Computable accurate upper and lower error bounds for approximate solutions of linear algebraic systems", ACM TOMS, 1(3)1975, 217-231.

5. Stewart, G. W., Introduction to Matrix Computations, Academic Press, New York, 1973.

```
IMSL ROUTINE NAME   - LEQT1B

PURPOSE             - LINEAR EQUATION SOLUTION - BAND STORAGE
                        MODE - SPACE ECONOMIZER SOLUTION

USAGE               - CALL LEQT1B (A,N,NLC,NUC,IA,B,M,IB,IJOB,XL,
                        IER)

ARGUMENTS    A      - INPUT/OUTPUT MATRIX OF DIMENSION N BY
                        (NUC+NLC+1). SEE PARAMETER IJOB.
             N      - ORDER OF MATRIX A AND THE NUMBER OF ROWS IN
                        B. (INPUT)
             NLC    - NUMBER OF LOWER CODIAGONALS IN MATRIX A.
                        (INPUT)
             NUC    - NUMBER OF UPPER CODIAGONALS IN MATRIX A.
                        (INPUT)
             IA     - ROW DIMENSION OF MATRIX A EXACTLY AS
                        SPECIFIED IN THE DIMENSION STATEMENT IN THE
                        CALLING PROGRAM. (INPUT)
             B      - INPUT/OUTPUT MATRIX OF DIMENSION N BY M.
                        ON INPUT, B CONTAINS THE M RIGHT-HAND SIDES
                        OF THE EQUATION AX = B. ON OUTPUT, THE
                        SOLUTION MATRIX X REPLACES B. IF IJOB = 1,
                        B IS NOT USED.
             M      - NUMBER OF RIGHT HAND SIDES (COLUMNS IN B).
                        (INPUT)
             IB     - ROW DIMENSION OF MATRIX B EXACTLY AS
                        SPECIFIED IN THE DIMENSION STATEMENT IN THE
                        CALLING PROGRAM. (INPUT)
             IJOB   - INPUT OPTION PARAMETER. IJOB = I IMPLIES WHEN
                        I = 0, FACTOR THE MATRIX A AND SOLVE THE
                          EQUATION AX = B. ON INPUT, A CONTAINS THE
                          COEFFICIENT MATRIX OF THE EQUATION AX = B,
                          WHERE A IS ASSUMED TO BE AN N BY N BAND
                          MATRIX. A IS STORED IN BAND STORAGE MODE
                          AND THEREFORE HAS DIMENSION N BY
                          (NLC+NUC+1). ON OUTPUT, A IS REPLACED
                          BY THE U MATRIX OF THE L-U DECOMPOSITION
                          OF A ROWWISE PERMUTATION OF MATRIX A. U
                          IS STORED IN BAND STORAGE MODE.
                        I = 1, FACTOR THE MATRIX A. A CONTAINS THE
                          SAME INPUT/OUTPUT INFORMATION AS IF
                          IJOB = 0.
                        I = 2, SOLVE THE EQUATION AX = B. THIS
                          OPTION IMPLIES THAT LEQT1B HAS ALREADY
                          BEEN CALLED USING IJOB = 0 OR 1 SO THAT
                          THE MATRIX A HAS ALREADY BEEN FACTORED.
                          IN THIS CASE, OUTPUT MATRICES A AND XL
                          MUST HAVE BEEN SAVED FOR REUSE IN THE
                          CALL TO LEQT1B.
             XL     - WORK AREA OF DIMENSION N*(NLC+1). THE FIRST
                        NLC*N LOCATIONS OF XL CONTAIN COMPONENTS OF
                        THE L MATRIX OF THE L-U DECOMPOSITION OF A
                        ROWWISE PERMUTATION OF A. THE LAST N
                        LOCATIONS CONTAIN THE PIVOT INDICES.
```

```
            IER      - ERROR PARAMETER. (OUTPUT)
                       TERMINAL ERROR
                         IER = 129 INDICATES THAT MATRIX A IS
                           ALGORITHMICALLY SINGULAR. (SEE THE
                           CHAPTER L PRELUDE).

PRECISION/HARDWARE   - SINGLE AND DOUBLE/H32
                     - SINGLE/H36,H48,H60

REQD. IMSL ROUTINES  - UERTST,UGETIO

NOTATION             - INFORMATION ON SPECIAL NOTATION AND
                         CONVENTIONS IS AVAILABLE IN THE MANUAL
                         INTRODUCTION OR THROUGH IMSL ROUTINE UHELP
```

Algorithm

For a given N by N band matrix (stored in band storage mode), LEQT1B factors the matrix A into the L-U decomposition of a rowwise permutation of A and/or solves the system of equations AX=B.

LEQT1B utilizes row equilibration and partial pivoting.

See reference:

Martin, R.S. and Wilkinson, J.H., "Solution of symmetric and unsymmetric band equations and the calculation of eigenvectors of band matrices", Numerische Mathematik, 9(4)1967, 279-301.

Programming Notes

1. When IJOB=1, parameters B, M, and IB are not used in the program.

2. Input matrix A is destroyed when IJOB=0 or 1. When IJOB=0 or 2, B is destroyed.

3. The determinant of A can be computed after LEQT1B has been called as follows:

```
      DET = 1.0
      IXL = NLC*N
      DO 10 J=1,N
        IXL = IXL+1
        IP = XL(IXL)
        DET = DET*A(J,1)
        IF(IP .NE. J) DET=-DET
   10 CONTINUE
```

4. LEQT1B can be used to compute the inverse of a band matrix. This is done by calling LEQT1B with M=N, B=the N by N identity matrix and IJOB=0. When N is large, it may be more practical to compute the inverse a column at a time. To do this, first call LEQT1B with IJOB=1, to factor A. Then, make succeeding calls with M=1, B=a column of the identity matrix and IJOB=2. B will be replaced by the corresponding column of A inverse.

Example

This example inputs the 3 by 3 matrix A and solves the equation AX=B for B.

Input:

```
INTEGER N,NLC,NUC,IA,M,IB,IJOB,IER
REAL    A(3,3),B(3,3),XL(6)
```

$$A = \begin{bmatrix} 0. & 1. & 2. \\ 2. & 5. & 1. \\ 1. & 17. & 0. \end{bmatrix}$$

```
N    =  3
NLC  =  1
NUC  =  1
IA   =  3
```

$$B = \begin{bmatrix} 1. & 0. & 0. \\ 0. & 1. & 0. \\ 0. & 0. & 1. \end{bmatrix}$$

```
M    =  3
IB   =  3
IJOB =  0
CALL LEQT1B(A,N,NLC,NUC,IA,B,M,IB,IJOB,XL,IER)
   :
END
```

Output:

$$B = \begin{bmatrix} 5.25 & -2.125 & .125 \\ -2.125 & 1.065 & -.0625 \\ .125 & -\ .0625 & .0625 \end{bmatrix}$$

```
IER  =  0
```

```
IMSL ROUTINE NAME   - LEQT1F

PURPOSE             - LINEAR EQUATION SOLUTION - FULL STORAGE
                        MODE - SPACE ECONOMIZER SOLUTION.

USAGE               - CALL LEQT1F (A,M,N,IA,B,IDGT,WKAREA,IER)

ARGUMENTS     A     - INPUT MATRIX OF DIMENSION N BY N CONTAINING
                        THE COEFFICIENT MATRIX OF THE EQUATION
                        AX = B.
                      ON OUTPUT, A IS REPLACED BY THE LU
                        DECOMPOSITION OF A ROWWISE PERMUTATION OF
                        A.
              M     - NUMBER OF RIGHT-HAND SIDES. (INPUT)
              N     - ORDER OF A AND NUMBER OF ROWS IN B. (INPUT)
              IA    - ROW DIMENSION OF A AND B EXACTLY AS SPECIFIED
                        IN THE DIMENSION STATEMENT OF THE CALLING
                        PROGRAM. (INPUT)
              B     - INPUT MATRIX OF DIMENSION N BY M CONTAINING
                        RIGHT-HAND SIDES OF THE EQUATION AX = B.
                      ON OUTPUT, THE N BY M SOLUTION X REPLACES B.
              IDGT  - INPUT OPTION.
                      IF IDGT IS GREATER THAN 0, THE ELEMENTS OF
                        A AND B ARE ASSUMED TO BE CORRECT TO IDGT
                        DECIMAL DIGITS AND THE ROUTINE PERFORMS
                        AN ACCURACY TEST.
                      IF IDGT EQUALS ZERO, THE ACCURACY TEST IS
                        BYPASSED.
              WKAREA - WORK AREA OF DIMENSION GREATER THAN OR EQUAL
                        TO N.
              IER   - ERROR PARAMETER. (OUTPUT)
                      TERMINAL ERROR
                        IER = 129 INDICATES THAT MATRIX A IS
                          ALGORITHMICALLY SINGULAR. (SEE THE
                          CHAPTER L PRELUDE).
                      WARNING ERROR
                        IER = 34 INDICATES THAT THE ACCURACY TEST
                          FAILED.  THE COMPUTED SOLUTION MAY BE IN
                          ERROR BY MORE THAN CAN BE ACCOUNTED FOR
                          BY THE UNCERTAINTY OF THE DATA.  THIS
                          WARNING CAN BE PRODUCED ONLY IF IDGT IS
                          GREATER THAN 0 ON INPUT.  (SEE CHAPTER L
                          PRELUDE FOR FURTHER DISCUSSION).

PRECISION/HARDWARE  - SINGLE AND DOUBLE/H32
                    - SINGLE/H36,H48,H60

REQD. IMSL ROUTINES - LUDATF,LUELMF,UERTST,UGETIO

NOTATION            - INFORMATION ON SPECIAL NOTATION AND
                        CONVENTIONS IS AVAILABLE IN THE MANUAL
                        INTRODUCTION OR THROUGH IMSL ROUTINE UHELP
```

Algorithm

LEQT1F solves the set of linear equations AX=B for X, given the N by N matrix A (in full storage mode). The N by M solution X overwrites B. The chief advantage of this program is that it uses less space than LEQT2F.

This routine performs Gaussian elimination (Crout algorithm) with equilibration and partial pivoting.

See reference: Forsythe, George and Moler, Cleve B., Computer Solution of Linear Algebraic Systems, Englewood Cliffs, N. J., Prentice-Hall, Inc., 1967, Chapter 9.

Note: This routine uses a Crout algorithm for decomposition (as opposed to the elimination routine in the above reference).

Accuracy

If IDGT is greater than zero, elements of A are assumed to be correct to IDGT decimal digits. The solution X will be the exact solution - without any roundoff error - to a matrix $\bar{A}$ which agrees with A in the first IDGT decimal digits. If such a solution is not obtainable in the accuracy with which we are working, a warning is given (IER=34). If IDGT equals zero, this accuracy test is bypassed.

Example

This example solves the set of linear equations AX=B for X where A is a 3 by 3 matrix and B is a 3 by 4 matrix. Since IDGT≠0, an accuracy test is performed.

Input:

```
REAL A(4,4),B(4,4),WKAREA(16)
INTEGER M,N,IA,IDGT,IER

N     =   3
M     =   4
IA    =   4
IDGT  =   3
```

$$A = \begin{bmatrix} 33.000 & 16.0 & 72.0 & x \\ -24.000 & -10.0 & -57.0 & x \\ -8.000 & -4.0 & -17.0 & x \\ x & x & x & x \end{bmatrix}$$

$$B = \begin{bmatrix} 1.0 & 0.0 & 0.0 & -359.0 \\ 0.0 & 1.0 & 0.0 & 281.0 \\ 0.0 & 0.0 & 1.0 & 85.0 \\ x & x & x & x \end{bmatrix}$$

```
CALL LEQT1F (A,M,N,IA,B,IDGT,WKAREA,IER)
      .
      .
      .
END
```

Output:

IER = 0

$$A = \begin{bmatrix} -8.0 & -4.0 & -17.0 & x \\ 3.0 & 2.0 & -6.0 & x \\ -4.1250 & -0.25 & 0.375 & x \\ x & x & x & x \end{bmatrix}$$

$$B = \begin{bmatrix} -9.6666 & -2.6666 & -32.0 & 1.0 \\ 8.0 & 2.5 & 25.5 & -2.0 \\ 2.6666 & .6666 & 9.0 & -5.0 \\ x & x & x & x \end{bmatrix}$$

Note: x indicates elements not used by LEQT1F.

APPENDIX

D

THE NAG LIBRARY PROGRAMS FOR SIMULTANEOUS LINEAR EQUATIONS

NAG stands for Numerical Algorithms Group, Ltd., which markets a large mathematical software library. Their philosophy is that a low cost and a resultant high volume will achieve commercial success. The library has over 300 subroutines and specific versions are available for computers from Burroughs, CDC, Cray, DEC, Harris, Hewlett-Packard, Honeywell, IBM, ICL, Interdata, Mudcomp, Nord, Philips, Prime, Siemens, Telefunken, Univac, and Xerox. The library is leased for about $100 per month and updated every 12 to 18 months. An Algol 60 version of the library is available as well as an Algol 68 version of a subset. For further information about the library and its contents see *NAG Library Manual*, published by Numerical Algorithms Group, Ltd., NAG Central Office, 7 Banbury Rd., Oxford OX2 6NN, United Kingdom, telephone: 44-865-511245; or NAG, Inc., 1250 Grace Court, Downers Grove, IL 60515, U.S.A., telephone: (312) 971-2337.

D.1 THE NAG CHAPTER INTRODUCTION

The reference manual for a library should be a self-contained user's guide. We reproduce the introductory material for Simultaneous Linear Equations here to illustrate their approach to providing user documentation.†

F04 - SIMULTANEOUS LINEAR EQUATIONS

CHAPTER INTRODUCTION

1. Scope of the Chapter

This chapter is concerned with the solution of the matrix equation AX=B, where B may be a single vector or a multiple right hand side and where A may be real, complex, symmetric, positive definite, banded, m×n (m>n) or sparse.

2. Background to the Problems

A set of linear equations may be written in the form

$$Ax = b$$

where the known matrix A, with real or complex coefficients, is of shape (m×n), (m rows and n columns), the known right hand vector b has m components (m rows and one column), and the required solution vector x has n components (n rows and one column). There may also be p vectors b_i, $i = 1,2,\ldots,p$ on the right hand side and the equations may then be written as

$$AX = B,$$

the required matrix X having as its p columns the solutions of $Ax_i = b_i$, $i = 1,2,\ldots,p$. Most routines deal with the latter case, but for clarity only the case p = 1 is discussed here.

The most common problem, the determination of the unique solution of Ax = b, occurs when m = n and A is not singular, that is rank(A) = n. This is discussed in Section 2.1 below. The next most common problem, discussed in Section 2.2 below, is the determination of the least squares solution of Ax = b required when m > n and rank(A) = n ≠ rank(A,b), where (A,b) is an m×(n+1) matrix formed by adding the column b to the matrix A. All other cases are in some sense "singular", and they are treated briefly in Section 2.3.

2.1. Unique Solution of Ax = b

Most routines in this chapter solve this particular problem. The computation starts with the triangular decomposition A = LU, where L and U are respectively lower and upper triangular matrices. The solution is then obtained by solving in succession the simpler equations

$$Ly = b$$
$$Ux = y$$

the first by forward substitution and the second by back substitution.

2.1. Unique Solution of Ax = b (contd)

In the particular case in which A is real, symmetric and positive definite, $U = L^T$ (so that $A = LL^T$, the Cholesky Decomposition). In all other cases, including the symmetric but not positive definite case, U has unit diagonal elements (the Crout Decomposition). If A is a band matrix then L and U have corresponding band widths.

Due to rounding errors the computed "solution" x_0, say, is only an approximation to the true solution x. This approximation will sometimes be satisfactory, agreeing with x to several figures, but if the problem is ill-conditioned then x and x_0 may have few or even no figures in common, and at this stage there is no means of estimating the "accuracy" of x_0.

To obtain this information, and to "correct" x_0 when this is meaningful (see next paragraph), the residual vector $r = b-Ax_0$ is computed in extended precision arithmetic, and a correction vector d is obtained by solving LUd = r. The new approximate solution x_0+d is usually more accurate and the correcting process is repeated until:

(a) further corrections are negligible or

(b) they show no further decrease.

It must be emphasised that the "true" solution x may not be meaningful, that is correct to all figures quoted, if the elements of A and b are known with certainty only to say p figures, where p is smaller than the word-length of the computer. The first correction vector d will then give some useful information about the number of figures in the "solution" which probably remain unchanged with respect to maximum possible uncertainties in the coefficients. Alternative useful information is obtained by solving two sets of equations, one with the given coefficients and one with the coefficients rounded to p-1 figures, and counting the number of figures to which the two solutions agree. In ill-conditioned problems this can be surprisingly small and even zero.

2.2. The Least Squares Solution of Ax = b, m > n, rank A = n

The least squares solution is the vector $\hat{x}$ which minimises the sum of the squares of the residuals,

$$S = (A\hat{x}-b)^T(A\hat{x}-b) = \|A\hat{x}-b\|_2^2$$

2.2. The Least Squares Solution of $Ax = b$, $m > n$, Rank $A = n$ (contd)

The solution is obtained in two steps:

(i) Householder Transformations are used to reduce A to "simpler form" via the equation $QA = R$, where R has the appearance

$$\begin{pmatrix} \hat{R} \\ \hline O \end{pmatrix}$$

with $\hat{R}$ a non-singular upper triangular $n \times n$ matrix and O a null matrix of shape $(m-n) \times n$. Similar operations convert b to $Qb = c$, where

$$c = \begin{pmatrix} c_1 \\ \hline c_2 \end{pmatrix}$$

with c_1 having n rows and c_2 having m-n rows.

(ii) The required least squares solution is obtained by back substitution in the equation

$$\hat{R}\hat{x} = c_1 .$$

Due to rounding errors the computed $\hat{x}_0$ is only an approximation to the required $\hat{x}$, but as in Section 2.1 this can be improved by "iterative refinement". The first correction d is the solution of the least squares problem

$$Ad = b - A\hat{x}_0 = r$$

and since the matrix A is unchanged this computation takes less time than that of the original $\hat{x}_0$. The process can be repeated until further corrections are (a) negligible or (b) show no further decrease.

2.3. Singular cases

(a) Whatever the shape $(m \times n)$ of the matrix A, the equations have no solution unless $\text{rank}(A,b) = \text{rank}(A)$. If these ranks are equal the solution is unique only if $m \geq n$ and $\text{rank}(A) = n$. (The routines of case 2.1, with $m = n$ check that $\text{rank}(A) = n$ and otherwise go into a failure exit.) For if $\text{rank}(A) = r < n$ the homogeneous linear equations $Ax = 0$ have n-r independent non-trivial solutions v_i, and if x_0 is any solution of $Ax = b$ then

3. Recommendations on Choice and Use of Routines

3.1. General Discussion

Most of the routines in this chapter solve linear equations **Ax** = b when A is (n×n) and a unique solution is expected (case 2.1). If this turns out to be untrue the routines go to a failure exit. The matrix A may be "general" real or complex, or may have a few special forms (a) real, symmetric and positive definite (all eigenvalues greater than zero), (b) as (a) but also banded and (c) real and sparse. Some routines produce just a first approximation , and others correct this by the method of iterative refinement discussed in 2.

Those routines that calculate a first approximation only are said to calculate an "approximate" solution while those that use iterative refinement are said to calculate an "accurate" solution.

It must be emphasized that it is wasteful of computer time and space to use an inappropriate routine, for example one for the complex case when the equations are real. It is also unsatisfactory to use the special routines for a positive definite matrix if this property is not known in advance.

Routines are given for calculating the approximate solution, that is solving the linear equations just once, and also for obtaining the accurate solution by successive iterative corrections of this first approximation. The latter, of course, are more costly in terms of time and storage, since each correction involves the solution of n sets of linear equations and since the original A and its LU decomposition must be stored together with the first and successively corrected approximations to the solution. In practice the storage requirements for the "corrected" routines are about double those of the "approximate" routines, though the extra computer time is not prohibitive since the same matrix and the same LU decomposition is used in every linear equation solution.

Despite the extra work of the "corrected" routines, they are overwhelmingly superior to the "approximate" routines. For without at least one correction it is impossible to give any estimate either of the number of accurate figures in the solution or the number of "meaningful" figures relating to the degree of uncertainty in the coefficients of the matrix. (See Section 2.)

The routine for a real sparse matrix should be used only when the number of non-zero elements is very small, less than 10% of the n^2 elements of A, and the matrix does not have a relatively small band width.

3.1. General Discussion (contd)

For case 2.2, when $m > n$ and a unique least squares solution is expected, there are two routines for a real A, one of which computes a first approximation and the other computes iterative corrections. If it transpires that rank(A) < n, so that the least squares solution is not unique then the routine goes to the failure exit. Again as in case 2.1 the "correcting" routine is superior in all respects (other than time and storage) to the "approximate" routine. If it turns out that rank(A,b) = rank(A) = n, this least squares solution is the unique solution of Ax = b, that is $\|Ax-b\|_2^2 = 0$.

If the routine for case 2.2 fails because rank(A)=r < n, then the routine for calculating the "minimal length least squares solution" can be used. Currently there is only a routine for the "approximate" solution. This routine also attempts to calculate the rank, r, of the matrix given a tolerance to decide when elements can be regarded as zero. However, only the singular value decomposition method described below gives a reliable indication of rank.
All other "singular" cases (case 2.3) are covered by one routine, F01BHA/F, which uses the singular value decomposition of A. This gives either the minimal length solution of Ax = b or the minimal length least squares solution, (as explained in 2), and also produces the vectors v_i which are the non-trivial solutions of the homogeneous equations Ax = 0 (case p = 0).

One difficulty about this routine is the determination of rank(A) = r. The failure cases of 2.1 and 2.2 show that rank(A) ≠ n but do not give the value of r. This is theoretically determinable via the singular value decomposition, but in difficult cases rounding errors can be troublesome.

The routines in this chapter fail into two easily defined categories.

(i) Black Box Routines

Commonly the equations $Ax_i = b_i$, $i = 1,2,\ldots,p$ are to be solved when p and all the b_i are known in advance. The black box routines should then be used and they call routines in the next category (ii) and chapters F01 and F03.

(ii) General Purpose Routines

It may happen in some problems that the number p is not known in advance, extra right hand sides being "generated" in the course of the computation. Since the matrix A is unchanged, it is convenient and economic to perform the triangular decomposition once only. This is done by using routines in chapters F03 or F01 and the relevant information is used in subsequent calls of routines in this category.

3.3. Decision Trees

If at any stage the answer to a question is 'Don't know' this should be read as 'No'.

(i) Black Box Routines

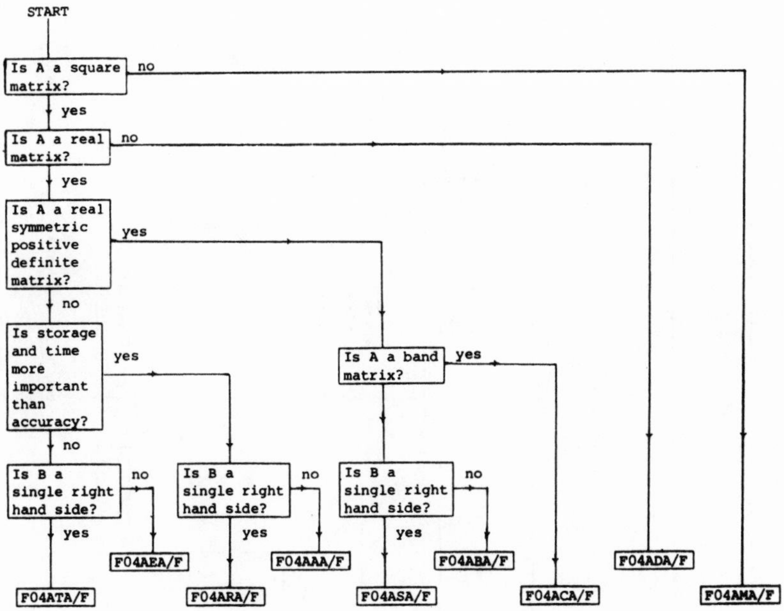

(ii) General Purpose Routines

The name of the routine that should be used to decompose the matrix A into triangular matrices is given in brackets under the name of the routine for solving the set of linear equations.

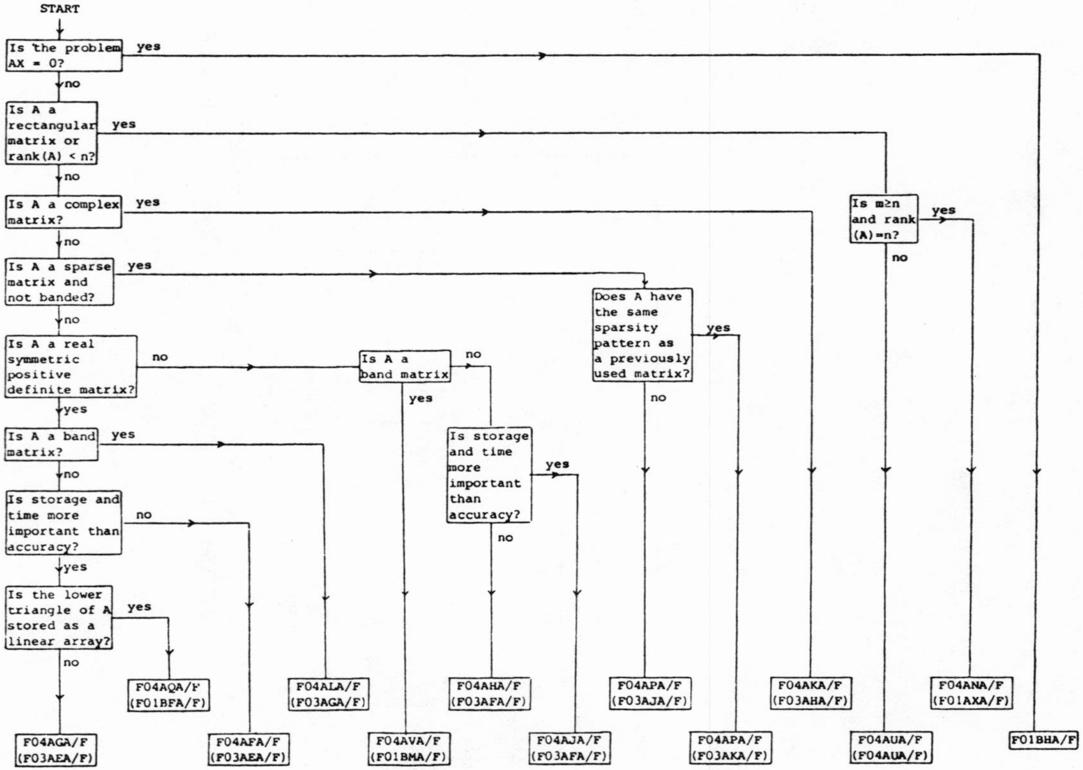

CHAPTER CONTENTS - F04

IMPORTANT: refer to the appropriate implementation document to check that a routine is available in the required language and implementation.

a) Black Box Routines

These routines solve the matrix equation AX=B:

Routine name	Purpose	Mark of introduction
F04AAA/F	Approximate solution of a set of real linear equations with multiple right hand sides AX = B by Crout's Factorisation Method.	2
F04ABA/F	Accurate solution of a set of real symmetric positive definite linear equations with multiple right hand sides AX = B, by Cholesky's Decomposition Method.	2
F04ACA/F	Approximate solution of a set of real symmetric positive definite band linear equations AX = B with multiple right hand sides by Cholesky's Decomposition Method.	2
F04ADA/F	Approximate solution of a set of complex linear equations with multiple right hand sides AX = B by Crout's Factorisation Method.	2
F04AEA/F	Accurate solution of a set of real linear equations with multiple right hand sides AX = B by Crout's Factorisation Method.	2
F04AMA/F	Accurate least squares solution of a set of m linear equations in n unknowns, $m \geq n$, with multiple right hand sides, AX = B.	2
F04ARA/F	Approximate solution of a set of real linear equations with a single right hand side, Ax = b, by Crout's Factorisation Method.	4
F04ASA/F	Accurate solution of a set of real symmetric positive definite linear equations with a single right hand side, Ax = b, by Cholesky's Decomposition Method.	4

a) Black Box Routines (contd)

Routine name	Purpose	Mark of introduction
F04ATA/F	Accurate solution of a set of real linear equations with a single right hand side, Ax = b, by Crout's Factorisation Method.	4

b) General Purpose Routines

These routines solve the matrix equation AX = B. A must be previously decomposed.

Routine name	Purpose	Mark of introduction
F04AFA/F	Accurate solution of a set of real symmetric positive definite linear equations with multiple right hand sides, AX = B, where A has been decomposed into triangular matrices using F03AEA/F.	2
F04AGA/F	Approximate solution of a set of real symmetric positive definite linear equations with multiple right hand sides, AX = B, where A has been decomposed into triangular matrices using F03AEA/F.	2
F04AHA/F	Accurate solution of a set of real linear equations with multiple right hand sides, AX = B, where A has been decomposed into triangular matrices using F03AFA/F.	2
F04AJA/F	Approximate solution of a set of real linear equations with multiple right hand sides, AX = B, where A has been decomposed into triangular matrices using F03AFA/F.	2
F04AKA/F	Approximate solution of a set of complex linear equations with multiple right hand sides, AX = B, where A has been decomposed into triangular matrices using F03AHA/F.	2

b) General Purpose Routines (contd)

Routine name	Purpose	Mark of introduction
F04ALA/F	Approximate solution of a set of real symmetric positive definite band linear equations with multiple right hand sides, AX = B, where A has been decomposed into triangular matrices using F03AGA/F.	2
F04ANA/F	Approximate least squares solution of a set of m linear equations in n unknowns, $m \geq n$, with a single right hand side, Ax = b, where A has been decomposed into triangular matrices using F01AXA/F.	2
F04APA/F	Approximate solution of a set of real sparse linear equations with one right hand side, Ax = b or $A^T x = b$, where A has been decomposed into triangular matrices using F03AJA/F or F03AKA/F. (Also evaluates Ab or $A^T b$.)	3
F04AQA/F	Approximate solution of a set of real symmetric positive definite linear equations with one right hand side Ax = b where A has been decomposed into LDL^T using F01BFA/F. Economical storage.	3
F04AUA/F	Approximate minimal least squares solution of a set of real $m \times n$ ($m \geq n$) linear equations (rank$\leq$n) with multiple right-hand sides, AX = B where A has been factored using F01BKA/F	5
F04AVA/F	Approximate solution of a set of real band linear equations with multiple right hand sides AX = B, where A has been decomposed into triangular matrices, using F01BMA/F.	6

NOTATION: routine names ending in A/F indicate either the Algol 60 routine, ending in A, or the FORTRAN routine, ending in F; for example, A02AAA/F means either A02AAA (Algol 60) or A02AAF (FORTRAN).

1. Purpose

F04ARF calculates the approximate solution of a set of real linear equations with a single right hand side, Ax=b, by Crout's factorisation method.

IMPORTANT: before using this routine, read the appropriate machine implementation document to check the interpretation of italicised terms and other implementation-dependent details.

2. Specification (FORTRAN IV)

```
      SUBROUTINE F04ARF(A,IA,B,N,C,WKSPCE,IFAIL)
C     INTEGER IA,N,IFAIL
C     real A(IA,N),B(N),C(N),WKSPCE(N)
```

3. Description

Given a set of linear equations, Ax=b, the routine first decomposes A using Crout's factorisation with partial pivoting, PA=LU, where P is a permutation matrix, L is lower triangular and U is unit upper triangular. The approximate solution x is found by forward and backward substitution in Ly=Pb and Ux=y, where b is the right hand side. *Additional precision* accumulation of innerproducts is used throughout the calculation.

4. References

[1] WILKINSON, J.H. and REINSCH, C.
Handbook for Automatic Computation.
Volume II, Linear Algebra.
Springer-Verlag, 1971, pp. 93-110.

5. Parameters

A - *real* array of DIMENSION (IA,p) where $p \geq N$.
Before entry, A should contain the elements of the real matrix. On successful exit, it will contain the Crout factorisation with the unit diagonal of U understood.

IA - INTEGER.
On entry, IA specifies the first dimension of array A as declared in the calling (sub)program ($IA \geq N$). Unchanged on exit.

B - *real* array of DIMENSION at least (N).
Before entry, B should contain the elements of the right hand side. Unchanged on exit but see Section 11.

N - INTEGER.
On entry, N specifies the order of matrix A.
Unchanged on exit.

C - *real* array of DIMENSION at least (N).
On successful exit, C will contain the solution vector.

WKSPCE - *real* array of DIMENSION at least (N).
Used as working space.

IFAIL - INTEGER.
Before entry, IFAIL must be assigned a value. For users not familiar with this parameter (described in Chapter P01) the recommended value is 0. Unless the routine detects an error (see Section 6), IFAIL contains 0 on exit.

6. Error Indicators

Errors detected by the routine:-

IFAIL = 1 The matrix A is singular, possibly due to rounding errors.

7. Auxiliary Routines

This routine calls the NAG Library routines F03AFF, F04AJF, P01AAF and X02AAF.

8. Timing

The time taken is approximately proportional to N^3.

9. Storage

There are no internally declared arrays.

10. Accuracy

The accuracy of the computed solution depends on the conditioning of the original matrix. For a detailed error analysis see [1], page 107.

11. Further Comments

If the routine is called with the same name for parameters B and C then the solution vector will overwrite the right hand side.

12. Keywords

Approximate Solution of Linear Equations.
Crout Factorisation.
Real Matrix.
Single Right Hand Side.

13. Example

To solve the set of linear equations Ax=b where

$$A = \begin{pmatrix} 33 & 16 & 72 \\ -24 & -10 & -57 \\ -8 & -4 & -17 \end{pmatrix} \qquad \text{and} \quad b = \begin{pmatrix} -359 \\ 281 \\ 85 \end{pmatrix}$$

Program

This single precision example program may require amendment
 i) for use in a DOUBLE PRECISION implementation
ii) for use in either precision in certain implementations.
The results produced may differ slightly.

```
C     F04ARF EXAMPLE PROGRAM TEXT
C     NAG COPYRIGHT 1975
C     MARK 4.5 REVISED
C
      REAL A(4,4), B(6), C(6), WKS(18)
      INTEGER NIN, NOUT, I, N, J, IA, IFAIL
      DATA NIN /5/, NOUT /6/
      READ (NIN,99999) (WKS(I),I=1,7)
      WRITE (NOUT,99997) (WKS(I),I=1,6)
      N = 3
      READ (NIN,99998) ((A(I,J),J=1,N),I=1,N), (B(I),I=1,N)
      IA = 4
      IFAIL = 1
      CALL F04ARF(A, IA, B, N, C, WKS, IFAIL)
      IF (IFAIL.EQ.0) GO TO 20
      WRITE (NOUT,99996) IFAIL
      STOP
   20 WRITE (NOUT,99995) (C(I),I=1,N)
      STOP
99999 FORMAT (6A4, 1A3)
99998 FORMAT (3F5.0)
99997 FORMAT (4(1X/), 1H , 5A4, 1A3, 7HRESULTS/1X)
99996 FORMAT (25HOERROR IN F04ARF IFAIL = , I2)
99995 FORMAT (10HOSOLUTIONS/(1H , F4.1))
      END
```

Data

```
F04ARF EXAMPLE PROGRAM DATA
   33   16   72
  -24  -10  -57
   -8   -4  -17
 -359  281   85
```

Results

```
F04ARF EXAMPLE PROGRAM RESULTS

SOLUTIONS
 1.0
-2.0
-5.0
```

APPENDIX

E

THE LAWSON-HANSON LEAST-SQUARES PROGRAMS

These Fortran programs are documented and listed in Appendix C from Lawson and Hanson (1974). Persons wishing to purchase the code and data in machine readable form may do so by contacting IMSL. The programs are available at a nominal charge from IMSL, Inc., Sixth Floor, GNB Building, 7500 Bellaire Blvd., Houston, TX 77036; telephone: (713) 772-1927.

These programs are applicable to most least-squares problems, linear or nonlinear. The basic ideas of least squares are presented in Chap. 11 of this book but, as we note there, anyone who has serious least-squares problems should consult the text by Lawson and Hanson.

The programs are organized under six main programs which are designed to demonstrate the various algorithms and usage of the software modules. The organization of the programs is given in Fig. E.1.

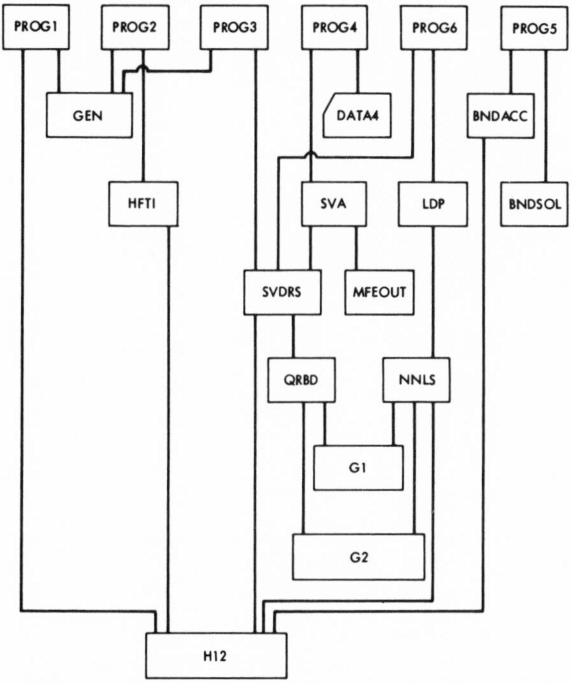

Figure E.1 Organization of the Lawson-Hanson programs. In addition, DIFF is called by HFTI, QRBD, LDP, and NNLS. (Reproduced by permission from C. L. Lawson and R. J. Hanson, *Solving Least Squares Problems*, p. 251. Copyright © 1974 by Prentice Hall, Inc., Englewood Cliffs.)

A directory of the main Lawson-Hanson programs is presented in Table E.1 and of their subprograms in Table E.2. The set includes six main programs (drivers), one data set, and fourteen basic modules. The definitions are given in terms of the names introduced in Lawson and Hanson (1974). An independent presentation could be much longer and, in any case, a user of these programs should have access to that book.

Table E.1 Directory of main programs and the data element DATA4

Name of Program	Fortran Code Page Number	Purpose of Program
PROG1	279	Demonstrates Algorithms HFT, HS1, and COV of Chapters 11 and 12. Calls subprograms **H12** and **GEN**.
PROG2	281	Demonstrates Algorithms HFTI and COV of Chapters 14 and 12, respectively. Calls subprograms **HFTI** and **GEN**.
PROG3	283	Demonstrates the singular value decomposition algorithm of Chapter 18. Calls subprograms **SVDRS** and **GEN**.
PROG4	285	Demonstrates singular value analysis including computation of Levenberg–Marquardt solution norms and residual norms as described in Chapters 18, 25, and 26. Calls subroutine **SVA** and reads the data element **DATA4**.
DATA4	285	This is not a program. It is a set of 15 card images containing data to be read by **PROG4**. This example is discussed in Chapter 26.
PROG5	286	Demonstrates the band-limited sequential accumulation algorithm of Chapter 27, Sections 2 and 4. The algorithm is used to fit a cubic spline (with uniformly spaced breakpoints) to a table of data. Calls subroutines **BNDACC** and **BNDSOL**.
PROG6	288	Computes the constrained line-fitting problem given as an example in Chapter 23. The program illustrates a typical usage of the subroutine **LDP**, which in turn uses the subroutine **NNLS**. **PROG6** also calls **SVDRS**.

Source: C. L. Lawson and R. J. Hanson, *Solving Least Squares Problems*, pp. 249. Copyright © 1974 by Prentice Hall, Inc., Englewood Cliffs; reprinted by permission.

Table E.2 Directory of subprograms

Name of Subprogram	User's Guide Page Number	Fortran Code Page Number	Purpose of Subprogram
HFTI	254	290	Implements Algorithm HFTI of Chapter 14. Calls subprograms **H12** and **DIFF**.
SVA	256	292	Implements singular value analysis and Levenberg–Marquardt analysis as described in Chapters 18 and 25. Produces printed output of quantities of interest. Calls subroutines **SVDRS** and **MFEOUT**.
SVDRS	260	295	Computes the singular value decomposition as described in Chapter 18. Calls subroutines **H12** and **QRBD**.
QRBD	262	298	Computes the singular value decomposition of a bidiagonal matrix as described in Chapter 18. Calls subprograms **G1**, **G2**, and **DIFF**.
BNDACC and **BNDSOL**	264	301 and 302	Implements the band-limited sequential accumulation algorithm of Chapter 27, Section 2. Calls subroutine **H12**.
LDP	267	303	Solves the least distance programming problem as described in Chapter 23. Calls subprograms **NNLS** and **DIFF**.
NNLS	269	304	Computes a least squares solution, subject to all variables being nonnegative, as described in Chapter 23. Calls subprograms **H12**, **G1**, **G2**, and **DIFF**.
H12	271	308	Constructs and applies a Householder transformation as described in Chapter 10.
G1 and **G2**	274	309	Constructs and applies a Givens rotation as described in Chapter 10.
MFEOUT	275	310	Prints a two-dimensional array in a choice of two pleasing formats.
GEN	277	311	Generates a sequence of numbers for use in constructing test data. Used by **PROG1**, **PROG2**, and **PROG3**.
DIFF	278	311	Computes the difference between two floating point arguments.

Source: C. L. Lawson and R. J. Hanson, *Solving Least Squares Problems*, pp. 249–250. Copyright © 1974 by Prentice Hall, Inc., Englewood Cliffs; reprinted by permission.

The user's guide† for one module, HFTI, is given to illustrate the approach used by these authors. The user's guide is not incorporated into the initial comments of these programs.

USER'S GUIDE TO HFTI: SOLUTION OF THE LEAST SQUARES PROBLEM BY HOUSEHOLDER TRANSFORMATIONS

Subroutines Called **H12, DIFF**

Purpose

This subroutine solves a linear least squares problem or a set of linear least squares problems having the same matrix but different right-side vectors. The problem data consists of an **M** × **N** matrix A, an **M** × **NB** matrix B, and an absolute tolerance parameter τ. The **NB** column vectors of B represent right-side vectors b_j for **NB** distinct linear least squares problems.

$$Ax_j \cong b_j \qquad j = 1, \ldots, \mathbf{NB}$$

This set of problems can also be written as the matrix least squares problem:

$$AX \cong B$$

where X is the **N** × **NB** matrix having column vectors x_j.

Note that if B is the **M** × **M** identity matrix, then X will be the pseudo-inverse of A.

Method

This subroutine first transforms the augmented matrix $[A: B]$ to a matrix $[R: C]$ using premultiplying Householder transformations with column interchanges. All subdiagonal elements in the matrix R are zero and its diagonal elements satisfy $|r_{ii}| \geq |r_{i+1,i+1}|$, $i = 1, \ldots, l - 1$, where $l = \min\{\mathbf{M}, \mathbf{N}\}$.

The subroutine will set the pseudorank **KRANK** equal to the number of diagonal elements of R exceeding τ in magnitude. Minimal length solution vectors $\hat{x}_j$, $j = 1, \ldots, \mathbf{NB}$, will be computed for the problems defined by the first **KRANK** rows of $[R: C]$.

If the relative uncertainty in the data matrix B is ρ, it is suggested that τ be set approximately equal to $\rho \|A\|$.

For further algorithmic details, see Algorithm HFTI in Chapter 14.

Usage

DIMENSION A(MDA, n_1), {B(MDB, n_2) or **B(m_1)}, RNORM(n_2), H(n_1), G(n_1)**
INTEGER IP(n_1)
CALL HFTI (A, MDA, M, N, B, MDB, NB, TAU, KRANK, RNORM, H, G, IP)

The dimensioning parameters must satisfy **MDA** ≥ **M**, n_1 ≥ **N**, **MDB** ≥ max {**M**, **N**}, m_1 ≥ max {**M**, **N**}, and n_2 ≥ **NB**.

The subroutine parameters are defined as follows:

† C. L. Lawson and R. J. Hanson, *Solving Least Squares Problems*, pp. 254–256. Copyright © 1974 by Prentice Hall, Inc., Englewood Cliffs; reprinted by permission.

A(,), MDA, M, N — The array **A(,)** initially contains the **M** $\times$ **N** matrix A of the least squares problem $AX \cong B$. The first dimensioning parameter of the array **A(,)** is **MDA**, which must satisfy **MDA** $\geq$ **M**. Either **M** $\geq$ **N** or **M** $<$ **N** is permitted. There is no restriction on the rank of A. The contents of the array **A(,)** will be modified by the subroutine. See Fig. 14.1 for an example illustrating the final contents of **A(,)**.

B( ), MDB, NB — If **NB** $=$ **0** the subroutine will make no references to the array **B( )**. If **NB** $>$ **0** the array **B( )** must initially contain the **M** $\times$ **NB** matrix B of the least squares problem $AX \cong B$ and on return the array **B( )** will contain the **N** $\times$ **NB** solution matrix $\hat{X}$. If **NB** $\geq$ **2** the array **B( )** must be double subscripted with first dimensioning parameter **MDB** $\geq$ max {**M, N**}. If **NB** $=$ **1** the array **B( )** may be either doubly or singly subscripted. In the latter case the value of **MDB** is arbitrary but some Fortran compilers require that **MDB** be assigned a valid integer value, say **MDB** $=$ **1**.

TAU — Absolute tolerance parameter provided by user for pseudorank determination.

KRANK — Set by the subroutine to indicate the pseudorank of A.

RNORM( ) — On exit, **RNORM(J)** will contain the euclidean norm of the residual vector for the problem defined by the jth column vector of the array **B(,)** for $j =$ **1, . . . , NB**.

H( ), G( ) — Arrays of working space. See Fig. 14.1 for an example illustrating the final contents of these arrays.

IP( ) — Array in which the subroutine records indices describing the permutation of column vectors. See Fig. 14.1 for an example illustrating the final contents of this array.

Example of Usage

See **PROG2** for an example of the usage of this subroutine.

APPENDIX

F

EISPACK—MATRIX EIGENSYSTEM ROUTINES

The calculation of eigenvalues and eigenvectors of a matrix is much more difficult than solving a linear system of equations. In fact, no reliable (numerically stable) method was known before the 1960s when the QR-algorithm was discovered. The analysis and implementation of good eigenvalue algorithms normally require a numerical analyst, if not a specialist in matrix computations. The EISPACK programs are a premier example of the idea of an expert embedding his knowhow in computer programs for the rest of the world to use.

These routines originate from a set of Algol programs prepared by J. H. Wilkinson and C. Reinsch in the late 1960s. The use of Algol limited their applicability in the United States and therefore a project was started to implement the procedures in Fortran, in order to produce highly efficient versions for specific machines, to test them in depth, to certify the programs and, in general, to produce the highest quality software possible. The principal people in this project (NATS—National Activity to Test Software) were B. T. Smith, J. M. Boyle, J. J. Dongarra, B. S. Garbow, Y. Ikebe, V. C. Klema, and C. B. Moler. The EISPACK programs are presented and documented in Smith et al. (1976) and Garbow et al. (1977). These programs are available at a nominal cost from IMSL, Inc., Sixth Floor, GNB Building, 7500 Bellaire Blvd., Houston, TX 77036.

The approach used was to create a systematized collection of programs, each one a module which implements a particular phase of the solution process. These modules are then assembled in various ways for particular eigenvalue computations. There is a large number of cases; the first level of breakdown is shown in the following table:

Basic cases of the eigensystem problems

Class of Matrix / Problem Classification	Complex General	Complex Hermitian	Real General	Real Symmetric	Real Symmetric Tridiagonal	Special Real Tridiagonal
All Eigenvalues & Corresponding Eigenvectors	XX	XX	XX	XX	XX	XX
All Eigenvalues	XX	XX	XX	XX	XX	XX
All Eigenvalues & Selected Eigenvectors	XX		XX			
Some Eigenvalues & Corresponding Eigenvectors		XX		XX	XX	XX
Some Eigenvalues		XX		XX	XX	XX

Boxes containing XX have recommended basic paths described in the EISPACK Guide.
SOURCE: EISPACK Guide, Table 4; reprinted by permission.

Recommended *basic paths* are given for 22 of the 30 cases in this table. For some cases there is a further breakdown based on other characteristics of the matrix (e.g., size). The large number of modules in EISPACK makes it imperative (at least for the typical user) that these basic paths be assembled into single subprograms for the more common cases. A knowledgeable person can assemble the modules to handle almost any particular matrix well. A control program has been written for the IBM OS/360-370 version which, in effect, creates a problem-oriented, special purpose language for eigensystem computations.

APPENDIX

G

THE LOCAL COMPUTING CENTER LIBRARY—PURDUE EXAMPLE

The typical computing center gets software from a variety of sources. These include

1. Locally written programs
2. Programs from other locations obtained through friends, word-of-mouth advertising, and other informal means
3. Programs published in the scientific literature; for example, the BLAS and Lawson-Hanson least squares programs
4. Collections of programs (usually concentrated in one area) available from nonprofit sources such as the government (EISPACK and LINPACK) or user groups (SHARE for IBM users)
5. General libraries from commercial sources such as IMSL, Inc., and NAG, Ltd.
6. At one time all major computer manufacturers provided substantial software libraries free with their computers. These are now sold separately; the SL-MATH library of IBM is still widely available.
7. Specialized applications programs from various sources

Matrix computation software is by nature widely used and hundreds of programs are available from all these sources. Furthermore, many people write their own matrix computation programs on the theory (generally mistaken) that they can do it quicker that way.

We examine the linear equations software in the Purdue University Computing Center as an example of what is available in a good computing center library. It has the IMSL library, the LINPACK programs plus seven locally written programs. Four of the local programs are similar and named LINEQ1, LINEQ2, LINEQ3, and LINEQ4. The library write-up for LINEQ1 is shown below. LINEQ2 is for double-precision systems and LINEQ4 is for complex systems. LINEQ3 is a variant of LINEQ2 which uses triple-precision for the iterative improvement. These routines have two system-dependent features: The inner loop of the elimination is done in assembly language and dynamic storage allocation is used to generate the workspace needed for the algorithm. They also take advantage of a common, but nonstandard, Fortran complier feature to avoid passing the column dimension declarations to the subroutines. The arrays are declared

REAL A(N,1), B(N,1), X(N,1)

inside the subroutine which works properly (because of the Fortran storage scheme for arrays) even though it produces subscripts out of bounds.

There are two programs for special matrices: SYMEQ1 for symmetric matrices and GELB for band matrices (not necessarily the same bandwidth on each side of the diagonal). The library write-up for GELB is also shown. Finally, there is an unusual program BOUNDS which is a very accurate implementation of the Aird-Lynch error estimates (discussed in Chap. 9). It uses interval arithmetic and double precision in order to obtain true bounds very precisely. The library write-up for BOUNDS is the final example shown.

The computing center library has one of the common frustrating properties: there are too many alternatives for the same application. There are close to 100 linear equation solvers from which to choose: 12 from IMSL, 65 from LINPACK, 6 local, plus many contained in packages or systems like SPSS, SOUPAC, BMD, etc. While many of these are not applicable to the same problem, many users are at a loss as to how to decide which is most appropriate for their application. The result is frequently an almost random selection.

PURDUE UNIVERSITY COMPUTING CENTER

SUBROUTINE LINEQ1

SYSTEMS LIBRARY

Purpose:

(1) Solves the real matrix equation AX=B with NR right-hand sides.
(2) Computes the inverse of a real matrix A.
(3) Evaluates the real matrix expression $A^{-1}B$.

Usage: CALL LINEQ1 (A,B,X,ND,N,NR,S)

Description of parameters:

A - (N x N) real coefficient matrix.
B - (N x NR) real right-hand side array.
X - (N x NR) real array for return of solution vectors.
ND - the number of rows for the arrays A, B, and X in the dimension statement in the user program
N - the number of equations to be solved.
NR - the number of right-hand sides to be solved.
S - integer variable returned non-zero only if matrix A is singular to machine accuracy.

This routine may be used to invert a matrix A by solving the system of equations AX=B where B is the (N x N) identity matrix. In this case, NR is N and the inverse of A is returned in X. The (N x N) identity matrix may be formed by the following FORTRAN statements:

```
      DO   2  I=1,N
      DO   1  J=1,N
    1 B(I,J)=0.0
    2 B(I,I)=1.0
```

The matrix expression $X=A^{-1}B$ may be formed by noting that X is the solution of the matrix equation AX=B which this routine can compute directly. This method will produce more accurate answers faster than can be obtained by computing A^{-1} and then multiplying A^{-1} by B.

Remarks: Arrays A and B are not destroyed. At execution time, the field length of your program will be increased for temporary storage needed by this subroutine.

Method: The matrix A is factored into lower and upper triangular matrices L and U and then the equations LZ=B and UX=Z are solved in turn. Double precision accumulation of inner products and iterative refinement are used so solutions are very accurate whenever S is returned equal to zero.

Ralston and Wilf Mathematical Methods for Digital Computers
Volume 2 Wiley 1967.

Written by David S. Dodson

PURDUE UNIVERSITY COMPUTING CENTER

SUBROUTINE GELB

DECKS USED: GELB

Purpose: To solve a system of simultaneous linear equations with a coefficient matrix of band structure.

Usage: CALL GELB (R,A,M,N,MUD,MLD,EPS,IER)

Description of Parameters:

R - M by N right hand side matrix (destroyed).
On return R contains the solution of the equations.
A - a vector of dimension MA which contains the band of the coefficient matrix stored rowwise in the first ME successive storage locations (see remarks below).
M - the number of equations in the system.
N - the number of right hand side vectors.
MUD - the number of upper codiagonals (that means codiagonals above main diagonal).
MLD - the number of lower codiagonals (that means codiagonals below main diagonal).
EPS - an input constant which is used as relative tolerance for test on loss of significance.
IER - resulting error parameter coded as follows

IER=0 - no error
IER=-1 - no result because of wrong input parameters M, MUD, MLD or because of pivot element at any elimination step equal to 0.
IER=K - warning due to possible loss of significance indicated at elimination step K+1, where pivot element was less than or equal to the internal tolerance EPS times absolutely greatest element of matrix A.

Remarks: The band of width MUD+MLD+1 of the coefficient matrix is assumed to be stored rowwise in the first ME successive storage locations of totally needed MA storage locations, where

MA=M*MC-ML*(ML+1)/2 and ME=MA-MU*(MU+1)/2 with
MC=MIN(M,1+MUD+MLD), ML=MC-1-MLD, MU=MC-1-MUD.

Right hand side matrix R is assumed to be stored columnwise in N*M successive storage locations. On return solution matrix R is also stored columnwise.

Input parameters M, MUD, MLD should satisfy the following restrictions

MUD not less than zero
MLD not less than zero
MUD + MLD not greater than 2*M-2.

No action besides error message IER=-1 takes place if these restrictions are not satisfied.

A relative tolerance of EPS between .00001 and .000001 is suggested.

The procedure gives results if the restrictions on input parameters are satisfied and if pivot elements at all elimination steps are different from 0. However warning IER=K - if given - indicates possible loss of significance. In case of a well scaled matrix A and appropriate tolerance EPS, IER=K may be interpreted that matrix A has the rank K. No warning is given if matrix A has no lower codiagonal.

Method: Solution is done by means of GAUSS elimination with column pivoting only, in order to preserve band structure in remaining coefficient matrices.

PURDUE UNIVERSITY COMPUTING CENTER

TITLE: BOUNDS

AUTHORS: T. J. Aird and Robert E. Lynch

DECKNAME: Bounds

PURPOSE: To compute error bounds for solutions of systems of linear equations. The error bounds account for specified uncertainties in the elements of both the coefficient matrix A and the right hand side B for the approximate solution X.

USAGE: CALL BOUNDS (AA,BB,X,A,ND,N,NR,BND)

In the discussion given below, X is considered to be an approximate solution of the system of linear equations with coefficient matrix A and right hand side B. Also, the elements of A and of B are assumed to have been obtained by previous computations or by experimental measurements of physical data. Thus, they are subject to certain errors. The problem is to determine the effect that these errors have on the solution.

Error bounds are computed which account for the maximum possible deviation between X and the solution of any system with coefficient matrix AO which satisfies:

AA(1,I,J) ≤ AO(I,J) ≤ AA(2,I,J)
for I, J = 1,...,N;

and right hand side BO which satisfies:

BB(1,I,K) ≤ BO(I,K) ≤ BB(2,I,K)
for I = 1,...,N and
for K = 1,...,NR.

In this case, AO and BO are said to satisfy the conditions given by AA and BB respectively.

Specifically, BND(1,K) and BND(2,K) are computed for K = 1,...,NR so that:

BND(1,K) ≤ MAX[ABS(T(I,K) - X(I,K)), I=1,...,N] ≤ BND(2,K)

holds for the solution T of AO*T = BO whenever AO and BO satisfy the conditions given by AA and BB respectively.

DESCRIPTION OF PARAMETERS:

AA - (2 by N by N) matrix which specifies the uncertainty in A.

BB - (2 by N by NR) matrix which specifies the uncertainty in B.

X - (N by NR) matrix of NR approximate solutions X (.,1),...,X(.,NR) corresponding to the NR right hand sides B(.,1),...,B(.,NR).

A - (N by N) coefficient matrix representative.
I.e., A matrix which satisfies
AA(1,I,J) ≤ A(I,J) ≤ AA(2,I,J).
A is destroyed during the computation.

ND - Dimension bound for AA, BB, X, and A.
AA must have dimension bounds (2,ND,N),
BB must have dimension bounds (2,ND,NR),
X must have dimension bounds (ND,NR),
A must have dimension bounds (ND,N).

N - number of equations.

NR - number of right hand sides.

BND - (2 by NR) matrix in which the computed lower and upper error bounds will be stored.

REMARKS:

1) The intervals given by AA and BB may also be in reverse order. That is AA(1,I,J) ≥ AA(2,I,J) or BB(1,I,K) ≥ BB(2,I,K) is permitted for any I, J, K.

2) Usually the matrix A is used to compute the approximate solution X and then used to compute the elements of AA.

For example,

AA(1,I,J) = A(I,J)*(1-1.0E-8)
AA(2,I,J) = A(I,J)*(1+1.0E-8)

would indicate that A(I,J) is known to 8 digits. The same is true for B and BB.

3) BND(1,K)=BND(2,K)=-1.0 indicates that error bounds could not be computed by the subroutine. When this condition arises either A has been determined to be singular, or C (the approximate inverse of A) did not satisfy the basic inequality:

NORM(I - C*AO) < 1

for all matrices AO which satisfy the conditions given by AA.

4) Rounding errors are taken into account during the computation of the error bounds.

METHOD:

The basic error bound formula is

NORM(C*R)/(1+D) ≤ NORM(ERROR) ≤ NORM(C*R)/(1-D)

where C is an approximate inverse for A which must satisfy

D = NORM(I - C*AO) < 1

and R = BO - AO*X. The MAX norm is used in the subroutine. Interval arithmetic is used to compute intervals which contain the quantities in the error bound formula. Thus, lower and upper bounds are computed for NORM(C*R) based on AA and BB, and an upper bound is computed for D based on AA.

REFERENCES

Aird, T. J., and R. E. Lynch (1975): Computable accurate upper and lower error bounds for approximate solutions of linear algebra systems. *ACM Trans. Math. Software*, **1**, pp. 217–231.

Bjorck, A. (1967): Solving linear least squares problems by Gram-Schmidt orthogonalization. *BIT*, **7**, pp. 1–21.

Blue, J. L. (1975): Automatic numerical quadrature—DQUAD. *Bell Laboratories Report*, Murray Hill, N.J.

deBoor, C. W. (1971): CADRE: An algorithm for numerical quadrature, in J. Rice (ed.), *Mathematical Software*. Academic Press, New York, pp. 417–450.

Dongarra, J. J., J. R. Bunch, C. B. Moler, and G. W. Stewart (1979): *LINPACK Users Guide*. Soc. Indust. Appl. Math., Philadelphia, 368 pages.

Faddeev, D. K., and V. N. Faddeeva (1963): *Computational Methods in Linear Algebra*. Freeman, San Francisco, 621 pages. Translated from the Russian.

Forsythe, G. E., and W. R. Wasow (1960): *Finite Difference Methods for Partial Differential Equations*. John Wiley, New York, 444 pages.

Fox, L. (1965): *Introduction to Numerical Linear Algebra*. Oxford University Press, Oxford, 327 pages.

Garbow, B. S., J. M. Boyle, J. J. Dongarra, and C. B. Moler (1977): *Matrix Eigensystem Routines—EISPACK Guide Extensions*. Lecture Notes in Computer Science, vol. 51. Springer Verlag, Berlin, 343 pages.

Gentleman, M. (1973): Least squares computations by Givens transformations without square roots. *J. Inst. Math. Appl.*, **12**, pp. 329–336.

Lawson, C. L., R. J. Hanson, D. R. Kincaird, and F. T. Krogh (1979): Basic linear algebra subprograms for Fortran usage. *ACM Trans. Math. Software*, **5**, pp. 308–323.

Lawson, C. L., and R. J. Hanson (1974): *Solving Least Squares Problems*. Prentice-Hall, Englewood Cliffs, 340 pages.

Oettle, W., and W. Prager (1964): Compatibility of approximate solutions of linear equations with given error bounds for coefficients and right-hand sides. *Numer. Math.*, **6**, pp. 405–409.

Parlett, B. N., and Y. Wang (1975): The influence of the compiler on the cost of mathematical software—in particular on the cost of triangular factorization. *ACM Trans. Math. Software*, **1**, pp. 35–46.

Rice, J. R. (1976): Parallel algorithms for adaptive quadrature III: program correctness. *ACM Trans. Math. Software*, **2,** pp. 1–30.

Rice, J. R. (1976*a*): The algorithm selection problem, in M. Rubicoff and M. Yovits (eds.), *Advances in Computers*, vol. 15. Academic Press, New York, pp. 65–118.

Rice, J. R. (1966): Experiments with Gram-Schmidt orthogonalization. *Math. Comp.*, **20,** pp. 325–328.

Rice, J. R. (1966*a*): A theory of condition. *SIAM J. Num. Anal.*, **3,** pp. 287–310.

Ryder, B. G. (1974): The PFORT verifier. *Software Practice and Experience*, **4,** pp. 359–378.

Smith, B. T., J. M. Boyle, J. J. Dongarra, B. S. Garbow, Y. Ikebe, V. C. Klema, and C. B. Moler. (1976): *Matrix Systems Routines—EISPACK Guide*. Lecture Notes in Computer Science, vol. 6 (2d ed.). Springer Verlag, Berlin, 551 pages.

Stewart, G. W. (1973): *Introduction to Matrix Computations*. Academic Press, New York, 441 pages.

Varga, R. S. (1962): *Matrix Iterative Analysis*. Prentice-Hall, Englewood Cliffs, 322 pages.

Von Neumann, J., and H. H. Goldstine (1947): Numerical inverting of matrices of high order. *Bull. Amer. Math. Soc.*, **53,** pp. 1021–1089.

Wilkinson, J. H. (1963): *Rounding Errors in Algebraic Processes*. Prentice-Hall, Englewood Cliffs, 161 pages.

Young, D. M. (1971): *Iterative Solution for Large Linear Systems*. Academic Press, New York, 563 pages.

INDEX

INDEX